Java™ Programming

Step-by-Step

™ Programming

Step-by-Step

Tony Bevis

Ability First Limited
Essex, United Kingdom

AbilityFIRST

Java Programming Step-by-Step

British Library Cataloguing in Publication Data. A catalogue record for this book is available from the British Library.

First published: January 2012

Published by: Ability First Limited

Dragon Enterprise Centre, 28 Stephenson Road

Leigh-on-Sea, Essex SS9 5LY, United Kingdom

www.abilityfirst.co.uk/books

ISBN: 978-0-9565758-2-1

Cover image by kuroji, copyright Fotolia.

Table of Contents

Preface

This book is intended for the new or inexperience programmer who wishes to become familiar with the Java programming language, and in particular to learn good design and implementation principles. You will be taken step-by-step through the creation and implementation of a desktop application that models a virtual zoo, complete with animals, zoo keepers and visitors, and its user interface will look like this:

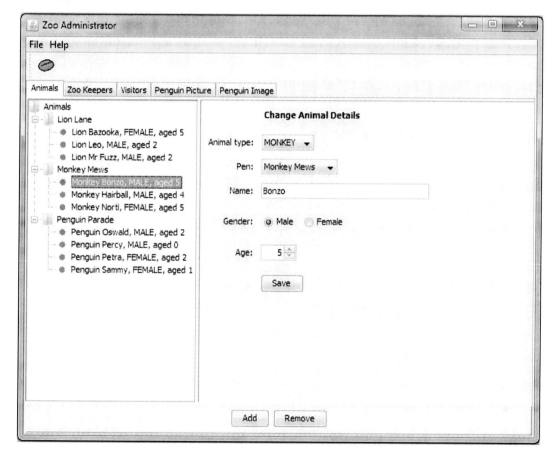

Rather than follow any particular development methodology this book instead uses concepts and techniques which are common to many. In particular, it is *iterative*; that is, small parts of the application are built and then continually improved upon as the full application is developed, with frequent modifications and enhancements along the way.

Java is a huge language with many facilities, and a book such as this can only provide a subset of such knowledge. It is hoped that you will be able to use the techniques and knowledge gleaned from this book as a solid foundation upon which you can extend your knowledge as you gain experience in developing your own applications.

Prerequisite knowledge

In order to make best use of this book you should be confident in using a computer, know and understand common computer terminology, and know how to download and install software. If you have prior programming experience then you are likely to gain additional benefit from this book.

How this book is organised

Because this book develops a complete application from scratch, each chapter builds on the knowledge of the previous chapters and continues the application's development. Therefore, it is recommended that you read the chapters in order, especially if you are a complete beginner.

Chapters 1 to 3 provide an introduction to Java and basic object-oriented concepts, together with how to create classes, attributes and methods.

Chapters 4 and 5 show how to partition your application and control when things should happen.

Chapter 6 demonstrates how to handle groups of items, process them consecutively and arrange them in particular sequences.

Chapters 7 and 8 how you how to handle unexpected occurrences, how to improve how your code is structured, and how to make parts of your system more reusable.

Chapters 9 and 10 provide additional ways of developing parts of your application, how you can produce documentation for it and test that it works correctly.

Chapters 11 and 12 introduce you to some more sophisticated ways of grouping items and shows how your application can perform more than one process concurrently.

Chapters 13 and 14 introduce the components that make up a graphical user interface.

Chapter 15 gives you a means of controlling access between the different parts of your application;

Chapters 16, 17 and 18 develop and complete the graphical user interface that makes up the sample application in this book.

Chapter 19 shows you some techniques of saving data to a file on your disk, and how this data can be retrieved at a later time.

Chapter 20 rounds off with a brief look at some additional features of Java that have not already been covered in this book.

A glossary and bibliography complete the book.

The software used in this book

This book makes use of the NetBeans development tool. This is a freely available application, download instructions for which are given in the first chapter. At the time of publishing NetBeans is at version 7, and ships with Java 6 built-in. However, it is possible that by the time you read this book that Java 7 will be in effect, and therefore this book points out the enhancements that are available with Java 7 for you convenience.

Conventions used in this book

New terms are given in **bold**, and these will generally also be defined in the glossary.

Java code that you need to enter, or that is shown as output, is shown in a fixed-width font as follows:

```
anObject.doSomething();
```

Often, a piece of additional or modified code is provided, and these are indicated in **bold**:

```
anObject.doSomethingElseInstead();
anObject.alsoDoThis();
```

Also marked in bold will be directions to use menu bar options, such as **File | New Project...**, where the vertical bar separates each option.

Names of classes, objects or Java statements will appear in the text using a fixed-width font such as `MyClass` or `someObject`, for example.

Where some useful or important additional information about a topic is included it will be shown in a note-box, like the following:

> This is some additional information in a note-box.

This book's resources

You can download all of the Java source code from this book, and view or tell us about any errata from our website:

http://www.abilityfirst.co.uk/books

> This book occasionally includes hyper-links to external sites. These were correct at time of publishing, but are subject to change. We are not responsible for the content of any external sites.

1. Introduction

The Java programming language has become a successful and widely used language suitable for many different types of application, including business applications, games, utilities, networking tools, and many more.

In this chapter you will learn:

- *A brief history of the language;*

- *An overview of object-oriented programming;*

- *How to go about the process of programming;*

- *A simple example program.*

Brief history and usages of Java

Java dates back to the early 1990s as a research project undertaken at Sun Microsystems (now part of Oracle) to look at the application of computers to consumer electronic devices. The research team originally considered using C++ but decided the problem was best addressed by creating a new language with the following features:

- **Simple & familiar:** They wanted the language to be based on C++ so existing programmers would feel at home, but at the same time reduced in complexity;

- **Object-oriented:** They wanted to use the modern approach to software development that more closely models the real-world;

- **Robust:** The language should be strictly checked and omit the error-prone features of C++;

- **Secure:** There should be self-checking to ensure each program's own integrity;

- **Portable**: Programs should be capable of running unchanged "as-is" on a variety platforms & devices;

- **Sufficient performance**: Programs should run fast enough for practical use;

- **Multi-threaded**: Programs should be capable of handling different processes concurrently.

There are three main editions of Java suitable for different purposes:

- **Java SE (Standard Edition)**: used for general purpose desktop applications and browser based applets;

- **Java EE (Enterprise Edition)**: an extended edition used for large-scale enterprise applications, typically web based;

- **Java ME (Mobile Edition)**[1]: A cut-down edition used for mobile devices such as smartphones and PDAs.

This book will use Java SE (Standard Edition).

It is also necessary to distinguish between between the **Java Development Kit (JDK)** and the **Java Runtime Environment (JRE)**:

- The **Java Development Kit (JDK)** is a set of tools used to write Java programs;

- The **Java Runtime Environment (JRE)** needs to be installed if you just need to run a program that has been written in Java. Once installed, this creates a **Java Virtual Machine (JVM)** which is the component that actually runs any Java program on your platform, including those written on a different

---

1   Java ME is becoming less used now since the popularity of Google Android's own set of Java development tools.

platform. Common platforms are Windows, Linux and Macintosh, and a JRE is also available on some other platforms too.

The JDK automatically incorporates the JRE for convenience so that you don't need to download each separately.

Java can be used to develop the following types of program:

- **Application**: these are usually graphical and run from the desktop;

- **Applet**: these are always graphical and run inside a web page;

- **Servlet**: these are used by Java EE to serve web pages;

- **MIDlet**: these are used by Java ME to serve mobile applications;

- **Aglet**: these are "Java Agents" which can move from host to host;

- **Hardware embedded**: these are built in to devices, such as the Java Card.

This book will focus on desktop applications.

Note: Do not confuse Java with JavaScript – they are are two entirely separate languages which have different uses, although there is some degree of similarity in their syntax. Java is generally more comparable to C# and C++ than to JavaScript.

What is object-oriented programming?

Object-oriented programming is an attempt to more closely model the real world when developing software, compared to procedural languages. The two key terms you need to understand at this stage are **class** and **object**:

- *class*: this is a like a template or blueprint that models something from the real-world (such as a person, product, event, role, etc.);

- *object*: this is a specific instance of a class (such as a particular person, a particular product, a particular event, a particular role, etc.) and that is capable of storing its own data and responding to messages sent to it.

To give an example, suppose you want to model an animal. When naming a class it is conventional to use a singular noun with its initial letter capitalised, so you might call the class Animal.

Now you have decided to create an Animal class, you need to think about two types of things that are common to all animals; its *attributes* (i.e. what it is composed of) and its *behaviours* (i.e. what it can do in response to a request):

1. *What attributes will it need? You might consider the following:*

   - Each animal will have a name (e.g. Fido, Cuddles, etc.);

   - Each animal will have a gender (male or female);

   - Each animal will be a certain number of years old.

2. *What behaviours will it need? You might consider the following:*

   - Another object might want to know a particular animal's name;

- Another object might want to know a particular animal's gender;

- Another object might want to know a particular animal's age;

In Java, each attribute value is stored in an area of memory known as a **variable** and each aspect of its behaviour is defined in a **method**. Variables and methods are given unique names so that they can be identified.

How programs are generally developed

The majority of programming languages use a specific set of commands that resemble English but which have to follow a prescriptive set of rules. By using commands that loosely resemble English it makes it easer for human programmers to give the computer the required instructions. These commands as written by the programmer is known as **source code**.

Because computers do not (yet) understand English, there needs to be some sort of translation into the language computers do understand, namely binary numbers. This translation is carried out by specially written "translation" programs which can be either (or both) of the following types:

- *Compiler*: this type of translator is invoked by the programmer and reads all of the source code to produce a complete runnable version that will be directly understood by the computer, and which is known as **machine code**;

- *Interpreter*: this type of translator is invoked by the end user of the program, although they probably won't know about it as it will be done automatically. It reads the source code one (or more) command(s) at a time performing the translation to machine code on the fly and running the translated code immediately. It then carries on through the remainder of the source code doing the translation and running it until the end of the program.

Because interpreters translate and run on the fly they tend to run more slowly than equivalent programs that were compiled.

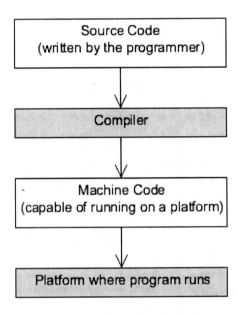

Figure 1.1: How programs are compiled

You should note that machine code is of necessity specific to particular platforms (e.g. Windows, Linux, Max, different processors, etc.). Because one of the primary goals of Java is portability (i.e. platform independence), Java uses a modified version of the above approach which is summarised in these steps:

1. The programmer writes the Java source code in the normal way. These source code files are typically given a file suffix of **.java**;

2. The programmer invokes the compiler to create what is known as **bytecode** (this can be thought of as platform independent machine code). The

bytecode is stored in a file with the same name as the source code except with a different file suffix, in this case **.class**;

3. The bytecode is delivered to the end user computer;

4. The end user needs to already have a **Java Virtual Machine (JVM)** installed on their machine. They can then run the bytecode (which is interpreted by the JVM).

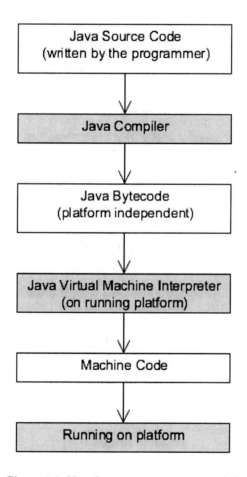

Figure 1.2: How Java programs are compiled

It can therefore be seen that Java programs are both compiled and interpreted.

There are separate JVMs for different platforms, but they are all capable of running the same compiled bytecode. It is this approach that gives Java its platform independence since the programmer only needs to develop, compile and deliver one version of the program.

Java syntax & naming conventions

In common with most languages Java programs have to adhere to a certain syntax in order for them to be successfully compiled. There are also certain conventions which ought to be complied with to aid understanding. This book will use the terms **must** and **should** to cover the most important aspects of syntax and conventions by stating whether you *must* do something a certain way (because otherwise your program won't compile), or whether you *should* do it a certain way (in order to adhere to conventions).

An important point to note is that capitalisation is significant in Java; that is; `Animal`, `animal` and `ANIMAL` all refer to different things as far as Java is concerned since they each have different letters capitalised.

Therefore, you must remember to be consistent in your use of capitalisation, and the built-in Java commands and keywords must be used using the correct capitalisation or else they will not be recognised.

There are lots of rules regarding syntax and conventions, but here are the important ones to get you started:

- The names of your classes **should** be in **camel-case**[1] and **should** always start with a capital letter (e.g., `Animal`, `Person`, `TelephoneNumber`, `HourlyPaidEmployee`).

- The names of your objects, variables and methods **should** be in camel-case and **should** always start with a lower case letter; examples:
    - object names: `fred`, `firstAccount`, `blueBoy`, `counter`;
    - variable names: `address`, `currentBalance`, `dateOfBirth`;
    - method names: `getName`, `setCurrentBalance`, `run`.

- The names of methods that retrieve and return information (such as the value of a variable) often begin with the word "get" (e.g. `getName` would return the value of the `name` attribute), although there are exceptions to this. Note that the 'n' for `name` becomes capitalised when appended to the "get".

- The names of methods that modify information (such as the value of a variable) often begin with the word "set" (e.g. `setName`), although again there are exceptions to this.

- Spaces are not allowed for class, variable or method names.

The book's example project

In this book you will learn the major facilities of the Java language through the gradual development of a "virtual zoo". This will entail developing classes that model different types of animal, zoo keepers, visitors, etc. and will incorporate a graphical user interface that allows you to simulate being the zoo's administrator.

The project will be developed in a step-by-step manner, in small incremental phases, where each phase builds on and extends the phases

---

1   This means that, because spaces are not allowed, if your name consists of more that one word then the initial letter of the second and subsequent words should be capitalised.

which came before. By the end of the book you will have a good working knowledge of the major facilities of the Java programming language.

How Java programs are entered

While it is possible to use a simple text editor to enter Java source code, and to use command line instructions to invoke the compiler, it is generally beneficial to use an **Integrated Development Environment (IDE)**[1]. Two very popular open source IDEs are Eclipse[2] and NetBeans[3]. Both are very capable and more similar than they are different.

This book will use NetBeans version 7, which is itself a Java application and which is sponsored by Oracle. The NetBeans download options allow you to either download NetBeans itself if you already have the Java JDK installed on your system, otherwise you can download a single bundle that incorporates the JDK and NetBeans together:

Go to the following site where you can select the appropriate download:
http://www.oracle.com/technetwork/java/javase/downloads/index.html

If you want to download and install both the JDK and NetBeans in one go then scroll down until you see the section headed **Java SE Development Kit (JDK) Cobundles**. Under this section you should see an option such as the following together with a **Download** button:

  JDK 6 Update 30 with NetBeans 7.1
  (it is possible that the respective product version numbers will be
  different when you view this)

If you know that you already have the JDK installed on your machine then you can get NetBeans separately from:
http://netbeans.org/downloads/index.html (select the Java SE version)

---

1   Sometimes called an Interactive Development Environment.
2   Available from the Eclipse Foundation website: http://www.eclipse.org/
3   Avaiable from the NetBeans website: http://netbeans.org/

Creating a simple Java program

Once NetBeans has been installed, start it and you should see the following screen:

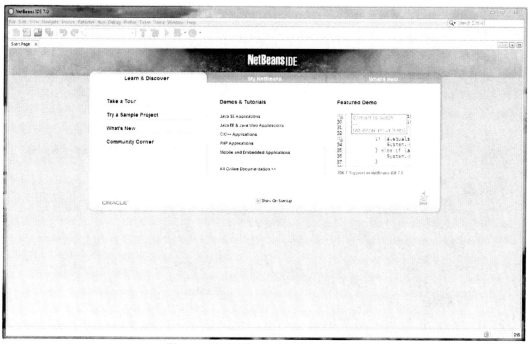

Figure 1.3: NetBeans startup window

Uncheck the **Show on Startup** checkbox and then choose **Help | Check for Updates**, following the prompts to download and install any updates that may exist. Depending upon which updates were needed you may be prompted to restart the IDE.

Select **File | New Project...** after which the following dialog will appear:

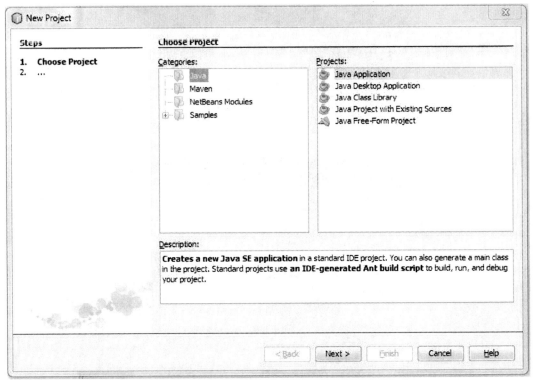

Figure 1.4: NetBeans New Project dialog

Ensure that **Java** is highlighted in the **Categories** list and that **Java Application** is highlighted in the **Projects** list, then click the **Next >** button.

The application that you will develop in this book will model a virtual zoo, so in the **New Java Application** dialog overtype the **Project Name** field so that it states `VirtualZoo`, ensure that the **Create Main Class** and **Set as Main Project** checkboxes are both checked. You can leave the **Project Location** entry to its default value unless you particularly wish to change it.

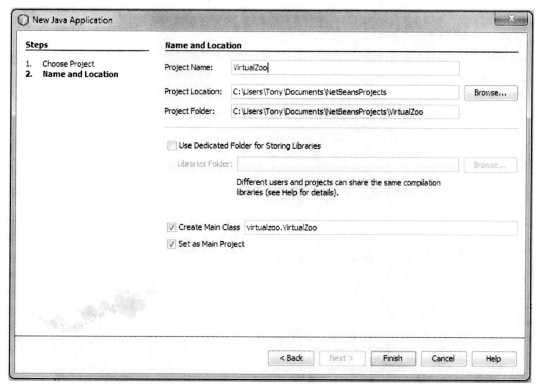

Figure 1.5: NetBeans New Java Application dialog

When you are ready, click **Finish**. The IDE should now look like this:

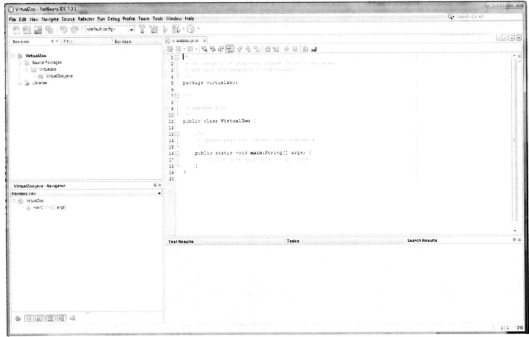

Figure 1.6: NetBeans window with new class

The window in the top left position shows three tabs; **Projects**, **Files** and **Services**, where the **Projects** tab is active. Within each of the tabs is an expandable tree, and each click-able element within the tree is known as a **node**:

- The `VirtualZoo` node at the top is the project name you created;

- Under the `Source Packages` node there exists the node `virtualzoo`, which is the name of a **package** that contains your Java source code files. Packages provide a means of grouping files in a similar way that your computer uses folders or directories to group various files[1]. Generally, each separate package will correspond to a directory or folder on your disk. Note that packages are by convention named using all lower-case letters; NetBeans converted your entered project name for you to follow this convention;

---

1   While it is not mandatory to place your Java source files in packages it is strongly recommended that you do so, since it makes your application more manageable as it becomes more complex.

- Under the `virtualzoo` package node is the Java source code file `VirtualZoo.java`, which was generated by NetBeans when you created the package.

The larger window in the central location contains the source code for `VirtualZoo` (i.e. the `VirtualZoo.java` file as listed under the `virtualzoo` package node). This contains Java code generated by NetBeans as a starting point for your application:

1. The lines that start with the characters **/*** and which continue until ***/** are all comments, being notes for the benefit of programmers and which are ignored by Java;

- The first actual Java statement is `package virtualzoo;`

  ○ The `package` statement specifies the name of the package where this particular Java file is located;

  ○ The `package` statement must always be the first non-comment line in a Java source file;

  ○ Note that the statement ends with a semi-colon – all Java statements need to end with a semi-colon unless it comprises a **block**, to be explained shortly.

- There then follows another set of comment lines indicating the name of the author, which will be set to your system's default value;

- The statement `public class VirtualZoo` declares that this Java source file is for a *class*:

  ○ You saw earlier that a class can be through of as a template or blueprint that models something. This particular class is modelling the application's starting point;

  ○ The keyword `public` means that the class will be available for use outside of this package as well as within it. Large applications can have several packages defined, and by default objects within each package can only communicate with other objects within the same package, unless the `public` modifier is used;

- o `VirtualZoo` is the name of the class. Its source code will be stored in a file named `VirtualZoo.java`;

- o There is an opening brace (i.e. curly bracket) at the end of the line. This signifies the starting point of a **block** of other Java statements contained within the block until the closing brace character, which signifies the end of the block.

Blocks of code exist between an opening and closing brace, like this:
```
a Java block statement {
        other Java statements go here
}
```

Some programmers prefer this format with the opening brace on its own line:
```
a Java block statement
{
        other Java statements go here
}
```

This book will use the first format with the opening brace on the same line as its preceding statement.

You can therefore see that for the `VirtualZoo` class the block is in this format:

```
public class VirtualZoo {

    rest of class goes here

}
```

Inside the class block is a second block that looks like this:

```
public static void main(String[] args) {
    // TODO code application logic here
}
```

Note the following:

- The statement `public static void main(String[] args)` will seem rather cryptic if you are new to the language. For now, all you need to know is that all Java applications need at least one class containing a block with this particular **signature** as the starting point of the application. As you learn about Java in this book you will become familiar with the meaning of each of the terms;

- Inside the block the two forward slash characters mean a single-line comment follows. Again, these comments are for the benefit of the programmer and are ignored by Java.

For reasons of brevity this book will often not show the multi-line comments that exist within a source file, since the book's narrative will contain a more detailed explanation. Without the multi-line comments (which you can delete if you wish) the Java source looks like this:

```java
package virtualzoo;

public class VirtualZoo {

    public static void main(String[] args) {
        // TODO code application logic here
    }
}
```

The `public static void main(String[] args)` block is said to be **nested** inside the `public class VirtualZoo` block. Indentation has been used purely to aid readability.

To see the application do something, change the comment line above to the following, as marked in **bold**:

```
package virtualzoo;

public class VirtualZoo {

    public static void main(String[] args) {
        System.out.println("Hello World");
    }
}
```

The `System.out.println("Hello World");` statement sends the text you specify (i.e. "Hello World") to the **Output** window. To get it to run, you can use any of the following options:

- Click the green arrow icon in the toolbar (its hover text is **Run Main Project**); or

- Select the menu options **Run | Run Main Project**; or

- Right-click the `VirtualZoo` project node in the **Projects** window and select **Run**; or

- Right-click the `VirtualZoo.java` source code node and select **Run**.

> If you receive error notifications when entering the above or trying to run it, check that you have entered the statement exactly as specified – common mistakes include not using the correct capitalisation or forgetting to include a semi-colon at the end of the statement.

Whichever method you choose run it, NetBeans automatically compiles the source code for you, and you should see the output appear in the bottom section of NetBeans known as the **Output** window:

Figure 1.7: NetBeans Output window

Later, you will modify the code so that instead of it sending "Hello World" to the **Output** window it launches the application you will be developing in this book.

An example class to model an animal

Earlier a class called Animal was specified capable of storing an animal's name, gender and age, and also capable of providing that information upon request. You will therefore start to write the Java source code for such a class. This new class, along with other related classes you will also develop in this book to represent zoo keepers and visitors, can be thought of as being part of the **core system** of the zoo application. For reasons which will become clear later, it is useful to separate the core system classes (which are non-graphical) from those which will be part of the graphical user interface[1]. You will therefore create two sub-packages under virtualzoo called core and ui to contain these classes respectively.

Right-click on the virtualzoo package node, select **New I Java Package...** and enter virtualzoo.core in the **Package Name** entry field:

---

1   You will start to develop the graphical user interface starting in Chapter 16.

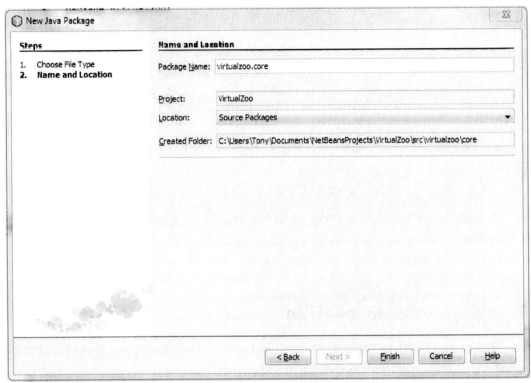

Figure 1.8: NetBeans New Java Package dialog

Click the **Finish** button. Now repeat the same process by right-clicking the `virtualzoo` package node again and creating another package called `virtualzoo.ui`, after which the IDE should look similar to that shown below:

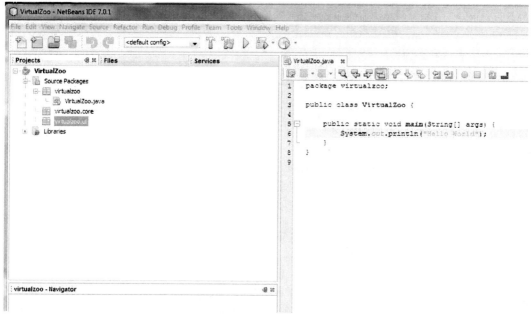

Figure 1.9: Updated NetBeans window

Ensure your package structure matches that in the illustration above before continuing. To summarise, you currently have three separate packages which will be used throughout this book for the following purposes:

- Package `virtualzoo` will only contain the class `VirtualZoo`. This class will become the "launcher" of your application;

- Package `virtualzoo.core` will contain the various non-graphical "core" classes which model the zoo application;

- Package `virtualzoo.ui` will contain the various graphical user interface classes which liaise with the core system classes.

> Even though `core` and `ui` are sub-packages of `virtualzoo` you should still think of them as being separate packages from `virtualzoo` in their own right.

You are now in a position to create the `Animal` class, so right-click on the `virtualzoo.core` package node, select **New | Java Class...** and enter the class name `Animal` into the **Class Name** box:

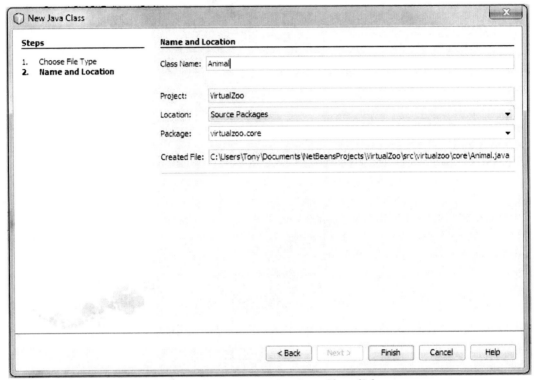

Figure 1.10: NetBeans New Java Class dialog

When you click the **Finish** button a new tab will appear for the Java source code for the new class:

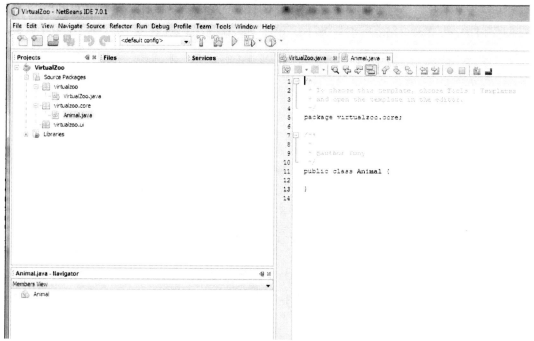

Figure 1.11: Updated NetBeans window

The source code for `Animal` currently looks like this:

```java
/*
 * To change this template, choose Tools | Templates
 * and open the template in the editor.
 */
package virtualzoo.core;

/**
 *
 * @author Tony
 */
public class Animal {

}
```

You will recall that so far there are three required attributes (i.e. name, gender and age) and three behaviours (i.e. being able to provide each of the three attribute values to other objects that can make use of it).

Declaring attributes

The attributes of a class are stored in **instance variables**.

- The term **instance** refers to the fact that there are potentially any number of animals that may need to exist, and each individual animal object will be an instance of the Animal class (i.e. an actual entity in its own right where its values may be different to other instances);

- The term **variable** refers to the fact that its value can be set to something, and possibly change over time (its age, being a prime example).

You can think of a variable as being a storage location for a value of some kind. In Java there are two categories of variable, as follows:

- **Primitive variables**: This kind of variable holds values directly. The most commonly used primitives are:

  - int: used to store an integer value (i.e. a whole number), which may be either positive or negative. *Examples: 3, 187, -2408;*

  - double: used to store a numerical value with decimal places, which may be either positive or negative. *Examples: 4.5, 527.0, -56.9;*

  - boolean: used to store a "true/false" or "yes/no" value. The value of a boolean[1] variable can only be either true or false[2].

- **Reference variables**: This kind of variable holds a reference, which you can think of as a "pointer") to an object (i.e. an instance) of a

---

1   Named after George Boole, an English mathematician.
2   Some other languages allow numerical values for boolean types (e.g. 1 for true and 0 for false) but Java does not allow this. You therefore cannot use booleans in arithmetic computations.

class. This could be either an object of a class supplied with Java or an object of a class that was written by you or someone else. Some example Java supplied classes are:

○ `String`: objects of this type contain a "string" of characters, i.e. a piece of text;

○ `Date`: objects of this type contain a calendar date value;

○ `File`: objects of this type provide a means of gaining access to a file or directory.

Note the different naming convention to distinguish between primitive and reference types; primitive types start with a lower-case letter (e.g. `int`) while reference types start with an upper-case letter (e.g. `String`). This is because reference types are always classes, which should start with a capital letter according to Java conventions.

While most of Java revolves around classes and objects, primitive types exist primarily for efficiency reasons for frequently used numerical and logical types.

When you declare an instance variable you have to decide which type to use; firstly whether it should be a primitive or a reference type, and then which specific primitive or reference type. An animal's name is always a string of characters, so the `String` class would be a natural choice. An animal's age, measured in whole years, would most readily be stored using the primitive `int` type. For an animal's gender you will, for the time being, also use a `String` (which will be either "m" or "f").

Type the statements marked in bold below inside the class block part of the `Animal` source file:

```
package virtualzoo.core;
```

```
public class Animal {

    // Declare instance variables to hold an animal's attributes
    private String name;          // the animal's name
    private String gender;        // the animal's gender ("m" or "f")
    private int age;              // the animal's age in years

    // Rest of class will go here...


}
```

- The keyword `private` means that the instance variable is only available from within this particular class – nothing else has direct access to it. This is very important to prevent another part of the application from modifying its value to a nonsensical value (for example, by making `age` a negative amount). The majority of your instance variables **should** be private, although there are occasional exceptions to this;

- The term `String` refers to the **type** of value that this variable will contain. `String` is itself a class that is built-in to the Java language and which is capable of storing a piece of text. Therefore, this variable is a **reference** to a `String` object. As previously noted because `String` is a class it adheres to the convention of starting with a capital letter. You will use other built-in classes later in the book;

- The term `name` is simply the identifying name of this instance variable, which will be used to store the animal's name. The other two instance variables are named `gender` and `age`. Note the initial letters are lower-case in compliance with the naming conventions for variables;

- The semi-colon character `;` signifies the end of a Java statement. As mentioned, you **must** end all Java statements (except those which comprise a block) with a semi-colon;

- Some comments, indicated by two forward slashes, have been included for each instance variable. These are completely optional, but if you include them they must be either after the semi-colon or on a separate line of their own;

- The int keyword means that the instance variable named age will contain an integer value, that is, a whole number. Remember that int is a primitive type rather than an object reference type.

You will now define a **constructor** for the class. Constructors are used to actually create individual instances (i.e objects) of the Animal class to represent each separate animal that you need to so something with. When creating an instance, you can also specify the initial values of its variables. Add the statements marked in bold:

```
package virtualzoo.core;

public class Animal {

    // Declare instance variables to hold an animal's attributes
    private String name;        // the animal's name
    private String gender;      // the animal's gender ("m" or "f")
    private int age;            // the animal's age in years


    // Define constructor
    public Animal(String myName, String myGender, int myAge) {
        name = myName;
        gender = myGender;
        age = myAge;
    }


    // Rest of class will go here...

}
```

- The keyword public means this this constructor is allowed to be invoked from objects in any package;

- The term `Animal` matches the name of the class – you **must** do this when defining a constructor;

- You then **must** have a pair of normal brackets ( ), although it is possible for there to be nothing inside them. In this case, however, there is a comma-separated list of **arguments** (sometimes called **parameters**) that define the incoming variables with each preceded by their type, into the constructor. In other words, when some other part of the application needs to create an `Animal` object they must supply two `String` objects (for the name and gender) followed by an `int` value (for the age). These incoming objects and value are supplied in the variables named `myName`, `myGender` and `myAge`;

- There is another pair of opening and closing braces to mark the beginning and end of the **constructor block**;

- The statement `name = myName;` is known as an **assignment**. The `String` object referenced by `myName` (which was the first argument passed into the constructor) is assigned to the instance variable `name`. This is done so that the incoming value is remembered once the constructor block has finished;

- Likewise, `myGender` is assigned to the instance variable `gender`, and `myAge` is assigned to the instance variable `age`;

- The references and values for `myName`, `myGender` and `myAge` only exist for the duration of the constructor and are lost once it completes. They are said to be **local** to the constructor. However, `name`, `gender` and `age` were defined as instance variables outside of the constructor and are therefore **global**, that is, available throughout the class (but not outside the class because they were defined to be `private`);

So far, you have written a class which is capable of instantiating (i.e. creating) one or more objects (i.e. instances) of the `Animal` class, and you can supply the values for each instance.

To show how you could use this new class, modify the `VirtualZoo` class as follows (changes marked in bold):

```
package virtualzoo;

import virtualzoo.core.Animal;

public class VirtualZoo {

    public static void main(String[] args) {
        Animal bruno;
        bruno = new Animal("Bruno", "m", 4);
    }
}
```

Note the following:

- The statement `import virtualzoo.core.Animal;` is needed to import the `Animal` class you just developed because it exists within a different package to the `VirtualZoo` class. If `Animal` was defined in the same class then an `import` statement would not be needed. You will learn more about importing classes later;

- The statement `Animal bruno;` declares a variable called `bruno` of type `Animal`, although at this point an object for it does not yet exist;

- The statement `bruno = new Animal("Bruno", "m", 4);` creates an `Animal` object and assigns it to the reference variable `bruno`. The `new` keyword tells Java to invoke the constructor of the class which follows. Inside the brackets two `Strings` and an `int` are sent to the constructor, representing the actual name, gender and age for this particular object. Strings are always defined by enclosing them inside double-quotation marks, although these do not form part of the string. Here, you have specified that the animal's name is Bruno, that it is male, and that it is four years old;

- At this stage, it is not obvious what type of animal Bruno is, but for the time being this does not matter. Later in the book you will see how to specify different kinds of animal.

If is very common to combine the two declaration and instantiation statements into a single line, as follows:

```
public static void main(String[] args) {
    Animal bruno = new Animal("Bruno", "m", 4);
}
```

You can run this application right now (by clicking the green arrow button in the toolbar) and the **Output** window should show that it completed successfully.

Figure 1.12: NetBeans Output window

The `Animal` object referenced by `bruno` existed for the duration of the run, and was then discarded when the program ended.

At this stage, of course, the program is not very useful as there is currently no way of getting the values out since the instance variables were declared to be `private`.

You will now add the functionality needed to retrieve the data from each instance.

Declaring functionality

The behaviours of a class are defined by writing **methods**[1], where each method performs one piece of functionality. In an application, different objects send messages to each other, where each message results in a method being invoked. Some methods retrieve and return information while other methods might perform some internal processing such as modify some data.

You will now write a method to retrieve the animal's name. In the `Animal` class add the lines marked in bold:

```
package virtualzoo.core;

public class Animal {

    // Declare instance variables to hold an animal's attributes
    private String name;        // the animal's name
    private String gender;      // the animal's gender ("m" or "f")
    private int age;            // the animal's age in years


    // Define constructor
    public Animal(String myName, String myGender, int myAge) {
        name = myName;
        gender = myGender;
        age = myAge;
    }


    // Define instance methods

    // Return the animal's name
    public String getName() {
        return name;
    }


    // Rest of class will go here...

}
```

---

1   In some other languages methods are known as functions. Java always uses the term *method*.

- The keyword `public` means that the method is available to be invoked by other objects from any package;

- The term `String` means that this method returns a reference to a `String` object. Not all methods have to return something, but if they do you must define the type of thing that is being returned. If nothing is to be returned you must instead use the keyword `void`;

- The term `getName` defines the name of the method; it is followed by a pair of empty opening and closing brackets since this particular method does not need any arguments to be passed into it. If you have a method that does require arguments to be passed in, you would follow a similar syntax as was used for the constructor earlier;

- Note that since the method returns an instance variable it follows the naming convention of starting with `get` followed by the name of the instance variable (name), except that the 'n' of name is now capitalised since it is not the very first letter of the method name;

- Inside the method block the keyword `return` is a built-in command used to return (i.e. pass back) something to whoever made the request. In this case you are passing back a reference to the name instance variable object.

You will now define two additional methods to return the gender and the age:

```
public class Animal {

    // Declare instance variables to hold an animal's attributes
    private String name;        // the animal's name
    private String gender;      // the animal's gender ("m" or "f")
    private int age;            // the animal's age in years


    // Define constructor
    public Animal(String myName, String myGender, int myAge) {
```

```
        name = myName;
        gender = myGender;
        age = myAge;
    }



    // Define instance methods

    // Return the animal's name
    public String getName() {
        return name;
    }

    // Return the animal's gender
    public String getGender() {
        return gender;
    }

    // Return the animal's age
    public int getAge() {
        return age;
    }


    // Rest of class will go here...

}
```

- The getGender() method is very similar to getName() except that it returns the gender instance variable, which is also an object of type String;

- The getAge() method is likewise similar, returning the int value of the age instance variable.

Trying out the new methods

Modify the VirtualZoo class to invoke the three methods you just defined after the bruno object has been instantiated:

```
public class VirtualZoo {

    public static void main(String[] args) {
        Animal bruno = new Animal("Bruno", "m", 4);

        // Output bruno's details
        String brunoName = bruno.getName();
        System.out.println(brunoName);

        String brunoGender = bruno.getGender();
        System.out.println(brunoGender);

        int brunoAge = bruno.getAge();
        System.out.println(brunoAge);
    }
}
```

- The statement `String brunoName = bruno.getName();` causes the `getName()` method to be invoked upon the `bruno` object. Since this method returns a `String` you need to assign it to a `String` object, which here is called `brunoName`:

  o The notation to invoke a method is to specify the name of the object, followed by a dot, followed by the name of the method including its brackets (which here are empty);

  o Once this completes the `String` it returns is assigned to the `String` reference `brunoName`.

- The statement `System.out.println(brunoName);` sends a line to the **Output** window containing the textual value of the variable `brunoName`;

- The `getGender()` method is similarly invoked and assigned to a `String` reference called `brunoGender`, which is then also sent to the **Output** window;

- The `getAge()` method is also similarly invoked and assigned to the `int` variable called `brunoAge`, which is sent to the **Output** window.

If you run the project you should see the following in the **Output** window:

Figure 1.13: NetBeans Output window

It is possible to combine the invocation of the getter methods inside the statements which send to output:

```
public static void main(String[] args) {
    Animal bruno = new Animal("Bruno", "m", 4);

    // Output bruno's data
    System.out.println(bruno.getName());
    System.out.println(bruno.getGender());
    System.out.println(bruno.getAge());
}
```

The way the above works is by processing methods from the inside out; that is, the inner most pair of brackets relates to the getName() method, which is nested inside another pair of brackets which relates to the println() method. The processing follows this sequence:

1. The getName() method is invoked upon the bruno object reference;

2. The getName() method returns a String reference (for the animal's name);

3. The `String` reference returned becomes the argument to the Java supplied `println()` method, so assuming the `String` "Bruno" was returned it would have the effect of doing this:

- `System.out.println("Bruno");`

4. The `String` Bruno is sent to the output window (which is what the `println()` method does).

You can enhance the output by combining the variables with some explanatory text:

```java
public static void main(String[] args) {
    Animal bruno = new Animal("Bruno", "m", 4);

    // Output bruno's data
    System.out.println("Name: " + bruno.getName());
    System.out.println("Gender: " + bruno.getGender());
    System.out.println("Age: " + bruno.getAge());
}
```

Note how you can use the + operator to **concatenate** together pieces of text, so the output should now show:

Figure 1.14: NetBeans output window

You can create as many `Animal` objects as you like:

```java
Animal bruno = new Animal("Bruno", "m", 4);
Animal cuddles = new Animal("Cuddles", "f", 2);
```

```
Animal someDog = new Animal("Fido", "m", 3);
Animal aGiraffe = new Animal("Gilly the Giraffe", "f", 7);
```

Each object so created has its own independent **state** (i.e. set of instance variable values), so you need to specify which one when invoking a method upon it:

```
String x = cuddles.getGender(); // what is cuddle's gender?
int ga = aGiraffe.getAge(); // how old is Gilly the Giraffe?
```

> As you have seen, you can name your objects anything you like, but it makes sense to use names which directly relate to the object and which are easily remembered.

Building your projects

When you run your projects NetBeans will automatically recompile any updated Java class files for you. Sometimes, however, it is helpful to run the compilation process without running the project, perhaps just to see if you have any errors. To do this, right-click on the `VirtualZoo` project node and select **Clean and Build**. Alternatively, there is an icon on the toolbar that looks like a hammer and brush that performs the same action.

You may want to clean and build your projects periodically as you work your way through this book. Make sure the last line of the **Output** window says BUILD SUCCESSFUL. If the build failed, then there will be some preceding lines pinpointing the classes and statements that are in error.

2. Object-Oriented Concepts

Java is an object-oriented programming language, providing you with a means of modelling your programs in a way that more closely models the real-world as compared to procedural languages.

In this chapter you will learn:

- *Some basic object-oriented concepts and terminology;*

- *How to define and use attributes and methods;*

- *What objects are and how to create and reference them;*

- *How to deal with errors which may occur;*

- *About the provided documentation for Java;*

- *About primitive data types.*

Object-oriented concepts

In the previous chapter you learned that that a **class** is defined as a template or blueprint to model something, and an **object** is an instance (i.e. a particular example) of a class.

You also learned that when you write a class you specify its **instance variables** in order to store its attributes and its **methods** and **constructors** in order to provide its functionality (i.e. behaviours).

This chapter will develop these concepts and introduce some additional terminology.

Each object consists of both **state** and **protocol**:

- An object's **state** is all of the data that it stores. This corresponds to the values of all of its instance variables taken as a whole;

- An object's **protocol** is all the things it can do. This corresponds to its methods taken as a whole, which you can think of as its **behaviour**.

Encapsulation describes the concept that each individual object consists of both its state and its protocol.

It is a good idea to prevent an object's state from being modified in nonsensical ways; for example, you might have an instance variable that stores an animal's age and it would make no sense for this to contain a negative value. To prevent this kind of thing from happening you can define the **visibility** of each instance variable, and it is recommended that in the majority of cases you declare instance variables to be `private`. This keyword means that only the class in which they are declared has direct access to the variable.

But what if you need other classes to be able to update a animal's age, but still need to prevent nonsensical values? To accomplish this, a method can be defined that contains Java code; it can verify that the age value is sensible before actually updating the instance variable value. It is common for many methods to be declared `public`, meaning that any other object can invoke it.

You can think of methods as providing a protective layer around the variables; the only way other parts of the application can get at the variables' data is through its methods.

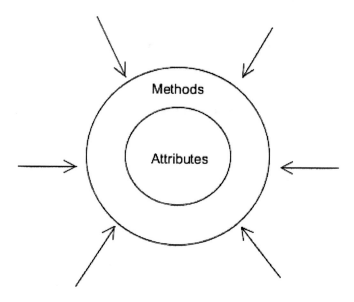

Figure 2.1: Encapsulation and data-hiding

Attributes

The **attributes** (also known as **properties**, or sometimes **fields**) of a class are defined by declaring **instance variables**. These are defined within the class block but outside of any constructors or methods.

A good rule-of-thumb is to declare instance variables to be **private** in order accomplish **data-hiding**.

All instance variables should be given meaningful names and follow the convention of camel-case but starting with a small letter. You should avoid abbreviations (unless they are in common use).

```
// Example instance variables
```

```
private String name;
private String placeOfBirth;
private String copyOfHtmlPage;
```

Methods

When an object sends a message to another object, it causes a method to be invoked:

```
// Example method defined in a particular class returns a String
public String sayHello() {
    return "Hello";
}

// Somewhere else we send a message to the above...
String s = sayHello(); // if sending from same class
String s = anObject.sayHello(); // if sending from a different class

// The variable named s should now contain "Hello";
```

Methods names should also adhere to camel-case and start with a small letter. The first word in a compound word method name (or the only word in a single word method name) should normally be a verb. The name is always followed by an opening and closing bracket to contain its required arguments, but the brackets may be empty if no arguments are needed.

In the above example method sayHello() the pair of brackets are empty. This signifies that no arguments (also known as parameters) are being sent along with the message. An argument is a value that the method might use to do something useful, for example to say hello to a particular person:

```
// Modified version of method that has a method argument
public String sayHello(String name) {
        return "Hello " + name;
}

// Somewhere else we send a message to the above...
```

```
String s = sayHello("Fred");

// The variable s should now contain "Hello Fred";
```

Note how you need to specify the type of argument being sent (String above). You can send multiple arguments separated by commas:

```
// Modified version of method that has 3 method arguments
public String sayHello(String firstName, String lastName,
                                                    int age) {
       return "Hello " + firstName + " " + lastName +
                ", you are" + age + " years old";
}

// Somewhere else we send a message to the above...
String s = sayHello("Fred", "Bloggs", "50");

// The variable s should now contain "Hello Fred Bloggs, you are 50
years old";
```

- Each argument type is declared on the method signature (String, String, int);

- It is permissible to write each Java statement over more than one line, as in the two places above;

- The + symbol is used to concatenate String objects into larger String objects;

- Spaces are included in the strings to aid formatting;

- The method call must specify all of the arguments in the correct order (two String objects followed by an int primitive value in the above example).

The above example method returns a String reference. You can return any recognised class or primitive type, or if you don't need to return anything just specify the keyword void:

```
// Return a sum
public int sum(int firstNumber, int secondNumber) {
```

```
        int total = firstNumber + secondNumber;
        return total;
    }


    // Nothing to return
    public void outputWord(String word) {
        System.out.println(word);
    }
```

Inside the sum() method above, the + symbol is being used for its usual arithmetical purpose of adding the two values contained in the argument variables firstNumber and secondNumber. The sum of these is then stored in a local method int variable called total. The value of total is then returned to the caller. You could use this method as follows:

```
// Add two numbers
int value = sum(3, 6);

// At this stage, value will contain 9
```

> The term **member** is sometimes used to refer to either a variable or a method. Therefore a class's members is all of its attributes and methods.

Creating objects

Object instances are created using the new keyword, which is followed by the constructor name[1] and arguments (if applicable). Here is an example where a Date object is created[2]:

```
Date rightNow = new Date(); // defaults to today's date
```

It is also possible to write the above in two separate statements:

```
Date rightNow;             // define reference of type Date
rightNow = new Date();     // create new Date object
```

---

1   Remember that constructors always have the same name as the class in which it is defined.
2   Date is a Java supplied class that exists in a package called java.util.

Note how you must specify the type of object that will contain the reference.

> Java is a **strongly typed** language. This means that you need to declare each variable's type and can only store compatible values in that variable.

Object references

In the `Date` object created above called `rightNow`, the variable is actually a **reference** to the object rather than the object itself. You can think of a reference as being a **handle** or **pointer**. You can point other references to the same object provided they have the same type:

```
Date date1 = new Date();
Date date2 = date1; // both date1 & date2 reference the same object

Date date3 = new Date(); // this is a different object
Date date4 = date3; // both date3 & date4 reference the same object

// You now have two objects of type Date:
// - date1 and date2 both reference one of the Date objects
// - date3 and date4 both reference the other Date object
```

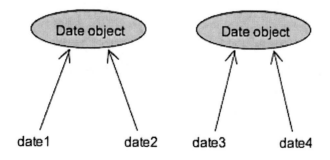

Figure 2.2: Two Date objects and four references

Dealing with errors in programs

Errors in Java programs can be categorised into two types:

1. Errors that stop the class from being compiled;

2. Errors where the program compiles successfully but does the wrong thing when it runs.

There are two categories of reason why a class won't compile; **syntax** errors and **semantic** errors:

```
// Example syntax error - missing semi-colon at end of statement
Date today = new Date()

// Example semantic error - should be getTime() not getTimes()
int time = today.getTimes();
```

To resolve a syntax or semantic error you need to look at the message(s) provided by the compiler. It is generally caused by a typing error or spelling mistake.

Errors where the class compiles but does the wrong thing when run are known as **logical** errors:

```
// Example logical error - should be adding not subtracting
int numberOfMen = 7;
int numberOfWomen = 5;
int total = numberOfMen - numberOfWomen; // should use + not -
```

To resolve a logical error is often harder, and you may have to trace through each statement to spot where it is going wrong. See if you can spot the error in the following method:

```
// This method should return a value that is twice the product
// of the three arguments
public int twiceProduct(int firstNumber, int secondNumber,
                                        int thirdNumber) {
        // Add the three argument values
        int sum = firstNumber + secondNumber + thirdNumber;
```

```
        // double the sum just calculated
        int twiceSum = sum * 3; // * means multiply
        return twiceSum;
    }
```

Hopefully you can see that the sum is being multiplied by 3 when it should instead be multiplied by 2. If you are unable to spot the logical error by just looking at the code then a good technique is to send pertinent values to output at particular stages using `System.out.println()`:

```
    // This method should return a value that is twice the product
    // of the three arguments
    public int twiceProduct(int firstNumber, int secondNumber,
                                                  int thirdNumber) {
        // Add the three argument values
        int sum = firstNumber + secondNumber + thirdNumber;
        System.out.println("sum = " + sum);

        // double the sum just calculated
        int twiceSum = sum * 3; // * means multiply
        System.out.println(" twiceSum = " + twiceSum);

        return twiceSum;
    }
```

Doing the above should help you locate where the error is, since you will see that `sum` is correct but `twiceSum` is incorrect, so you only need to look at the line(s) of code that precede the incorrect location.

An logical error in a piece of software is known as a **bug**, so resolving errors is know as **debugging**. There are more sophisticated debugging techniques involving **breakpoints** and **assertions**, which will be covered later in the book.

Using the Java APIs

Java contains many pre-built classes to facilitate programming for graphics, networking, multi-threading[1], etc. You can access the **Application Programming Interface (API)** documentation for all of Java supplied classes from the following link:

> http://download.oracle.com/javase/6/docs/api/
> (The above link is for Java SE version 6)

You can scroll through the alphabetical list of classes in the bottom left margin (under the heading **All Classes**) and select the required class. The currently selected class API appears in the main section.

The String class

Open the API in your browser and select the String class. Your screen should look something like this:

---

1   A thread is a separate line of execution, and multi-threading means running multiple threads at the same time within a single program.

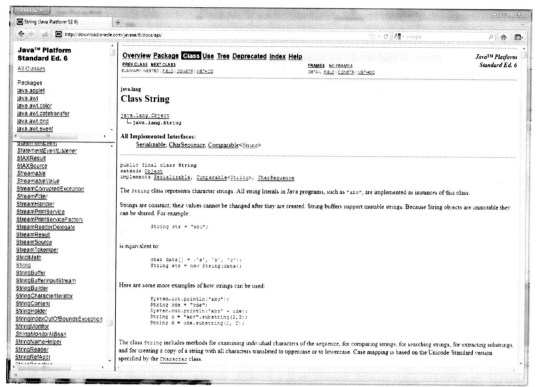

Figure 2.3: Javadoc for the String class

The above web-based documentation is known as **Javadoc**. After some header information you will see a description of the class. Scroll through the main body until you reach the section headed **Method Summary**, where you will see an alphabetic list of all available methods that can be invoked on `String` objects. Scroll to the method named `toUpperCase()` and click its link. You should now see a description of what the method does:

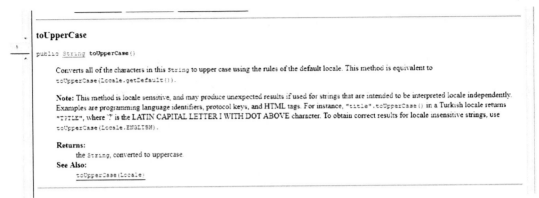

Figure 2.4: Method summary

This tells you that the method converts all of the characters to upper-case; but note that it doesn't actually modify the object on which it operates but instead returns a new `String` with its characters in upper-case; the original `String` object is unchanged!

```
String word = "banana";
String anotherWord = word.toUpperCase();


// At this point:
//    word still contains "banana"
//    anotherWord contains "BANANA"
```

If you want to modify the content of the original `String` you would need to assign the returned `String` reference to itself:

```
String word = "banana";
word = word.toUpperCase(); // Now word contains "BANANA"
```

In fact, there are no methods within the `String` class that modify the object on which it is applied; instead, a new `String` object is returned. It is therefore an **immutable** class. Immutable classes provide several advantages (including but not limited to being simple to use in multi-threaded applications), and many built-in Java classes are immutable.

In the examples just given note the way in in which the `String` object was created above – the `new` keyword was not used. This feature is unique to the String class; all other classes require new to instantiate objects. This feature exists for convenience to the programmer since strings are so frequently used. You are still still allowed to use new when instantiating, however:

```
String word1 = new String("apple"); // this is perfectly valid
String word2 = "orange"; // this is the shortcut technique
```

Another aspect of String that differs from other classes is the fact that Java pools unique Strings in memory:

```
String name1 = "Bob";
String name2 = "Bob";
// At this point there is only ONE object of type String in
// existence, and both name1 and name2 point to that same object.
// This is because name2 had the same content as name1 when created.
```

It is important to note, though, that when new is used for String (and all other classes) you always get separate objects, even if the values passed in are the same.

```
String name3 = new String("Thelma");
String name4 = new String("Thelma");
// name3 and name4 are TWO separate objects
```

Primitive data types

You have already seen that int is a primitive type that can store integer values. You should note the following about the int primitive:

- It is **signed**; meaning it can store negative as well as positive integers;

- It is stored using 32 bits (i.e. 4 bytes), so its range of values is -2^{31} to $2^{31} - 1$

There are three other signed integer primitives of different sizes:

- `byte`: 8 bits, range -128 to 127;

- `short`: 16 bits, range -32,768 to 32767;

- `long`: 64 bits, range -2^{63} to $2^{63} - 1$.

```
// Examples of byte, short and long integer types
byte b = 47;
short s = -12345;
long g = 1234567890;
```

> The default value of all of the primitive integer types is 0.

There is a separate primitive called `char` which is used to hold **Unicode**[1] characters. This is **unsigned** and 16 bits, holding the range of values \u0000 to \uFFFF (in hexadecimal[2]):

```
// Examples (note must use single quotes for char)
char letterA = 'A';        // the letter A
char tab = '\t';           // the tab character
char greekLetterPi = '\u03c0';
```

> The default value of the `char` primitive type is \0000.

There are two primitives which hold **floating-point** numbers and which allow decimal places to be stored:

- `float`: 32 bits, range $\pm 3.4 \times 10^{38}$ to $\pm 1.4 \times 10^{-45}$;

- `double`: 64 bits, range $\pm 1.8 \times 10^{308}$ to $\pm 4.9 \times 10^{-324}$.

```
// Examples
float f = 123.45f; // the 'f' is required for floats
double d = 123.45; // 'd' at end is optional so is omitted here
```

---

1   Unicode is a standardised character set where each character has a unique code number. See
    http://www.unicode.org
2   Base 16 numbering.

> The default value of the floating-point primitive types is 0.0.

An important point to note about the floating-point types `float` and `double` is that they are intended for scientific and engineering uses and as such are not suitable for storing or doing calculations with monetary amounts. This will be explored in a later chapter.

The final primitive type is `boolean`, which can only be one of the values `true` or `false`:

```
// Examples
boolean raining = true;
boolean sunny = false;
```

> The default value of the `boolean` primitive type is `false`.

Each of the eight primitives above have **wrapper** classes within Java, although they are not used anywhere near as frequently as the primitives. They can be distinguished due to their class names beginning with a capital letter (as per the normal Java naming conventions), and have similar but not always identical names:

Primitive type	Class wrapper type
boolean	Boolean
byte	Byte
char	Character
double	Double
float	Float
int	Integer
long	Long
short	Short

Enhancements in Java 7

If you are using Java 7 then you can use the underscore character as a separator for numeric literals, as a means of making the number easier to read. For example, to define an int with the value of one million, contrast the following two statements:

```
// Pre-Java 7...
int million = 1000000;

// Java 7...
int million = 1_000_000;
```

3. Using Classes and Methods

Methods provide the means of telling an object what it can do.

In this chapter you will learn:

- *Methods which change an object's state;*

- *Overloading and inheritance;*

- *Abstract classes and methods.*

Methods that modify an object's state

The `Animal` class allows its instance variables to be set from the constructor, but only currently provides methods which return those values to client objects[1]. Although it is unlikely that an animal's name or gender could change it is still a possibility (if, for example, the entries were wrongly entered to begin with) and the age value will naturally change on an annual basis.

To this end, you will now define three additional methods within `Animal` that enables these values to be changed, starting with a method to change the animal's name (marked in bold below):

```
public class Animal {

    // Declare instance variables to hold an animal's attributes
    private String name;        // the animal's name
    private String gender;      // the animal's gender ("m" or "f")
    private int age;            // the animal's age in years


    // Define constructor
    public Animal(String myName, String myGender, int myAge) {
        name = myName;
        gender = myGender;
```

---

1   A "client object" is any other object that invokes a method of the current object.

```
        age = myAge;
    }


    // Define instance methods

    // Return the animal's name
    public String getName () {
        return name;
    }

    // Change the animal's name
    public void setName (String newName) {
        name = newName;
    }

    // Return the animal's gender
    public String getGender () {
        return gender;
    }

    // Return the animal's age
    public int getAge () {
        return age;
    }


    // Rest of class will go here...

}
```

Note the following about the new method:

- The method is `public` so objects from any package can invoke it;

- The `void` keyword means that a value is not returned from this method. There is no need to return anything since its purpose is merely to modify an internal instance variable;

- The method is called `setName()` where the prefix "set" is a commonly adopted convention for naming methods that modify an object's state.

The methods to change the gender and age follow a similar pattern (from now on, surrounding code won't always be shown in order to save space):

```
// Change the animal's gender
public void setGender(String newGender) {
    gender = newGender;
}

// Change the animal's age
public void setAge(int newAge) {
    age = newAge;
}
```

The new methods can be invoked (for example from the `VirtualZoo` class) as follows:

```
Animal bruno = new Animal("Bruno", "m", 4);

// Change bruno's details
bruno.setName("Bruuuuno");
bruno.setGender("f"); // She was a girl all along!
bruno.setAge(5); // and now a year older

// Output bruno's details
System.out.println("Name: " + bruno.getName());
System.out.println("Gender: " + bruno.getGender());
System.out.println("Age: " + bruno.getAge());
```

Overloading

The `Animal` class currently defines a constructor which requires three argument values to be supplied (for the name, gender and age), and if when you invoke this constructor you supply the wrong number or the wrong type the compiler will give you an error message.

You may consider that it would be useful for client objects to create newly born animal objects (i.e whose age would be zero) without having to specify the third argument value, purely as a matter of convenience. Add the following constructor definition above the existing constructor in the `Animal` class:

```
public Animal(String myName, String myGender) {
    this(myName, myGender, 0);
}

public Animal(String myName, String myGender, int myAge) {
    name = myName;
    gender = myGender;
    age = myAge;
}
```

Note the following:

- This new constructor only requires two `String` arguments to be supplied;

- The `this()` statement inside the constructor body passes the two supplied `String`s along with the `int` value zero to the constructor that requires all three arguments to be specified. The zero effectively becomes a default value for the age. The process of one constructor forwarding to another is a useful technique that prevents you from having to duplicate code. Without it, you would have had to have coded the body as follows:

```
public Animal(String myName, String myGender) {
    // DON'T DO THIS - USE THE TECHNIQUE ABOVE IN PREFERENCE
    name = myName;
    gender = myGender;
    age = 0;
}
```

Defining more than one constructor within a class is known as **constructor overloading**, and is a common technique that allows client objects more flexibility in how they instantiate objects of your class. For example, to create a new-born animal you can now use either of the following two approaches, whichever is most convenient:

```
Animal aCat1 = new Animal("Tiddles", "f"); // age of zero assumed
```

```
Animal aCat2 = new Animal("Arthur", "m", 0); // age of zero specified
```

It is also possible to overload methods. For example, some animals may have a nickname, but instead of defining a separate instance variable for these odd cases you could instead overload the setName() method so that in addition to the current one which requires one String argument you define a second one which requires two:

```
public void setName(String newName) {
    name = newName;
}

public void setName(String newName, String nickName) {
    setName(newName + "(also known as " + nickName + ")");
}
```

Note the following:

- The second version of setName() requires two String arguments, and when supplied in this way will append the nickname to the proper name which is still supplied in the first argument value;

- The method body forwards to the setName() method which requires only one argument.

Try the following statements in the VirtualZoo class:

```
bruno.setName("Bruno", "The Beast");
System.out.println("Name: " + bruno.getName());
```

The output from the above should show:

```
Name: Bruno(also known as The Beast)
```

Inheritance

It was mentioned earlier that there is currently no obvious way of specifying what type of animal is being created. You might guess that Bruno could be a dog or that Tiddles could be a cat, but there is no guarantee of this.

For the zoo application the type of each animal is important to know, and a simplistic approach would be to introduce another instance variable within the Animal class to store its type (e.g. lion, monkey etc.). However, this approach is not very flexible; it is known, for example, that different animals have different feeding requirements, and trying to cater for all the different possibilities would become difficult to manage.

Object-oriented languages provide a feature known as **inheritance** whereby you can define a class as being "a kind of" a different class, and when you do this the inheriting class automatically adopts all of the capabilities of the class it inherits from.

In NetBeans, right-click on the virtualzoo.core package node and select **New | Java Class...**, and then enter Lion as the class name. After you click **Finish** the Java source should look as follows (ignoring comment lines):

```
package virtualzoo.core;

public class Lion {

}
```

To specify that a lion is a type of animal you need to make the Lion class inherit from the Animal class, which is done using the **extends** keyword:

```
package virtualzoo.core;

public class Lion extends Animal {

}
```

The class you inherit from (Animal in the above example) is known as the **superclass** and the one doing the inheriting (Lion in the above example) is known as the **subclass**.

The inheritance relationship between Animal and Lion can be shown diagrammatically by using a **class diagram**:

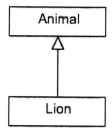

Figure 3.1: Inheritance:
Lion is a type of Animal

In a class diagram the subclass points toward the superclass to indicate that it inherits from it. The superclass does not have to be drawn above its subclasses, although it is common to do so. Class diagrams are an example of a range of diagramming techniques that form part of the **Unified Modeling[1] Language** (UML[2]).

Note that in Java a class can only extend **one** other class.

After entering the above you will note a red exclamation point in NetBeans to the left of the class declaration line. If you hover your mouse over this you will see an error message stating that no suitable constructor could be

---

1   Note the American spelling of "Modeling".
2   UML is beyond the scope of this book except for the occasional class diagram where it would help to clarify the relationship between certain classes.

found. This is because constructors are not inherited, and therefore always need to be specified.

Include two constructors for the `Lion` class as follows (they follow the same pattern as the constructors within `Animal`:

```
public class Lion extends Animal {

    public Lion(String myName, String myGender) {
        this(myName, myGender, 0);
    }

    public Lion(String myName, String myGender, int myAge) {
        super(myName, myGender, myAge);
    }

}
```

Note the following:

- The names of the constructors must match the class name (`Lion` in this case);

- The constructor that requires only two arguments forwards to the constructor that requires three, in the same way as was defined in the `Animal` class;

- The body for the constructor that requires three arguments does not assign to the instance variables in the same way as was the case within `Animal`. Instead, the `super()` statement causes the constructor of the class from which `Lion` is inheriting from (`Animal` in this case) to be invoked, and it passes along the three supplied argument values. The constructor within `Animal` assigns the supplied values and then passes control back to the `Lion` constructor;

- This process of a subclass constructor invoking a superclass constructor is in fact a requirement of Java, which enforces it in order to ensure that all state is properly initialised.

At this point, the `Lion` class is identical in terms of functionality to the `Animal` class. It automatically inherits all of its `public` methods without having to specify them: In `VirtualZoo` add the following `import` statement:

```
package virtualzoo;

import java.util.*;
import virtualzoo.core.Animal;
import virtualzoo.core.Lion;

public class VirtualZoo {
```

Now inside the `main()` method add the following:

```
Lion leo = new Lion("Leo", "m", 8);
System.out.println(leo.getName());
```

Note, however, that the instance variables defined within `Animal` are not directly available within `Lion` since they were declared to be `private`. Therefore, if within the `Lion` class you need access to these instance variables you need to invoke the appropriate methods that supply them, such as `getName()`, etc.

It is also possible to construct a `Lion` by specifying the reference type to be `Animal`:

```
Animal clarence = new Lion("Clarence", "m", 12);
```

The above approach works because `Lion` is a type of `Animal`. As you become more familiar with Java you will see that declaring the reference type using the superclass can provide some advantages, such as when you need a group of different types of animals.

Now that you know how to create subclasses you will create two more to represent penguins and monkeys. In NetBeans, ensure the virtualzoo.core package node is expanded and right-click on the Lion node, and then select **Copy**.

Now, right-click on the virtualzoo.core package node and select **Paste | Refactor Copy...**, and in the **Copy Class** dialog enter Penguin in the **New Name** field, and finally click **Refactor**.

Double-click the Penguin.java node in the **Projects** window to open the source code. You will see that NetBeans has adjusted the class and constructor names for you:

```java
package virtualzoo.core;

public class Penguin extends Animal {

    public Penguin(String myName, String myGender) {
        this(myName, myGender, 0);
    }

    public Penguin(String myName, String myGender, int myAge) {
        super(myName, myGender, myAge);
    }
}
```

Follow the same process to create another class called Monkey, which should look like this:

```java
package virtualzoo.core;

public class Monkey extends Animal {

    public Monkey(String myName, String myGender) {
        this(myName, myGender, 0);
    }

    public Monkey(String myName, String myGender, int myAge) {
        super(myName, myGender, myAge);
    }
}
```

At this stage you can create animals in any of the following ways:

```
Animal animal1 = new Animal("Fred", "m", 2);
Lion animal2 = new Lion("Leo", "m", 8);
Penguin animal3 = new Penguin("Oswald", "m", 3);
Monkey animal4 = new Monkey("Bonzo", "f", 5);
```

> You will need to import `virtualzoo.core.Lion`, `virtualzoo.core.Penguin` and `virtualzoo.core.Monkey`.

They are all types of animal, and it is also therefore possible to specify the above as follows:

```
Animal animal1 = new Animal("Fred", "m", 2);
Animal animal2 = new Lion("Leo", "m", 8);
Animal animal3 = new Penguin("Oswald", "m", 3);
Animal animal4 = new Monkey("Bonzo", "f", 5);
```

Overriding methods

The zoo would like to know which animal types are endangered, even though most types in the zoo aren't. Add the following method within the `Animal` class:

```
public boolean isEndangered() {
    return false;
}
```

> Note that for getter methods that return a `boolean` value the Java convention is to prefix the method name with `is` rather than `get`.

The above method takes a default view; each animal is not endangered. Remember, each subclass automatically inherits this method, and in the case of monkeys and penguins invoking the `isEndangered()` method will correctly return `false`. However, lions are endangered, so Java allows you to override its code to do something different.

Insert the following method in the `Lion` class:

```
public boolean isEndangered() {
    return true;
}
```

You will notice a small glyph to the left of the method declaration line in NetBeans which is a warning message. If you hover your mouse over it you will see **Add @Override Annotation**. Click on the glyph and then click the message which subsequently appears. You should see the following line inserted above the method:

```
@Override
public boolean isEndangered() {
    return true;
}
```

This is known as an annotation, and exists to remind the reader that this method overrides a method defined in a superclass. Including annotations is optional but recommended.

You can now invoke the `isEndangered()` method on any type of animal, and it will return false for each type except `Lion` objects.

```
boolean b1 = animal1.isEndangered();   // should return false
boolean b2 = animal2.isEndangered();   // should return true
boolean b3 = animal3.isEndangered();   // should return false
boolean b4 = animal4.isEndangered();   // should return false
```

Overriding produces an example of **polymorphism**. This refers to the capability of an object of a particular type to take the most appropriate action in response to a request, and which may be different to the action taken by an object of a different type to the same request. In the above example, a `Lion` object responds to `isEndangered()` in a different way to a `Monkey` object.

Abstract classes and methods

Now that you have created three subclasses of Animal you might like to consider what is meant by "animal" - does it ever make sense to instantiate an Animal object that isn't a specific type of animal? It seems natural to think that "animal" is in fact an abstract concept. In real-world terms, every animal in existence is actually a specific type of animal, and it is not possible for any animal to be born without it being a specific type.

Java lets you model this concept by marking classes as **abstract**. Once you do this, it is no longer possible to instantiate an object of type Animal unless you specify its actual type. Change the class declaration within Animal as follows:

```
public abstract class Animal {
```

If within VirtualZoo you still have lines which instantiate using new Animal you will find they now give rise to an error message:

```
// The following will no longer work...
Animal animal1 = new Animal("Fred", "m", 2);

// But these will work fine because a subclass of Animal is created
Animal animal2 = new Lion("Leo", "m", 8);
Animal animal3 = new Giraffe("Oswald", "m", 3);
Animal animal4 = new Monkey("Bonzo", "f", 5);
```

You have now successfully prevented client objects from creating an Animal object without specifying which specific type of animal it is.

It is often the case with abstract classes that there is some functionality which will differ for each subclass but which has no sensible default. An example for animals would be their favourite food; unlike the isEndangered() method where it was assumed that the animal was not endangered unless specifically overridden, there is no obvious foodstuff that can serve as a sensible default.

With abstract classes this presents no problem; simply define an **abstract method**. Insert the following inside the `Animal` class:

```
public abstract String favouriteFood();
```

Note the following:

- The `abstract` keyword specifies that this method is abstract; that is, it has no default processing;

- There is no method body and hence no braces – the method declaration ends with a semi-colon;

- Only classes declared to be `abstract` are allowed to have abstract methods;

- Subclasses **must** override the method to supply the missing body (unless the subclass is also abstract).

In the `Lion` class, override this method by inserting the following:

```
@Override
public String favouriteFood() {
    return "meat";
}
```

In the `Penguin` class, override this method by inserting the following:

```
@Override
public String favouriteFood() {
    return "fish";
}
```

In the `Monkey` class, override this method by inserting the following:

```
@Override
public String favouriteFood() {
    return "banana";
}
```

Tidying up the Animal constructors

Since making the `Animal` class abstract the only constructor that ever gets invoked within `Animal` is the one requiring three arguments, which is called by its subclasses using the `super()` statement. The two-argument constructors in these subclasses forward to the three-argument one in the same subclass – hence the two-argument constructor of `Animal` is now redundant.

Although not essential, to remove it would be good discipline. This enforces the idea to subclasses that they need to supply all three arguments. Therefore, the only remaining constructor that should remain within `Animal` is the following:

```
// Define constructor
public Animal(String myName, String myGender, int myAge) {
    name = myName;
    gender = myGender;
    age = myAge;
}
```

To round off this chapter you will see the updated class diagram that takes account of the fact that there are now three subclasses of `Animal` and that `Animal` is now an abstract class:

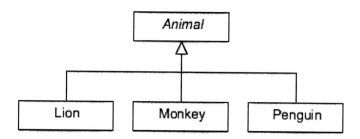

Figure 3.2: Abstract class with three concrete subclasses

You will notice that `Animal` is shown in italics to indicate that it is an abstract class. Non-abstract classes are commonly known as **concrete** classes, and are indicated in normal upright text.

4. Packages, the Object class and Interfaces

Packages allow you to partition your classes into sets of logical groups, and also enables you to protect parts of your application from other parts. The `Object` class provides the base from which all classes in Java, including your own, derive their functionality through inheritance. Interfaces provide a means of specifying types having particular capabilities.

In this chapter you will learn:

- *How to use packages;*

- *The `Object` class;*

- *Using the `this` and `super` keywords;*

- *Using interfaces.*

Packages and imports

A **package** is a named area used to group classes (or other files) that are logically related in some way. They are typically implemented by associating each with a unique folder or sub-folder (i.e. directory or subdirectory). While it is possible to create classes that are not in any package it is strongly recommended that you use packages for all your classes. All Java supplied classes are in packages, and all of the classes you have developed so far have been placed in one of the user-defined packages called `virtualzoo` or `virtualzoo.core`.

You have also previously learned that for all classes that are in a package there must be a `package` declaration statement as the first non-comment line, for example:

```
package virtualzoo.core;
```

- To follow naming conventions package names should be in all lower case, with compound words run together.

- You can define packages within other packages, using dots to separate them, for example `virtualzoo.core` would mean that within the `virtualzoo` package there exists a sub-package called `core`. This is useful for partitioning your classes into logically related areas, and later in the book when you develop graphical user interface classes you will make use of package `virtualzoo.ui` for these classes.

If you look at the Java APIs you will be able to see all of the supplied packages and their contents. If you select `String` from the bottom left hand frame you will see in the main section that the `String` class is within package `java.lang`.

Other supplied packages are `java.io` (for input/output classes), `java.math` (for mathematical classes), `java.util` (for utility classes), and many more.

In order to use a Java supplied class you need to **import** its package into your source file, except for classes which exist within `java.lang` which contains those classes so frequently used that it is automatically imported. An example of such a class is `String` – you didn't need to specify an import since it is defined within `java.lang`.

Suppose the zoo wishes to record the date each animal is admitted to the zoo, which for simplicity you can assume will always be the date the animal's object is instantiated. There is a `Date` class supplied within the `java.util` package that will serve to store this date, so the first step is to import it into the `Animal` class. Insert the line marked in bold in the specified location:

```
package virtualzoo.core;
```

```
import java.util.Date;
```

```
public abstract class Animal {
... rest of class...
```

Note that the `import` statement must be placed after the `package` statement but before the class declaration statement. Now that you have specified the `import` your class can make use of the `Date` class. `Date` is just one of a number of classes within the `java.util` package. If you need to use several classes from the same package it is possible to specify a wild-card import in the following format:

```
import java.util.*; // makes any class within java.util available
```

The asterisk indicates that you might want to use any class within the `java.util` package. Java only imports the classes you actually use, however, so there is no penalty associated with using the wild-card technique.

At this stage, it would be useful to modify the `import` statement that appears in class `VirtualZoo` to use the wild-card technique, as follows:

```
import virtualzoo.core.*;
```

The above change will allow `VirtualZoo` to access any class in `virtualzoo.core` rather than having to import `Animal`, `Lion`, `Penguin` and `Monkey` individually. You can therefore delete the following statements from within `VirtualZoo`:

```
import virtualzoo.core.Animal;
import virtualzoo.core.Lion;
import virtualzoo.core.Monkey;
import virtualzoo.core.Penguin;
```

And replace them with this one statement:
```
import virtualzoo.core.*;
```

and modifies the admission year value to be 2050. This actually modifies the `dateAdmitted` instance variable since its reference points to the same object which has just been modified.

In the above code the `getDateAdmitted()` method is invoked a second time. This is not actually necessary but done here to demonstrate that the the value inside the `Animal` object was indeed modified.

You will remember, though, that the intention was not to allow this date to change – it should be set to today's date inside the constructor and remain unchanged thereafter. The instance variable is defined as `private` and there is no setter method for it. The problem has arisen because the `Date` class is **mutable**, that is, it has methods which modify its own state. So when your `getDateAdmitted()` method returned a reference to it you were also returning the capability of modifying it.

This problem does not occur with the previous getter methods defined within `Animal` because:

- The `name` and `gender` instance variables are of type `String`, and `String` objects are **immutable**, that is, there are no methods that can modify its value after it has been constructed;

- The `age` instance variable is of the primitive `int` type. When you return a primitive type the caller gets its own copy of its contents so again the variable inside the `Animal` object cannot be modified.

The solution is for the `getDateAdmitted()` method to return a **defensive copy** of the `dateAdmitted` object in order to prevent a **privacy leak**. This requires constructing and returning a completely new object, although it will be set to have the same value as `dateAdmitted`.

If you look at the `Date` API you will see two things:

1. There is a constructor for the `Date` class which accepts a `long` primitive argument type representing the date in milliseconds.

2. There is a method called `getTime()` which returns a `long` primitive value containing the date value represented in milliseconds.

Therefore, if you get the date in milliseconds from the `dateAdmitted` instance variable you can use that value to create a separate object set to that value. Modify the `getDateAdmitted()` method as follows:

```
public Date getDateAdmitted() {
    // Return defensive copy
    long time = dateAdmitted.getTime();
    return new Date(time);
}
```

It is possible to combine the two statements into one and remove the need to allocate a named variable:

```
public Date getDateAdmitted() {
    // Return defensive copy
    return new Date(dateAdmitted.getTime());
}
```

If you run `VirtualZoo` again you should find that the same date is output both times. The `setYear()` method is operating on a separate copy and therefore has no impact upon the state of your `Animal` object.

The Object class

You saw earlier that any class can **extend** (i.e. inherit from) any other class, and this can be another class written by you or someone else, or a Java supplied class.

In fact, every class always inherits from a special Java supplied class called `Object`, and this happens even if you don't specify it. Your `Animal` class declaration could be written as follows:

```
public abstract class Animal extends Object {
```

There is no need to specify extends Object, however. If you don't specify it then it is assumed by Java. The class diagram can therefore be more accurately given as follows:

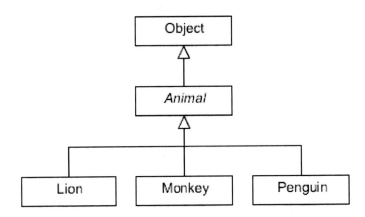

Figure 4.1: Class hierarchy for Object, Animal, Lion, Monkey and Penguin

The above diagram shows that the Animal class **directly** extends from Object whereas Lion, Monkey and Penguin only extend it **indirectly** (since they directly extend from Animal). Objects of type Animal can do anything an Object can do, and objects of type Lion, Penguin and Monkey can do anything an object of type Animal can do, which includes what Object can do.

The Java API documentation tells you the inheritance hierarchy near the top of its page, for example the FileReader class page looks like this:

Overview Package **Class** Use Tree Deprecated Index Help
PREV CLASS   NEXT CLASS   FRAMES   NO FRAMES
SUMMARY: NESTED | FIELD | CONSTR | METHOD   DETAIL: FIELD | CONSTR | METHOD

java.io
Class FileReader

```
java.lang.Object
  └ java.io.Reader
      └ java.io.InputStreamReader
          └ java.io.FileReader
```

All Implemented Interfaces:
    Closeable, Readable

```
public class FileReader
extends InputStreamReader
```

This shows that `FileReader` extends class `InputStreamReader`, which in turn extend class `Reader`, which in turn extends `Object`. The first three of these classes exist in the `java.io` package while `Object` exists within `java.lang`. (You will use the `FileReader` class in Chapter 19 – you don't need to understand it now).

The purpose of class `Object` is to provide certain basic functionality that is potentially useful for any class. The most important methods you need to know about that are defined within `Object` (and which therefore every class automatically inherits) are `equals()`, `hashCode()` and `toString()`. You will learn about the first two of these in a later chapter, but for now look at the API for `Object` and the description of its `toString()` method:

---

toString

```
public String toString()
```

Returns a string representation of the object. In general, the toString method returns a string that "textually represents" this object. The result should be a concise but informative representation that is easy for a person to read. It is recommended that all subclasses override this method.

The toString method for class Object returns a string consisting of the name of the class of which the object is an instance, the at-sign character '@', and the unsigned hexadecimal representation of the hash code of the object. In other words, this method returns a string equal to the value of:

```
getClass().getName() + '@' + Integer.toHexString(hashCode())
```

Returns:
   a string representation of the object.

Figure 4.2: Javadoc API for toString() method

Since all classes inherit this method you can invoke it already. Change the `main()` method in `VirtualZoo` to contain the following statements:

```
Animal leo = new Lion("Leo", "m", 4);
System.out.println(leo.toString());
```

The output will show something similar to the following:

```
run:
virtualzoo.core.Lion@2e471e30
BUILD SUCCESSFUL (total time: 0 seconds)
```

The first part shows the **qualified class name** (i.e. prefixed by the package the class is within) followed by an @ symbol. After the @ symbol is a series of characters, and note that the characters you see will probably be different to those shown above, since they may, for example, relate to the memory location (expressed in hexadecimal[1]) where the object reference is located.

The primary use of `toString()` is to provide for each object a useful textual representation of that object. As it stands with the default implementation of this method inherited from `Object`, only the piece before the @ symbol is useful. Of more use would be for the method to list the values of its instance variables. Therefore, within the `Animal` class, override the `toString()` method as follows:

```
@Override
```

---

1   Base 16 numbering system.

```
public String toString() {
    return name + ", " + gender + ", aged " + age;
}
```

If you run `VirtualZoo` again you should see the following :

```
Leo, m, aged 4
```

Hopefully you will agree that this provides much more useful information than the default implementation defined in `Object`.

The `toString()` method is also implied when not stated, when used with the `println()` method, so you could write the code in `VirtualZoo` as:

```
Animal leo = new Lion("Leo", "m", 4);
System.out.println(leo);
```

There is no need to override the method again within classes `Lion`, `Monkey` or `Penguin` since they all inherit from the overridden one in `Animal`.

Because of the different types of animal it would be useful for `toString()` to return the actual type as well as the name, gender and age. Modify it as follows:

```
@Override
public String toString() {
    return getClass().getSimpleName() + " " +
            name + ", " + gender + ", age " + age;
}
```

- The `getClass()` method is another method inherited from `Object`, and which returns the `Class` object associated with the class that the current object pertains to.

- The `Class` object has invoked upon it a `getSimpleName()` method, which returns the textual name of the class (e.g. `Lion`, `Monkey`, etc, without its package prefix).

- The above two methods are chained together. They could have been written as separate statements as follows:

```
Class c = getClass();
String className = c.getSimpleName();
```

When methods are chained together it saves the need to define temporary variable names. The chained methods are invoked from left to right, so firstly `getClass()` is executed to obtain a `Class` object, and then the `getSimpleName()` method is invoked upon this `Class` object. This returns a `String` object which becomes part of the text description.

The output should now be:

```
Lion Leo, m, aged 4
```

A class to model a zoo keeper

Your zoo will of course require a number of zoo keepers to help look after the animals, so you will now develop a `ZooKeeper` class. Just as you did with the `Animal` class, you need to think about the attributes and methods that each zoo keeper object will require, and you can assume that this results in the following list:

Attributes

For each zoo keeper you need to store their name, their address, their email address, and their annual salary.

Methods

For each zoo keeper you need methods that get and set their name, home address, email and salary. You will also override the `toString()` method to provide a user-friendly summary of this state.

Using NetBeans, create a new class in the `virtualzoo.core` package called `ZooKeeper`, and declare its instance variables:

```
package virtualzoo.core;
```

```
public class ZooKeeper {

    private String name;
    private String address;
    private String email;
    private double salary;


}
```

As shown above, the `String` class has been specified as the type to use for name, address and email, and the primitive `double` type for the salary (on the assumption that a salary could potentially include decimal places). But are these the best types to use?

You may recall from a previous chapter that `double` is not the best choice for storing or doing calculations for monetary values. The problem can be demonstrated with the code below:

```
// Demonstrate problem with floating-point arithmetic
double valueA = 2.0;                                      // statement 1
double valueB = 1.1;                                      // statement 2
double difference = valueA - valueB;                      // statement 3
System.out.println("difference = " + difference);         // statement 4
```

- Statement 1 creates a `double` variable named `valueA` containing `2.0`;

- Statement 2 creates a `double` variable named `valueB` containing `1.1`;

- Statement 3 subtracts `valueB` from `valueA` and stores the answer in a variable named `difference`;

- Statement 4 sends the `difference` variable value to the **Output** window.

Instead of resulting in an answer of 0.9, you will see 0.8999999999999999. This is not a bug with Java. It is instead an artefact of the way the `double` type is implemented as a floating-point value, and the same issue exists with the `float` primitive type.

The solution is to store financial value fields as type `BigDecimal`. This is a Java supplied class that exists within the package `java.math`, and it allows you to specify the exact number of decimal places required and what rounding rules should apply. A short demonstration follows (you will need to import `java.math.*` if you want to try this):

```
// Calculation with BigDecimal
BigDecimal valueX = new BigDecimal("2.0");      // statement 1
BigDecimal valueY = new BigDecimal("1.1");      // statement 2
BigDecimal result = valueX.subtract(valueY);    // statement 3
System.out.println("Difference = " + result);   // statement 4
```

- Statement 1 instantiates a `BigDecimal` object called `valueX` with the `String`[1] value `2.0`. The `String` is converted internally to a numeric value.

- Statement 2 instantiates a `BigDecimal` object called `valueY` with the `String` value `1.1`.

- Statement 3 performs the subtraction and stores the result in a new `BigDecimal` object called `result`.

- Statement 4 sends the `result` reference to the **Output** window.

The `setScale()` method can be used to specify the number of decimal places and the rounding rule to apply:

```
// Using BigDecimal with setScale()
BigDecimal valueZ = new BigDecimal("123.456");
valueZ = valueZ.setScale(2, RoundingMode.HALF_UP);
System.out.println("valueZ = " + valueZ);
```

- The first argument passed to `setScale()` specifies the number of decimal places required and the second argument the rounding rule

---

[1] It is also possible to pass a `double` to the `BigDecimal` constructor, but this is not recommended since it may result in similar problems as previously demonstrated. When you need to specify a specific value you should pass it as a `String`.

to apply. `RoundingMode.HALF_UP` means round to the nearest neighbour unless it is exactly half way, in which case it will round up. This is generally the most suitable mode to use for financial calculations, although the alternative `RoundingMode.HALF_EVEN` rounds toward the even neighbour when exactly half way may be preferred in some cases[1];

- Note that `BigDecimal` is, like `String`, an immutable class, and therefore the `setScale()` method returns a new `BigDecimal` object rather than modifying its own state. This is why its returned reference is assigned back to the variable `valueZ`.

The output from the above should be:

```
valueZ = 123.46
```

Make sure that package `java.math.*` is imported in the class `ZooKeeper` and then change the instance variable type for salary:

```
package virtualzoo.core;

import java.math.*;

public class ZooKeeper {

    private String name;
    private String address;
    private String email;
    private BigDecimal salary;

}
```

NetBeans contains a useful facility to assist with imports. Delete the above `import` statement and notice that an error glyph appears to the left of the `private BigDecimal salary;` statement. If you hover over this it will state that it cannot find the the `BigDecimal` symbol, so click with your mouse and select from the resulting pop-up the option to **Add import for java.math.BigDecimal**. The `import` statement will be added for you.

---

1   This is known as "Bankers rounding".

An alternative approach, especially useful if you have several such imports needed, is to right-click somewhere in the source code editor and select **Fix Imports** from the pop-up menu. You will note, however, that it imports the specific class rather than using the wild-card import.

You will now define a constructor that requires arguments for all four attributes:

```
package virtualzoo.core;

import java.math.BigDecimal;

public class ZooKeeper {

    private String name;
    private String address;
    private String email;
    private BigDecimal salary;

    public ZooKeeper(String myName, String myAddress, String myEmail,
                                    BigDecimal mySalary) {
        name = myName;
        address = myAddress;
        email = myEmail;
        salary = mySalary;
    }

}
```

You need to create setter and getter methods for each of these attributes:

```
package virtualzoo.core;

import java.math.BigDecimal;

public class ZooKeeper {

    private String name;
    private String address;
    private String email;
```

```
    private BigDecimal salary;

    public ZooKeeper(String myName, String myAddress, String myEmail,
                                  BigDecimal mySalary) {
        name = myName;
        address = myAddress;
        email = myEmail;
        salary = mySalary;
    }

    public String getName() {
        return name;
    }

    public void setName(String myName) {
        name = myName;
    }

    public String getAddress() {
        return address;
    }

    public void setAddress(String myAddress) {
        address = myAddress;
    }

    public String getEmail() {
        return email;
    }

    public void setEmail(String myEmail) {
        email = myEmail;
    }

    public BigDecimal getSalary() {
        return salary;
    }

    public void setSalary(BigDecimal mySalary) {
        salary = mySalary;
    }

}
```

And finally override the `toString()` method to return the zoo keeper's name:

```
… rest of code omitted …

@Override
public String toString() {
    return getName();
}
```

You can test the `toString()` method (and the constructor) by specifying the following statements in `VirtualZoo`:

```
ZooKeeper alice = new ZooKeeper("Alice Smith", "Some City",
                "alice@example.com", new BigDecimal("20000"));
System.out.println(alice);
```

Note that for the fourth argument (the salary) a new `BigDecimal` object is instantiated itself using a `String` argument. You have to create a `BigDecimal` object because that is the type required on the signature of the `ZooKeeper` constructor. Running the above should result in the following output:

```
Alice Smith
```

Using the keywords "this" and "super"

this

The keyword `this` is used to refer to the current instance, sometimes known as the **receiver** object. You have previously used it when overloading constructors in order to delegate to a different constructor:

```
public Lion(String myName, String myGender) {
    this(myName, myGender, 0);
}
```

The `this` keyword can also be used as a prefix to variables and methods using dot notation in order to explicitly specify that the variable or method refers to the current object. Take a look at the three-argument constructor in `Animal`:

```
public Animal(String myName, String myGender, int myAge) {
    name = myName;
    gender = myGender;
    age = myAge;
    dateAdmitted = new Date(); // today's date is assumed
}
```

You will note that the argument variable names are different to the instance variable names (e.g. the argument variable reference `myName` is assigned to the instance variable reference `name`).

However, it is quite permissible, and also fairly common, for argument variable names to be given the same name as their instance variable counterparts; in this event, the constructor signature above would now look like this:

```
public Animal(String name, String gender, int age) {
```

If you make the above changes you would naturally need to modify their assignment to their instance variable counterparts, but look how this would appear in the case of the name attribute:

```
name = name;
```

So which version of `name` is being referenced above, the argument variable or the instance variable? In fact, when an argument variable has the same name as an instance variable, the argument variable *hides* the instance variable, so the answer to the above question is that it is the *argument* variable `name` which is being referenced, and the instance variable is not touched at all.

The solution is to prefix the keyword `this` to the variable name using dot-notation in order to tell Java to use the instance variable. Therefore change the above statement to:

```
this.name = name;
```

What the above will do is assign the *argument* variable reference `name` to the *instance* variable reference `name`; the `this` keyword lets you distinguish between the two.

Now modify the remainder of the constructor so that is looks like this:

```
public Animal(String name, String gender, int age) {
    this.name = name;
    this.gender = gender;
    this.age = age;
    dateAdmitted = new Date(); // today's date is assumed
}
```

Note the following:

- If the keyword `this` is not used then Java refers to the local argument variable instead of the instance variable;

- If there is no local argument variable having the same name as an instance variable then `this` is implied and is not required to be specified, such as `dateAdmitted`, above.

You could also change the `setName()` methods argument name to be the same as the instance variable `name`, requiring the use of the `this` keyword:

```
public void setName(String name) {
    this.name = name;
}

public void setName(String name, String nickName) {
    setName(name + " (also known as " + nickName + ")");
}
```

And you could change the `setGender()` and `setAge()` methods to do the same, although this would only be for the sake of consistency – not something required by Java.

```
public void setGender(String gender) {
    this.gender = gender;
}

public void setAge(int age) {
    this.age = age;
}
```

Note that you could change the getter methods to specify the `this` keyword as follows:

```
public String getName() {
    return this.name;
}
```

However, remember that in the absence of an argument variable with the same name the `this` keyword is not required, and normal practice is not to include it unless it is required.

super

The keyword `super` is used when you want to refer to an instance variable, instance method or constructor that is in a superclass of the current instance. You have previously used `super` in the `Lion`, `Monkey` and `Penguin` classes so that they invoke the correct constructor of their superclass, `Animal`. For example, in `Lion`:

```
public Lion(String myName, String myGender, int myAge) {
    super(myName, myGender, myAge);
}
```

In constructors, a call to `super()` (passing no arguments) is implied if you do not specify it, so the three-argument `ZooKeeper` constructor could be written as:

```
public ZooKeeper(String name, String address, String email) {
    super();
    this.name = name;
    this.address = address;
    this.email = email;
```

```
}
```

Note the following:

- `super()` invokes the constructor of the superclass.

- `super()` is implied; if you don't specify it Java will invoke it for you.

- You can pass arguments to `super()` as long as there is a constructor taking that combination of arguments in a superclass.

- If your constructor invokes `this()` then `super()` is not invoked.

- If you specify either `this()` or `super()` then it must be the first statement inside the constructor.

It is also common to use `super` when overriding a method. For example, suppose in class `Lion` you decide to suffix the lion's name with some additional text; you could override the `getName()` method as follows:

```
... Inside the Lion class ...

@Override
public String getName() {
    return super.getName() + " the lion";
}
```

The statement `super.getName()` invokes the `getName()` method of this class's superclass (which in this case, is `Animal`). The `String` that returns (such as "Leo"). then has the text " the lion" appended to it. Therefore, if you invoke the `getName()` method upon an object of type `Lion` it will return "Leo the lion" rather than just "Leo".

The application developed in this book does not require the `getName()` method of `Lion` to be overridden, so please remove the above code if you entered it.

A class to model a visitor to the zoo

To model a zoo visitor let's assume you establish that only three pieces of information are required; their name, email address and the animal they are sponsoring, although they might not be sponsoring one. Create a Visitor class in `virtualzoo.core` with these as instance variables:

```
package virtualzoo.core;

public class Visitor {

    private String name;
    private String email;
    private Animal sponsoredAnimal;

}
```

You will note that the `sponsoredAnimal` variable is declared to be of type Animal. This will enable it to hold any `Animal` object, i.e. any of the subclasses `Lion`, `Monkey` or `Penguin`.

NetBeans includes facilities to generate code based on your instance variables, and uses the `this` keyword in its generated code. In the Visitor class right-click on the source code area at the point where you want the constructor to be and select **Insert Code...**, followed by **Constructor...**

In the **Generate Constructor** dialog ensure all of the instance variable check-boxes are checked and click **Generate**:

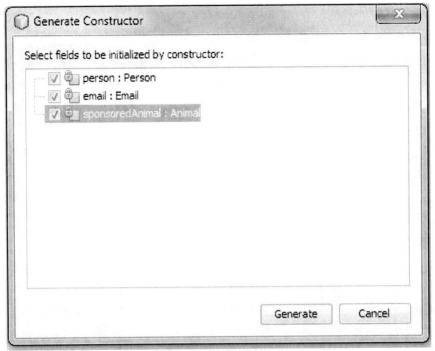

Figure 4.3: NetBeans Generate Constructor dialog

NetBeans will generate the following code:

```
public Visitor(String name, Email email, Animal sponsoredAnimal) {
    this.name = name;
    this.email = email;
    this.sponsoredAnimal = sponsoredAnimal;
}
```

Immediately after the constructor right-click the source code again, select **Insert Code...** followed by **Getter and Setter...**

Ensure the check-boxes are all checked and click **Generate** to produce the necessary methods. The source file should now look as follows:

```
package virtualzoo.core;

public class Visitor {

    private String name;
```

```
private String email;
private Animal sponsoredAnimal;

public Visitor(String name, String email, Animal sponsoredAnimal){
    this.name = name;
    this.email = email;
    this.sponsoredAnimal = sponsoredAnimal;
}

public String getEmail() {
    return email;
}

public void setEmail(String email) {
    this.email = email;
}

public String getName() {
    return name;
}

public void setName(String name) {
    this.name = name;
}

public Animal getSponsoredAnimal() {
    return sponsoredAnimal;
}

public void setSponsoredAnimal(Animal sponsoredAnimal) {
    this.sponsoredAnimal = sponsoredAnimal;
}

}
```

You can also use the code generator to generate a `toString()` method, although you should modify it to be as follows:

```
@Override
public String toString() {
    return getName();
}
```

Java interfaces

A Java **interface** (not to be confused with a user interface) is similar to a class in that it defines a named **type** that has a group of related method specifications. In an interface, however, there are no method bodies, that is, there is no code provided for the methods and there are no instance variables.

Interfaces are used to provide a reusable type that formalises what an object can do. They are also a means of overcoming the restrictions of Java of only being able to extend one class (through inheritance), since a class may **implement** any number of interfaces.

In your zoo application, the administrator envisages sending out email newsletters to both zoo keepers and visitors. The pertinent information needed in order to send out the email is simply the email address. Both the ZooKeeper class and the Visitor class have an email attribute, but the classes are independent.

You will now define a ZooAdministrator class in virtualzoo.core with a method called sendEmail() which takes a ZooKeeper object as its argument:

```
package virtualzoo.core;

public class ZooAdministrator {

    public void sendEmail(ZooKeeper zooKeeper) {
        System.out.println("Sending email to " + zooKeeper.getEmail());
    }

}
```

Note that you won't write any code to actually send emails, but just send some text to the **Output** window to simulate the process[1].

> Note also that in the ZooAdministrator class you have not defined a constructor. When this happens, Java will automatically assume that a public

---

1   There is an optional additional download called JavaMail that can be used for email management, but this is beyond the scope of this book.

constructor exists that takes no arguments and performs no action other than to invoke the no-arg constructor of its superclass. In other words, not specifying any constructor has the same effect as if you had specified the following constructor:

```
public ZooAdministator() {
    super();
}
```

In `VirtualZoo` enter the following statements:

```
// Create an administrator
ZooAdministrator admin = new ZooAdministrator();

// Create a zoo keeper
ZooKeeper alice = new ZooKeeper("Alice Smith", "Some City",
            "alice@example.com", new BigDecimal("20000"));

// Get the administrator to send an email to Alice
admin.sendEmail(alice);
```

Now suppose you have a visitor to whom an email should also be sent:

```
// Create a visitor
Visitor mary = new Visitor("Mary", "mary@example.com");

// Try to send Mary an email
admin.sendEmail(mary); // WON'T COMPILE
```

Java will not compile the class since the `sendEmail()` method only allows objects of type `ZooKeeper` to be passed as the argument. One solution would be to overload the `sendEmail()` method in `ZooAdministrator`, as follows:

```
public class ZooAdministrator {

    public void sendEmail(ZooKeeper zooKeeper) {
        System.out.println("Sending email to " + zooKeeper.getEmail());
    }
```

```
// DON'T DO THIS...
public void sendEmail(Visitor visitor) {
    System.out.println("Sending email to " + visitor.getEmail());
}

}
```

The above would work, but imagine that potentially there could be many otherwise unrelated classes with an email address attribute; you would have to define a new overloaded method for each class type.

A Java **interface** provides a neat solution to this. You can think of an interface as defining a capability (or set of capabilities) which you can add to a class's current capabilities. Using NetBeans, right-click on the virtualzoo.core package node and select **New | Java Interface...**, calling it Emailable[1]:

```
package virtualzoo;

public interface Emailable {

}
```

Note that the keyword **interface** is used where you have previously used **class**. Now enter the following method specification:

```
package virtualzoo.core;

public interface Emailable {

    public String getEmail();    // recipient's email address

}
```

As mentioned at the start of this section, method declarations in an interface have no bodies – they simply end in a semi-colon. To make use of the Emailable interface, modify the class declarations of both ZooKeeper and Visitor as follows:

---

1   Because interfaces are ofen used to add capabilities they are frequently named ending in "ible" or "able", although this is not a requirement of Java.

Firstly in `ZooKeeper`:

```
public class ZooKeeper implements Emailable {
```

And also in `Visitor`:

```
public class Visitor implements Emailable {
```

The `implements` keyword means that these classes now <u>must</u> include the method `getEmail()`, as was specified in the interface. You might want to think of an interface as being a kind of "contract", that implementing classes agree to abide by. Each implementing class can implement the required method(s) however they see fit, the only requirement is that they do so in some way.

As it happens, both `ZooKeeper` and `Visitor` already have defined a method called `getName()` so no further action is needed in these classes. However, to show you how the contract holds, try removing this method – you will find that Java will no longer compile these classes since they no longer abide by the "contract".

The final step is now to modify `ZooAdministrator` to take advantage of the interface. You now only need one `sendEmail()` method, and it takes an argument of type `Emailable`:

```
public class ZooAdministrator {

    public void sendEmail(Emailable emailable) {
        System.out.println("Sending email to " + emailable.getEmail());
    }

}
```

The `VirtualZoo` class will now send the email to both Alice and Mary, even though one is a zoo keeper and the other is a visitor. They are, however, now both `Emailable`.

Despite the apparent simplicity of interfaces they are in fact a very powerful feature of Java, especially when you consider that a single class may implement any number of them. You will see this done in a later chapter.

Using ZooAdministrator to manage the zoo

From this point in the book you will start to make more use of the `ZooAdministrator` class by using it to store example animals, zoo keepers, visitors, etc.

The `VirtualZoo` class, which is the entry point into the project, will be modified to simply instantiate a `ZooAdministrator` object and invoke certain of its functions. Later in the book, `VirtualZoo` will instead instantiate a graphical user interface which you will develop and which will allow manipulation of the various aspects of the zoo.

ZooAdministrator

Define new instance variables in the `ZooAdministrator` class to store some example zoo keepers and visitors:

```
private ZooKeeper alice, bob, charles;
private Visitor mary, peter, richard, tanya;
```

- The syntax rules of Java allow you to specify more than one instance variable as part of the same statement where each is separated by a comma, provided the variables are all of the same type. Hence:

  ○ `alice`, `bob` and `charles` will each be separate `ZooKeeper` objects; and

  ○ `mary`, `peter`, `richard` and `tanya` will each be separate `Visitor` objects.

Create a new `private` helper method called `createExampleZooKeepers()` to instantiate the zoo keepers:

```
private void createExampleZooKeepers() {
    alice = new ZooKeeper("Alice Smith", "Some City",
                "alice@example.com", new BigDecimal("20000"));
    bob = new ZooKeeper("Bob Jones", "2 The Road",
            "bob@example.com", new BigDecimal(22000));
    charles = new ZooKeeper("Charles Green", "3 The Avenue",
            "charles@example.com", new BigDecimal(18000));
}
```

- You will need to import the `java.math` package because the above code uses the `BigDecimal` class.

Create a new `private` helper method called `createExampleVisitors()` to instantiate the visitors:

```
private void createExampleVisitors() {
    mary = new Visitor("Mary Roberts", "mary@example.com");
    peter = new Visitor("Peter Harris", "peter@example.com");
    richard = new Visitor("Richard York", "richard@example.com");
    tanya = new Visitor("Tanya West", "tanya@example.com");
}
```

Define a constructor that invokes the two `private` methods you just entered:

```
public ZooAdministrator() {
    createExampleZooKeepers();
    createExampleVisitors();
}
```

VirtualZoo

All the `VirtualZoo` class needs to do for the moment is instantiate a `ZooAdministrator` object. Later, you will then invoke methods upon this object as new functionality is built in order to see the results. You will also define a new `Experiments` class which you can use to enter sample code.

The entire `VirtualZoo` class should look as follows:

```
package virtualzoo;
```

```
import virtualzoo.core.*;

public class VirtualZoo {

    public static void main(String[] args) {
        ZooAdministrator admin = new ZooAdministrator();

        // methods to be invoked on admin will go here...
    }

}
```

In package `virtualzoo` you should now create new class called `Experiments` where you can enter and test temporary code for the remainder of the book:

```
package virtualzoo;

import virtualzoo.core.*;

public class Experiments {

    public static void main(String[] args) {
        // experimental code will go here...
    }
}
```

5. Static Members, Constants and Conditionals

The static keyword enables you to define a variable or method that is not dependent upon any particular object. A constant is a variable whose value cannot be changed after it has been initialised. Conditional statements allow you to control when certain parts of your code are executed depending on whether a certain condition is met. Casting refers to the process of converting between compatible types.

In this chapter you will learn:

- *How to use static members;*

- *How to define constants;*

- *How to write conditional code;*

- *What casting is and how to use it.*

Static variables & methods

Sometimes it is useful to have a variable and/or method that is not associated with any particular instance of a class, either because it makes sense to "share" it among all instances or because it doesn't require an instance for its existence.

Suppose you want to keep a count of the combined age of all of the animals in the zoo. You could either calculate this externally to the Animal class or make it an integral facility of the class itself. The latter approach can be achieved by defining a **static** variable inside Animal which will be called combinedAge. Static variables are also known as **class variables**, because they relate to the class as whole rather than to any particular instance.

It is common to declare static variables before the instance variables, so insert the statements below marked in bold:

```
public abstract class Animal {

    // Static variables
    private static int combinedAge;

    // Declare instance variables to hold an animal's attributes
    .. rest of code ommitted ..
```

Note the following:

- The `combinedAge` variable is defined as `static` meaning it is "shared" among all instances, and there need not even be any instances – the variable will still exist;

- It is defined as `private` to prevent other objects outside of this class from gaining direct access to it;

- Because it declared to be the primitive type `int` its default value will be zero.

You should now insert a line at the end of the constructor to add the age of the animal in the process of being created to the value of the static variable named `combinedAge`:

```
public Animal(String name, String gender, int age) {
    this.name = name;
    this.gender = gender;
    this.age = age;
    dateAdmitted = new Date(); // today's date is assumed

    // Add this animal's age to the combined age total
    combinedAge = combinedAge + this.age;

}
```

- Each instance, both within constructors and methods, has access to its `static` variables;

- The value of `combinedAge` is added to `this.age` to obtain a new total. This new total is then stored back inside variable `combinedAge`;

- There is a short-cut technique which can be used to add the age into the total, so you could replace the statement to be as follows:

```
combinedAge += this.age;
```

Because the variable is `private` you need to define a `public` getter method, which in this case you will call `getCombinedAge()`:

```
// Static methods
public static int getCombinedAge() {
    return combinedAge;
}
```

- The method is defined using the `static` keyword because it makes use of a `static` variable. In fact, instance methods can also make use of `static` variables so the method does not have to be marked as `static`. However, making it `static` has the benefit that client objects can invoke the method without needing to create any `Animal` object first, as you will see shortly.

To reference the method in other objects you should prefix the method name with the name of the class the method exits within. Define the following code in the `main()` method of `Experiments`:

```
// At this point no animals have been created
System.out.println("Combined age = " + Animal.getCombinedAge());

// Now create an animal aged 3
Animal leo = new Lion("Leo", "m", 3);
System.out.println("Combined age = " + Animal.getCombinedAge());

// Create another animal aged 4
```

```
// Constants
public static final String MALE = "m";
public static final String FEMALE = "f";

... rest of class omitted ...
```

- The variables are defined as `final`, which prevents their references from being changed after being initially set, and because the `String` class is immutable it is this which effectively makes them "constant";

- Because these constants can never change value it is safe to make them `public`. In fact, it is useful to do so as you will see shortly;

- They are defined as `static` because you only need one value which can be shared by all the animals. If you omit the `static` keyword then each instance would have its own copy of the same value, which would be wasteful of memory;

- Java naming conventions are that constant names are defined in upper-case, i.e. MALE and FEMALE;

- The value ("m" or "f") is assigned as part of the declaration. Had this not been done the `String` would default to `null` and it would be impossible to change thereafter (because it is a constant!);

- To use the constants in client objects you need to prefix the class name to the variable name (e.g. `Animal.MALE` or `Animal.FEMALE`). Within the `Animal` class itself you don't need to include the prefix since it is implied.

You can now make use of the constant as follows:

```
Animal leo = new Lion("Leo", Animal.MALE, 3);
leo.setGender(Animal.FEMALE);
```

Hopefully you can see that this makes it more obvious to the reader that you are referring to a gender. The solution is not perfect, however, since there is nothing to stop client objects from still passing "m" or "f" directly.

Also, client objects could still pass a nonsensical value such as "x", "abcdef" or "silly" because the argument type will accept any String. This will be addressed in the next section.

Using an enum for constants

You will commonly see the above technique of static final variables to define constants, including in the Java APIs. However, since Java version 5, a new and more powerful way of defining constants has been available, known as an **enum** (short for enumerated type). Enums are types in their own right (like classes and interfaces), so you should remove the following statements in Animal since they are no longer needed:

```
// Constants
public static final String MALE = "m";
public static final String FEMALE = "f";
```

At the location where those constants were defined, declare the following lines instead:

```
// Define enum called Gender
public enum Gender {MALE, FEMALE};
```

Note the following:

- It is public because it contains only constants and is therefore safe for use outside of this class.

- The keyword enum is a "type" (in the same way that that classes and interfaces are "types");

- The name Gender follows the standard naming convention for types.

- The constants follow standard naming conventions for constants, i.e. are capitalised.

You can now modify the Animal class to change the gender instance variable type from String to Gender:

```
private Gender gender;       // the animal's gender
```

You also need to modify the constructor to specify `Gender` in place of `String` for the second argument type:

```
public Animal(String name, Gender gender, int age) {
    this.name = name;
    this.gender = gender;
    this.age = age;
    dateAdmitted = new Date(); // today's date is assumed

    // Add this animal's age to the combined age total
    combinedAge += this.age;
}
```

You need to modify the `getGender()` and `setGender()` methods in a similar manner:

```
// Return the animal's gender
public Gender getGender() {
    return gender;
}

// Change the animal's gender
public void setGender(Gender gender) {
    this.gender = gender;
}
```

It would be useful for client objects to check whether an animal is male or female without having to invoke `getGender()` and do the check themselves. Define the following two methods in the `Animal` class:

```
public boolean isMale() {
    return gender.equals(Gender.MALE);
}

public boolean isFemale() {
    return gender.equals(Gender.FEMALE);
}
```

- The `equals()` method is defined in `Object` and is therefore inherited by all classes. It serves to compare two objects to determine whether or not they are "equal" to each other, returning a `boolean` result. The `equals()` method for any `enum` compares whether the constant values are the same. You will learn more about the `equals()` method in Chapter 9, since it plays an important role in Java.

Finally, you need to modify the constructors with the `Animal` subclasses `Lion`, `Monkey` and `Penguin` to specify `Gender` instead of `String`. For example, in class `Lion`:

```
public Lion(String myName, Gender myGender) {
    this(myName, myGender, 0);
}

public Lion(String myName, Gender myGender, int myAge) {
    super(myName, myGender, myAge);
}
```

> Ensure you also modify `Penguin` and `Monkey` in the same way as above.

Client objects (such as `Experiments`) now specify the `enum` for the gender:

```
Animal leo = new Lion("Leo", Animal.Gender.MALE, 3);
leo.setGender(Animal.Gender.FEMALE);
```

Note the syntax above. You can read this as; use the `MALE` (or `FEMALE`) constant which exists within the `Gender` enum type, which in turn exists within class `Animal`.

Java will now ensure that only a valid `Gender` constant is supplied as argument values, so you can no longer supply nonsensical values as was the case previously.

Using an enum independently

Because an enum is a type in its own right you can define them independently rather than having to exist only within another class. Consider whether you think the gender constants could be useful in more than just animals? It seems likely that it could serve use elsewhere, such as to record the gender of the zoo keepers or visitors (even though this is not currently recorded).

Therefore, you will now extract the Gender enum from inside the Animal class and make it a file in its own right.

First, remove the following lines from the Animal class:

```
// Define enum called Gender
public enum Gender {MALE, FEMALE};
```

Right-click on the virtualzoo.core package node and select **New | Other...** ensure **Java** is highlighted under **Categories** and select **Java Enum...** under **File Types**. Click **Next >**, enter Gender as the class name. Click **Finish**.

Complete the source code so that it looks as follows:

```
package virtualzoo.core;

public enum Gender {

    MALE, FEMALE;

}
```

The Animal class will now locate the Gender enum from its separate location without any further modifications. Also, no further changes are needed to Lion, Monkey or Penguin – when the classes are recompiled they will locate the Gender enum in its separate file.

You do, however, need to make a small change in `VirtualZoo`, since the enum is no longer defined inside `Animal`:

```
Animal leo = new Lion("Leo", Gender.MALE, 3);
leo.setGender(Gender.FEMALE);
```

> It is possible to do much more with enums than merely defining constants – you can also define instance variables, constructors and methods.

Logical operators and the "if" statement

Frequently in programming you need to check whether a certain condition is true, and perform different processing if the condition holds to when the condition does not hold. Java provides the `if` statement to help you achieve this:

There are several logical operators used primarily to compare **primitives**:

==	Equal to (note the double equal signs)
!=	Not equal to
<	Less than
<=	Less than or equal to
>	Greater than
>=	Greater than or equal to

The comparison operator from the above table to take particular note of is ==, where there are two consecutive equal symbols, and which means to check whether one value is equal to another value. A common mistake among beginners is to confuse this with the single equals operator = you used previously, and which means assignment.

- *Single equals sign means assignment;*

- *Double equals sign means comparison.*

The Java `if` statement is used to test whether a particular condition holds, where the conditional expression resolves to a `boolean` value of either `true` or `false`:

```java
// Using if for conditional statements
int a = 3;
int b = 4;

if (a == b) {
    System.out.println("a is equal to b");
}

if (a != b) {
    System.out.println("a is not equal to b");
}

if (a < b) {
    System.out.println("a is less than b");
}

if (a <= b) {
    System.out.println("a is less than or equal to b");
}

if (a > b) {
    System.out.println("a is greater than b");
}

if (a >= b) {
    System.out.println("a is greater than or equal to b");
}
```

Braces are used to demarcate a block of code that will be executed if the condition is met. In the above example, because variable `a` is 3 and variable `b` is 4, the three blocks marked in bold will be executed because the `if` conditions return `true`:

- a is not equal to b: `(a != b);`
- a is less than b: `(a < b);`
- a is less than or equal to b: `(a <= b).`

The other `if` conditions will return `false` and therefore the code inside those blocks will not be executed.

The above operators will work for any numeric primitive type: `byte`, `short`, `int`, `long`, `float`, `double` and `char`.

If your `if` condition is comparing two `booleans` you can only use `==` and `!=`:

```
// Using if with booleans
boolean sunny = true;
boolean raining = false;

if (sunny == true) {
    System.out.println("It is sunny");
}

if (sunny == false) {
    System.out.println("It is not sunny");
}

if (sunny != true) {
    System.out.println("It is not sunny");
}

if (sunny != false) {
    System.out.println("It is sunny");
}

if (sunny == raining) {
    System.out.println("It is either sunny and raining" +
                    " or not sunny and not raining");
}
```

```
if (sunny != raining) {
    System.out.println("It is either sunny and not raining" +
                       " or not sunny and is raining");
}
```

> If you only need to execute one statement when the condition is met then the braces are optional:
> ```
> if (sunny == true) System.out.println("It is
> sunny");
> ```
>
> However, for clarity it is suggested that you always include the braces:
> ```
> if (sunny == true) {
>     System.out.println("It is sunny");
> }
> ```

You can abbreviate boolean comparisons to remove the second operand, for example:

```
if (sunny)
```

Is equivalent to saying:

```
if (sunny == true)
```

You can use the ! (read as "not") symbol to negate the comparison, hence:

```
if (! sunny)
```

Is equivalent to saying:

```
if (sunny == false)
```

Examples in use:
```
// if statement with implied test for true
if (sunny) {
    System.out.println("It is sunny");
}
```

```
// if statement with implied test for false
if (! sunny) {
    System.out.println("It is not sunny");
}
```

Compound operators

If you need to test more than one condition at the same time you can use the **logical and** operator && or the **logical or** operator ||:

```
// Compound operators
int i = 3;
int j = 4;
double x = 8.4;
double y = 9.7;

// Logical and: both must be true
if ((i < j) && (x > y)) {
    // the first comparison is true and the second is false
    // therefore the final result is false and this block of
    // code will not be entered.
    System.out.println("Should not be output");
}

// Logical or: either (or both) must be true
if ((i < j) || (x > y)) {
    // the first comparison is true and the second is false
    // therefore the final result is true and this block of
    // code will be entered.
    System.out.println("Should be output");
}
```

Both of the above operators only make the second comparison if the first one does not preclude the final result. For example, in the first example above, had i not been less than j then the second comparison of x and y would not have taken place, since it would not affect the final outcome. Similarly, in the second example above, because i is less than j there is no need to test x and y.

Your condition expression may include several compound tests, and you can also include the ! symbol to negate the test:

```
// Using ! with compound comparisons
boolean sunny = true;
boolean raining = false;
boolean cold = false;
boolean windy = true;

if (sunny && !raining && !cold && windy) {
    System.out.println("It is sunny, not raining, " +
                        "not cold and is windy");
}
```

> Java also includes the logical operators & (for **and**) and | (for **or**) where they each always test all parts of the comparison, even if it is unnecessary. It is recommended that you use && and || for your comparisons.

If you have methods that return a boolean these can also be used as the conditional expression:

```
private int temperature = 27;

public boolean isHot() {
    return (temperature >= 25);
}

public void weatherCheck() {
    if (isHot()) {
        System.out.println("It is hot");
    }
}
```

To negate a conditional for a method you can prefix the ! symbol:

```
if (! isHot()) {
    System.out.println("It is not hot");
}
```

The if... else... statement

You can use the `else` statement when you need to specify what should happen if the condition is <u>not</u> met. For example, you could modify the `weatherCheck()` method above:

```
public void weatherCheck() {
    if (isHot()) {
        System.out.println("It is hot");
    } else {
        System.out.println("It is not hot");
    }
}
```

You can also use `else` to test several alternate conditions:

```
public String whatShouldIWear(int temperature) {
    String clothing;

    if (temperature < 2) {
        clothing = "winter coat";

    } else if (temperature < 10) {
        clothing = "wooly jumper";

    } else if (temperature < 15) {
        clothing = "suit";

    } else if (temperature < 21) {
        clothing = "t-shirt";

    } else if (temperature < 27) {
        clothing = "shorts";

    } else {
        clothing = "suncream";
    }

    return clothing;
}
```

The following snippet shows an example of using the above method:

```
String myClothes = whatShouldIWear(23);
// myClothes should contain "shorts"
```

The ternary operator

There is a short-cut technique you can sometimes use in place of simple if...else... blocks. Consider the following code:

```
int temperature = 27;
String weather = "?";
if (temperature > 25) {
    weather = "hot";
} else {
    weather = "not hot";
}
```

The ternary operator allows you to combine the comparison with the assignment thus:

```
// Using ternary operator
int temperature = 27;
String weather = temperature > 25 ? "hot" : "not hot";
```

The ternary operator consists of a number of parts:

- A variable to receive the result: i.e. `String weather =`;

- The condition to check: i.e. `temperature > 25`;

- The question mark symbol: `?`;

- The value to assign if the condition is `true`: i.e. the string "hot";

- A colon symbol `:`;

- The value to assign if the condition is `false`: i.e. the string "not hot";

Conditional statements using switch...case...

An alternative structure to `if...else...` is the `switch...case...` block. You can only use this when testing for equality and for the integer primitives (`byte`, `short`, `int`, `long` and `char`) and their wrapper classes (`Byte`, `Short`, `Integer`, `Long` and `Character`), and for `enum` types:

```java
public String dayName(int dayNumber) {
    String name;

    switch (dayNumber) {
        case 0:
            name = "Sunday";
            break;
        case 1:
            name = "Monday";
            break;
        case 2:
            name = "Tuesday";
            break;
        case 3:
            name = "Wednesday";
            break;
        case 4:
            name = "Thursday";
            break;
        case 5:
            name = "Friday";
            break;
        case 6:
            name = "Saturday";
            break;
        default:
            name = "* unknown *";
    }

    return name;
}
```

Note the following:

- The `switch` statement references a suitable variable to be tested, which in this example is the method argument. You need an opening and closing brace to mark out the entire **switch block**.

- The `case` statement tests whether the variable is equal to the value specified. Note that that this is followed by a colon.

- The line(s) following the `case` are executed if the condition is met.

- You need to specify the `break` statement to prevent the following lines from being executed.

> If you do not specify `break` then the following lines of code will be executed without any further conditional testing!

- The `default` statement is optional. It allows you to specify code to be executed if none of the preceding conditions were met.

Example use:

```
String day = dayName(3);
// day should contain "Wednesday"
```

> While there are many legitimate uses for `if...else...` and `switch...case...` blocks you should be aware that their use might possibly be an indication that you have not fully exploited the object-oriented facilities of Java, such as using inheritance and overriding methods.

Enhancements for switch in Java 7

Java 7 enables you to use the `String` type as the subject in a `switch` block:

```
String day = "Monday";

switch (day) {
```

```
    case "Monday":
        // do something for Monday
        break;
    default:
        // some other day
}
```

Casting

You previously learned about the different capacities of the numeric primitive types; i.e. `byte` (8 bits), `short` (16 bits), `int` (32 bits), `long` (64 bits), `char` (16 bits), `float` (32 bits), `double` (64 bits).

The Java compiler is happy for you to copy a value from one of the above to a primitive of a different type provided that the receiving type has a larger capacity:

```
// Casting primitives
byte b = 4;
int i = b; // allowed because int is bigger than byte
```

However, if you attempt to put the value of an `int` into a `byte` (or a `short`) the compiler will complain that the receiving variable might lose precision:

```
int i = 4;
byte b = i; // THIS WILL NOT COMPILE
```

To overcome this you need to **cast** the larger type into the smaller, which is achieved by specifying the receiving type in brackets:

```
int i = 4;
byte b = (byte) i; // This cast will allow compilation
```

In using the above syntax you are effectively telling Java that you are aware of the potential loss of precision and are prepared to accept the consequences. You would only actually get a loss of precision if the value of the `int` variable i falls outside the bounds of `byte`, i.e. either less than -128 or greater than 127.

A similar situation occurs if you want to store a floating-point variable in an integer type, since to do so would lose the decimal places. Hence a cast would be required:

```
double d = 2.8;
int i = (int) d; // i will contain the value 2
```

Casting may also be required for objects. **Implicit casting** you have used previously and can be a useful technique for increasing reuse and reducing maintenance:

```
Animal leo = new Lion("Leo", Gender.MALE, 3);
```

Note that the receiving type for variable `leo` is declared to be `Animal`, but an object of type `Lion` actually gets instantiated. This is allowed because `Lion` is a subclass of `Animal`, or expressed in more everyday language an lion is a kind of animal.

If you now try to assign reference `leo` to a different reference of type `Lion` a cast is required:

```
Lion leo2 = leo; // WON'T COMPILE
Lion leo2 = (Lion) leo; // explicit casting to Lion
```

The cast is effectively telling Java that although you defined reference `leo` to be of type `Animal`, you know that it is in fact a `Lion` reference.

Arithmetic operations on primitives

The arithmetic operators are:

- + for addition: e.g. a + b;

- - for subtraction: e.g. a - b;

- * for multiplication: e.g. a * b;

- **/** for division: e.g. a / b;

- **%** for modulus (i.e. the remainder after division) : e.g. a % b;

- **++** for increment by 1: e.g. a++ or ++a;

- **--** for decrement by 1: e.g. a-- or --a;

Take careful note of how the following calculations are performed:

```
// Division
double d = 3.0 / 4.0;     // d becomes 0.75
int i = 3 / 4;            // i becomes 0 (int has no decimals)
int j = 15 / 2;           // j becomes 7

// if either value is floating point, the result will be as well
double e = 15 / 2.0;      // e becomes 7.5

// here both operands are int so that is computed first
double f = 15 / 2;        // f becomes 7.0

// modulus (remainder after division)
int k = 34 % 5;           // k becomes 4
double g = 3.5 % 2.1;     // f becomes 1.4

// negation
int a = 2;
int b = -a;               // b becomes -2 (- is prefix op rather than
                                                subtraction here)

// precedence rules - use brackets to avoid ambiguity
int p = 3 + (4 * 5);      // p becomes 23
int q = (3 + 4) * 5;      // q becomes 35

// increment & decrement (++, --)
int r = 10;
int s = r++;              // r becomes 11, but s becomes 10...!!!

r = 10;
s = ++r;                  // now both r and s will be 11
```

6. Arrays, Loops and Sorts

Arrays provide a simple means of grouping like objects that they can be processed as a whole. Loops enable you to repeat parts of your code a certain number of times, while sorting enables you to modify the sequence in which groups of objects are processed.

In this chapter you will learn:

- *How to use single-dimensional and multi-dimensional arrays;*

- *How to loop over the elements in an array;*

- *How to sort the elements of an array into a particular sequence.*

Arrays

An **array** is a collection of objects or primitives of a particular type, capable of being referenced by the individual items that comprise that array. Each item in an array, whether an object or a primitive, is known as an **element**. Arrays are specified using square brackets [] with the number of elements required given inside the brackets. The number of elements must be defined before the array is first used, and may not be changed thereafter.

An example of using a primitive array would be If you need to store the average temperature values for each of the twelve months of a year (assuming the temperatures are rounded to the nearest integer), then you could declare and instantiate an array with twelve int elements:

```
// Define array of temperatures for 12 months
int[] monthlyTemperatures = new int[12];
```

- int[] declares that you are defining an array of int primitives;

- `monthlyTemperatures` is the variable name of the array. It is conventional (thought not required) to name variables which represent a collection of items in the plural form;

- `new int[12]` declares that there should be 12 elements in the array;

- Each of the 12 individual elements will default to a value of zero, because that is the default value for `int`.

An example of an object array would be If you wanted to store details of four animals, then you could declare and instantiate an array with four `Animal` elements:

```
// Define array of four Animal objects
Animal[] animals = new Animal[4];
```

- `Animal[]` declares that you are defining an array of `Animal` objects;

- `animals` is the variable name of the array;

- `new Animal[4]` declares that there should be 4 elements in the array;

- Each of the 4 individual elements will default to `null`, i.e. no actual `Animal` objects have been instantiated yet.

To access a particular element within an array you specify the required **index** (that is, its element number) inside square brackets. Index values start from zero and go up to one less than the number of elements:

```
// The following values will each be zero at this stage
int january   = monthlyTemperatures[0];
int february  = monthlyTemperatures[1];
int march     = monthlyTemperatures[2];
int april     = monthlyTemperatures[3];
int may       = monthlyTemperatures[4];
int june      = monthlyTemperatures[5];
int july      = monthlyTemperatures[6];
```

```
int august    = monthlyTemperatures[7];
int september = monthlyTemperatures[8];
int october   = monthlyTemperatures[9];
int november  = monthlyTemperatures[10];
int december  = monthlyTemperatures[11];
```

To change the value of a particular element you reference it using its index. For example, to set the temperature for March to 8 its index will be 2:

```
// Set temperature for March
monthlyTemperatures[2] = 8; // index 2 is third element in array
```

Object arrays are used in the same way but each element is `null` until it is specifically instantiated:

```
// The following references will each be null at this stage.
Animal firstAnimal  = animals[0];
Animal secondAnimal = animals[1];
Animal thirdAnimal  = animals[2];
Animal fourthAnimal = animals[3];
```

You need to instantiate each element as appropriate:

```
// Create objects for each element in animals array
animals[0] = new Lion("Leo", Gender.MALE, 3);
animals[1] = new Monkey("Bonzo", Gender.MALE, 2);
animals[2] = new Penguin("Petra", Gender.FEMALE, 1);
animals[3] = new Penguin("Oswald", Gender.MALE, 4);
```

• Note that for object arrays you can instantiate a subclass of the declared type, as shown above, where each array element is declared as type `Animal` but actually contain a `Lion`, `Monkey` or `Penguin` object.

To invoke a method on an object element of an array, specify the required element number after the variable name:

```
// Get name of first animal in the array
String name = animals[0].getName();
```

If you attempt to access an element of an array using a non-existent index (such as -1 or 4, above) you will receive an ArrayIndexOutOfBoundsException at runtime. Similarly, if you try to access a method of an element of a reference type array before an object has been instantiated for that element you will receive a NullPointerException at runtime. It is the programmer's responsibility to ensure this is prevented.

> The number of elements defined for an array is specified once and cannot be changed thereafter. If you need to change the number of elements you would have to copy each element to a different array, but this might suggest that it would be better to use one of the classes from the Java collections framework, such as ArrayList, rather than using an array.
>
> The Java collections framework will be covered in Chapter 11.

There is a short-cut technique that lets you declare an array together with its values by listing them inside braces and separated by commas:

```java
int[] numbers = {14, 896, -28};
String[] sentence = {"words", "in", "a", "sentence"};
Animal[] pets = {new Lion("Leo", Gender.MALE, 3),
                 new Penguin("Percy", Gender.MALE, 2)};
```

- In each case the first listed item becomes element zero, the second becomes element one, etc;

- Note how you still need to use the new keyword when instantiating each object in the pets example above.

Multi-dimensional arrays

The arrays shown so far are examples of **single-dimensional** arrays, but Java allows you to define arrays with any number of dimensions. For example, to model a two-dimensional array of integer values corresponding to ten rows of 5 columns, you could declare and instantiate an array, and then access elements of it, as follows:

```
// 10 rows, 5 columns
int[][] tabularData = new int[10][5];

// Set value for third row, fifth column
tabularData[2][4] = 123; // remember, indexes start from 0
```

Example class using an array

You will now develop a simple class that uses a single-dimensional array to model a pen that contains a group of animals.

Create a new class in `virtualzoo.core` called `Pen` as follows that declares a constant and three instance variables:

```
package virtualzoo.core;

public class Pen {

    public static final int CAPACITY = 10;

    private String name;
    private Animal[] animals;
    private int nextElementIndex;

}
```

- The `CAPACITY` constant is an `int` that holds the maximum capacity of the pen;

- The `name` instance variable is a `String` to hold the name of the pen (e.g. "Penguin Parade");

- The `animals` instance variable is declared to be an array of `Animal` objects, although at the moment the number of elements the array can hold has not been set;

- The `nextElementIndex` instance variable is a simple `int` whose purpose is to keep track of the next element index number. It will be used when adding a new animal to the pen.

Define a constructor that initialises the name of the pen (from the argument) and number of elements the array can hold:

```
public Pen(String name) {
    this.name = name;
    animals = new Animal[CAPACITY];
}
```

- The above is the equivalent of specifying `animal` = `new Animal[10];`, but using the constant is better practice since the number is liable to be required elsewhere as well, and if you ever need to change the capacity you would only need to change one line of code, that being where the constant is defined;

- The `nextElementIndex` variable is automatically initialised to zero so does not need to be explicitly initialised in the constructor.

When a `Pen` object is instantiated it contains no actual animals, just ten available elements. Therefore, define a method to add an animal to the pen:

```
public void add(Animal animal) {
    if (nextElementIndex < CAPACITY) {
        animals[nextElementIndex] = animal;
        nextElementIndex++;
    }
}
```

- You have defined an `add()` method which requires an argument of type `Animal`, which means it is capable of accepting any type of animal (i.e. any subclass of `Animal`);

- The `if` statement checks whether the next element index is less than the maximum capacity of the pen, in other words that the pen is not already full. Only if there is space will the animal be assigned to the next available slot.

- After the animal is added, the next element index variable is incremented by one ready for the next animal to be added. Note the short-cut technique used of two plus symbols after the variable name. Alternative ways of achieving the same thing would be:

  - `nextElementIndex = nextElementIndex + 1;`

  - `nextElementIndex += 1;`

- If the pen is full the animal is not added and `nextElementIndex` is not incremented.

Define a method that returns the array:

```
public Animal[] getAnimals() {
    return animals;
}
```

- Note the return type requires the square brackets to signify that you are returning an array of `Animals` rather than a single `Animal`.

Client objects will find it useful to know exactly how many animals are in the pen, so define a method which returns this value:

```
public int getCount() {
    return nextElementIndex;
}
```

Define a setter and getter for the `name` attribute:

```
public void setName(String name) {
    this.name = name;
}

public String getName() {
```

```
        return name;
    }
```

Finally, override `toString()`:

```
@Override
public String toString() {
    return name;
}
```

To see how to use the `Pen` class enter the following statements into Experiments:

```
Pen penguinPen = new Pen("Penguin Parade");
penguinPen.add(new Penguin("Petra", Gender.FEMALE, 1));
penguinPen.add(new Penguin("Oswald", Gender.MALE, 2));

System.out.println("The pen is called " + penguinPen.getName();
System.out.println("There are " + penguinPen.getCount() +
                " animals in the pen");
```

- A `Pen` object is created and two `Penguin` objects are added to the pen. Note how the penguins are instantiated directly inside the argument brackets of the `add()` method. You could, of course, have instantiated each penguin on a separate line assigning it to a reference variable, and then pass the variable to the `add()` method;

- The name and number of animals in the pen is then reported.

> To run the above you need to right-click the `Experiments.java` node in the **Projects** window and select **Run File**.

The next question is how to efficiently retrieve the individual animals in a pen, after you retrieve that array using the `getAnimals()` method. When you have items in an array (or other type of collection) you can iterate over them in a loop. This is the subject of the next section.

Using looping constructs with arrays

Java allows four different mechanisms for looping over the elements of an array. Looping is sometimes referred to as **iteration**.

The standard "for" loop

The standard **for** loop is in the following format:

```
for (initialiser; condition; increment) {
    // code to work on each element goes here…
}
```

Note the following:

- The **initialiser** defines a variable (usually of type int) to serve as the index within the loop. It is common to use the identifier i, although more meaningful variable names may be more appropriate in some cases;

- The **condition** is an expression that that involves the identifier specified in the initialiser, and returns a boolean to control whether the loop should continue;

- The **increment** simply changes the value of the initialiser identifier (often just by adding one) for the next pass of the loop.

Example: To iterate over the animals in the pen, first retrieve the array of animals:

```
Animal[] animalsInPen = penguinPen.getAnimals();
```

Now you can iterate over them with the following code:

```
for (int i = 0; i < penguinPen.getCount(); i++) {
    System.out.println(animalsInPen[i]);
}
```

Note the following:

- It is most common when iterating over an array to set the *initialiser* variable (i in this case) to zero, although you may in fact start from any element you wish. The variable i is local to the for block, so it ceases to exist as soon as all of the iterations complete;

- The *condition* checks whether the current value of the initialiser variable is less than the number of animals in the pen, which it can find out using the getCount() method on the pen;

- It is most common to *increment* the initialiser variable by one, but you may increment by any value you wish, or decrement instead if you are iterating in reverse order.

The above loop is only iterating the specific number of times corresponding to the actual number of animals in the pen (making use of the getCount() method), rather than iterating over all ten elements of the array. When you need to iterate over every array element then all arrays have a publicly available length attribute (not method) which will provide that number. Change the above for statement as indicated:

```
for (int i = 0; i < animalsInPen.length; i++) {
```

The above will iterate over all ten array elements, but be aware that you only added two animals to the pen so after the first two elements the remaining eight elements will all be null. To ignore these you would need an extra conditional check, as follows:

```
for (int i = 0; i < animalsInPen.length; i++) {
    if (animalsInPen[i] != null) {
        System.out.println(animalsInPen[i]);
    }
}
```

A better approach would be for the getAnimals() method to only return the array items that aren't null, so modify it as follows:

```
public Animal[] getAnimals() {
    return Arrays.copyOfRange(animals, 0, nextElementIndex);
}
```

> The Arrays class is in package java.util which you will therefore need to import.

The copyOfRange() static method of Arrays returns a new array based on a subset of a given array, using the first and last index range specified in arguments two and three. The check for null is no longer required in the loop:

```
for (int i = 0; i < animalsInPen.length; i++) {
    System.out.println(animalsInPen[i]);
}
```

The "for-each" loop

The "for-each" loop is a simplified version of the standard for loop and follows this format:

```
for (Type variableName : array) {
    // do something with variableName …
}
```

Note the following:

- **Type** must be the same primitive or reference type the array was defined to contain.

- **variableName** will contain the current primitive value or object reference.

- **array** is the name of the array you want to loop over.

You could use the "for-each" looping mechanism to iterate over the animalsInZoo array as in the following method:

```
for (Animal anAnimal : animalsInPen) {
```

```
       System.out.println(anAnimal);
    }
```

In the above, the variable `anAnimal` will contain each array element's `Animal` object reference in turn.

Although the syntax of the "for-each" mechanism is simpler than the standard for loop, the main disadvantage is that you do not now have the element index number during each iteration.

The "while" loop

The `while` looping mechanism repeats a block of code *while* a boolean condition is true, and follows this format:

```
while (condition) {
    // do something...
    // modify condition to avoid infinite loop
}
```

Applied to the `animalsInPen` array you could iterate as follows:

```
int index = 0;
while (index < penguinPen.getCount()) {
    System.out.println(animalsInPen[index]);
    index++;
}
```

Note the following:

- A local `int` variable called `index` is defined before the `while` loop;

- The condition is that the value of `index` must be less than the number of animals in the pen;

- The value of `index` is incremented inside the `while` loop block. Failure to do this would result in an infinite loop;

- It is possible that the code inside the `while` block may not be executed at all if the `boolean` condition is `false` to start with.

The "do-while" loop

The "do-while" loop is similar to the "while" loop except that the conditional check is performed at the end of the block. It follows this format:

```
do {
    // do something
    // modify condition to avoid infinite loop
} while (condition);
```

Applied to the `animalsInPen` array you could do this:

```
int index = 0;
do {
    System.out.println(animalsInPen[index]);
    index++;
} while (index < penguinPen.getCount());
```

The primary difference compared to the normal "while" loop is that "do-while" will always execute the code inside the block at least once, since the conditional check only occurs at the end of the block. You therefore need to reinstate the check for `null`, since if no animals at all are in the pen you need to prevent the access to the first element.

Sorting arrays

The `Arrays` class (which exists in package `java.util`) contains a number of `static` utility methods to facilitate the sorting of arrays.

Sorting primitive arrays

If you need to iterate over an array ensuring that the elements are processed in some particular order then this is straightforward for arrays of primitives. Insert the following code in `Experiments` to declare an array of five `int` primitives with some values assigned for each element:

```
int[] values = new int[5];
values[0] = 17;
values[1] = 12;
values[2] = 24;
values[3] = 97;
values[4] = 3;
```

At the moment if you iterate over the elements they will be output in the same sequence as above:

```
for (int v : values) {
    System.out.println(v);
}
```

To get the values listed in ascending numerical order insert the following statement before the `for` block:

```
Arrays.sort(values);
```

- The `sort()` method of `Arrays` simply sorts the values of the array passed as the argument;

- You will need to import `java.util`.

You will now find the values listed in ascending numerical order.

Sorting object arrays

> You may find this section more challenging as it includes some complex concepts.

You have seen how an array of `int` primitives can be sorted by simply passing the array to the `Arrays.sort()` method. This works because `int` (and the other numeric primitives) have a built-in **natural ordering**, being their numerical value.

However, objects do not have any built-in natural ordering, since they could consist of any user defined attributes, which may themselves be primitives or other objects, and Java cannot predict what the natural ordering of your classes might be. To see what happens if you attempt to sort an array of objects you will return to the array returned from the Pen class:

```
Pen penguinPen = new Pen("Penguin Pen");
penguinPen.add(new Penguin("Petra", Gender.FEMALE, 1));
penguinPen.add(new Penguin("Oswald", Gender.MALE, 2));

Animal[] animalsInPen = penguinPen.getAnimals();
Arrays.sort(animalsInPen);

for (Animal anAnimal : animalsInPen) {
    System.out.println(anAnimal);
}
```

When you run the above you will receive a ClassCastException. This is because, in order to sort an array of objects you need to define its natural ordering by changing the Animal class so that it implements the Comparable interface. This interface specifies a compareTo() method which you must implement, and in which you can write the necessary code to manage the ordering.

Change the class declaration in Animal to implement the Comparable interface:

```
public abstract class Animal implements Comparable<Animal> {
```

Note the following:

- The <Animal> part that immediately follows Comparable is known as the **formal type parameter**. It specifies that you only want to compare the current `Animal` object with other `Animal` objects. It is possible to omit the `<Animal>` part but this is not recommended.

The `compareTo()` method that you need to implement will provide the other `Animal` object to compare against. The method returns an `int` value, which gets interpreted as follows:

- If a negative value is returned, it means the current object should be sorted before the other object;

- If a positive value is returned, it means the current object should be sorted after the other object;

- If zero is returned then the current object and the other object are identical as far as sorting is concerned.

Armed with this knowledge you can now implement the required `compareTo()` method to first sort as follows:

1. Alphabetically by the animal's name;

2. If the names are the same, then by gender;

3. If the genders are the same, then by the animal's ages;

4. If the ages are the same then a tie-breaker is needed – see the later discussion for why.

Ad the following method to `Animal`:

```
@Override
public int compareTo(Animal otherAnimal) {
    // Sort alphabetically by name
    int result = getName().compareTo(otherAnimal.getName());
    if (result != 0) return result;

    // Names are the same, so sort by gender
    // TO DO
}
```

- The method argument must be of type `Animal` due to the fact you specified `Comparable<Animal>` on the class definition;

- The `getName()` method is used to obtain the name attribute of both the current `Animal` and the other `Animal` being compared against. This method returns a `String`, and therefore the `compareTo()` method being used is that defined for the `String` class, and compares the two strings alphabetically;

- If the result is not zero then you know that the two names are different, so you can therefore return straightaway. However if the result is zero then the names are the same so you need to add some additional code to compare the genders.

```
@Override
public int compareTo(Animal otherAnimal) {
    // Sort alphabetically by name
    int result = getName().compareTo(otherAnimal.getName());
    if (result != 0) return result;

    // Names are the same, so sort by gender
    result = getGender().compareTo(otherAnimal.getGender());
    if (result != 0) return result;

    // Genders are the same, so sort by age
    // TO DO
}
```

- This time the `getGender()` method returns the `enum` value of the animals, and therefore the `compareTo()` method being used is that defined for `enums`, which also sorts alphabetically by the constant values;

- If the result is not zero then you know that the two genders are different, so you can therefore return straight away. However if the result is zero then the genders are the same so you need to add some additional code to compare the ages.

```java
@Override
public int compareTo(Animal otherAnimal) {
    // Sort alphabetically by name
    int result = getName().compareTo(otherAnimal.getName());
    if (result != 0) return result;

    // Names are the same, so sort by gender
    result = getGender().compareTo(otherAnimal.getGender());
    if (result != 0) return result;

    // Genders are the same, so sort by age
    result = getAge() - otherAnimal.getAge();
    if (result != 0) return result;

    // If reached here name, gender and age are the same.
    // TO DO
}
```

- The `getAge()` method returns an `int` primitive value, and you cannot invoke methods on primitives. Therefore, a simple subtraction is used to determine whether the ages are the same value;

- If the result is not zero then you know that the two ages are different, so you can therefore return straightaway. However if the result is zero then the ages are the same, and for this class special provision needs to be made to correctly handle this situation.

If all the attributes of the other animal match those of the current animal then you need to ascertain if it is because they both point to the same single object or whether they are two independent objects which just happen to have the same attribute values. The reason you have to check for this is that the `compareTo()` method must be consistent with `equals()`, that is, if two objects are equal according to the `equals()` method then `compareTo()` should return zero; conversely, if two objects are not equal according to the `equals()` method then `compareTo()` should return a non-zero result.

> The `equals()` method is defined within `Object` and is therefore available to all classes through inheritance. By default it compares object identity; that is it returns true if the two object references point to the same object.
>
> The `hashCode()` method is also defined within `Object` and returns an `int` value. This method must be consistent with `equals()`; that is, if some object is equal to the current object according to the `equals()` method then their `hashCode()` methods should return the same value.
>
> You will learn more about these methods in Chapter 9. For now, just be aware that the three methods `equals()`, `hashCode()` and `compareTo()` must return consistent results.

The `equals()` method has not been overridden in `Animal`, so it uses the inherited version which compares object identity. Therefore, the only time the `equals()` method will return `true` is if the object references being compared are in fact pointing to the same single object. In this case, they will also have the same hash code and so `compareTo()` should return zero in order to be consistent. In all other cases the hash codes will be different and `compareTo()` should return a non-zero value, which will match the fact that `equals()` will return `false`. Had the `Animal` object overridden the `equals()` method then the `compareTo()` method would need to be based on only the same attributes as uses within `equals()`.

You can now add the appropriate code to the end of the method:

```
@Override
public int compareTo(Animal otherAnimal) {
    // Sort alphabetically by name
    int result = getName().compareTo(otherAnimal.getName());
    if (result != 0) return result;

    // Names are the same, so sort by gender
    result = getGender().compareTo(otherAnimal.getGender());
    if (result != 0) return result;

    // Genders are the same, so sort by age
```

```
        result = getAge() - otherAnimal.getAge();
        if (result != 0) return result;

        /* If reached here name, gender and age are the same.
         * So that method is consistent with equals() will now
         * sort on hash code.
         */
        return hashCode() - otherAnimal.hashCode();
    }
```

- You just return the result of deducting one hash code from the other. If the result is zero then the it should mean that the two references are in fact the same object, otherwise they must point to two different objects (that just happen to have the same attribute values). In either case, your `compareTo()` method is now consistent with the `equals()` method.

You should now find that the animal objects will be sorted.

You can take a similar approach so that that the natural ordering of `ZooKeeper` is by each zoo keeper's name, and if they happen to be the same then by their email address. Change the `ZooKeeper` class signature to implement `Comparable`:

```
    public class ZooKeeper implements Emailable, Comparable<ZooKeeper> {
```

And define its `compareTo()` method:

```
    @Override
    public int compareTo(ZooKeeper otherZooKeeper) {
        // Sort alphabetically by name
        int result = getName().compareTo(otherZooKeeper.getName());
        if (result != 0) return result;

        // Names are the same, so sort by email
        result = getEmail().compareTo(otherZooKeeper.getEmail());
        if (result != 0) return result;

        /* If reached here name and email are the same.
         * So that method is consistent with equals() will now
         * sort on hash code.
         */
```

```
        return hashCode() - otherZooKeeper.hashCode();
    }
```

The Visitor class can also be made `Comparable`:

```
public class Visitor implements Emailable, Comparable<Visitor> {
```

The natural ordering for the `Visitor` class will also be firstly by name and then by email address:

```
@Override
public int compareTo(Visitor otherVisitor) {
    // Sort alphabetically by name
    int result = getName().compareTo(otherVisitor.getName());
    if (result != 0) {
        return result;
    }

    // Names are the same, so sort by email
    result = getEmail().compareTo(otherVisitor.getEmail());
    if (result != 0) {
        return result;
    }

    // If reached here name and email are the same.
    // So method is consistent with equals() will now sort by hash
    return hashCode() - otherVisitor.hashCode();
}
```

Sorting in alternative sequences

You have seen that making your class implement the `Comparable` interface and implementing its `compareTo()` method lets you define a class's natural (or default) ordering. But what if in addition to this you need an alternative sorting order for a particular purpose?

To define alternative sorting criteria you can create a class which implements a related interface called `Comparator`. This interface specifies a `compare()` method which provides two arguments, being two objects to sort. While you could create a complete new class to implement Comparator there is a facility in Java to define **inner classes**, these being a class which exists inside another class. You would use an inner class when its purpose is directly related in some way such that it is logically part of the same class within which you define it.

Therefore, inside the Animal class, where you would otherwise define a new method, include the following code:

```
// Inner class to sort by age then name
public static class SortByAgeName implements Comparator<Animal> {


}
```

- For readability the code should be indented at the same level as methods;

- This inner class is declared to be static since it doesn't depend on any particular instance. Inner classes do not have to be static, but where they don't depend on a particular instance of the outer class then making it static means it can be instantiated without needing an instance;

- In a similar manner to the Comparable interface, Comparator can have a formal type parameter specified, i.e. <Animal>, to enforce the types of objects which are to be compared.

The Comparator interface requires you to implement the compare() method, which has the following signature:

```
// Inner class to sort by age then name
public class SortByAgeName implements Comparator<Animal> {

    @Override
    public int compare(Animal animal1, Animal animal2) {
        // comparison code will go here...
    }
}
```

You can now enter the following statements to sort firstly by age and then by name. If both are the same, the hash codes are then compared for the same reason as in the `compareTo()` method.

```java
// Inner class to sort by age then name
public static class SortByAgeName implements Comparator<Animal> {

    @Override
    public int compare(Animal animal1, Animal animal2) {
        // Sort by age
        int result = animal1.getAge() - animal2.getAge();
        if (result != 0) return result;

        // Sort by name
        result = animal1.getName().compareTo(animal2.getName());
        if (result != 0) return result;

        /* If reached here age and name are the same.
         * So that method is consistent with equals() will now
         * sort on hash code.
         */
        return animal1.hashCode() - animal2.hashCode();
    }
}
```

You will recall that within `Experiments` you specified the following statement to sort an array based on its natural ordering:

```java
Arrays.sort(animalsInPen);
```

The `sort()` method in the `Arrays` class is overloaded, and can accept a second argument that specifies a `Comparator` object on which to base the sort criteria. Change the above statement as follows:

```java
Arrays.sort(animalsInPen, new Animal.SortByAgeName());
```

Above, the inner class `SortByAgeName` of the `Animal` class is instantiated to provide the `Comparator` object that the `sort()` method will use.

7. Exceptions

Exceptions are Java's way of controlling unexpected occurrences, and which allows you can gain control over what to do in these circumstances.

In this chapter you will learn:

- *What exceptions are and how to use them;*

- *The different categories of exception;*

- *How to define your own exceptions.*

Exceptions

Methods and constructors can throw an **exception** if something occurs which would prevent the normal execution of the program. Several Java supplied classes can throw exceptions if you attempt to do something that is not appropriate. An Exception is actually an object, albeit one that the Java runtime applies special handling for. There are many Java supplied exception classes and you can define your own if need be.

There are three categories of exception that can be thrown by a constructor or by a method:

1. ***Unchecked exceptions***: These refer to situations which you as the programmer could have prevented but didn't do so, such as dividing a number by zero or invoking a method on an object reference that is null (maybe because you have not yet instantiated the object). Because this category of exception is preventable the Java compiler will not force you to handle the exception if you let it occur. It is strongly recommended that you use **defensive programming** techniques to prevent this type of exception occuring (see later example).

2. ***Checked exceptions***: These are situations which you as the programmer cannot prevent and therefore the Java compiler will force you to make provision for. Examples would be trying to open a file that does not exist (maybe because someone deleted the file), or being unable to connect to a remote server because it is unavailable. The Java compiler forces you to use the **exception handling mechanism** for these situations.

3. ***Errors***: These are situations which you as the programmer cannot prevent and that there would be little point in attempting to, such as an execution fault in the JRE or if your program runs out of memory.

Handling unchecked exceptions

To demonstrate the category where an exception can occur but the programmer has not prevented it, enter the following statements:

```
int numerator = 123;
int denominator = 0;

System.out.println("answer = " + (numerator / denominator));
```

If you attempt to run the above you will receive an `ArithmeticException` and the program will stop, due to the fact that division by zero is not a valid mathematical operation.

To use defensive programming, simply check that the denominator value is not zero before doing the calculation:

```
int numerator = 123;
int denominator = 0;

if (denominator != 0) {
    System.out.println("answer = " + (numerator / denominator));
} else {
```

```
            System.out.println("denominator is zero");
    }
```

One of the most common exceptions in this category is `NullPointerException`. Suppose you have the code:

```
ZooKeeper fred = null;
String fredName = fred.getName();
```

You would receive a `NullPointerException` at runtime and the program would stop. You need to prevent the exception by ensuring that either you check for `null` or by instantiating `fred` before attempting to invoke any methods upon it.

Checked exceptions

The `FileReader` class enables you to read from text files, and one of its constructors allows you to pass a `String` argument containing the path and file name you wish to read from. See what happens if you have the following line of code somewhere: *(note: to try this you need to import package **java.io**)*

```
FileReader someFile = new FileReader("filename.txt");
```

Your class will not compile because the `FileReader` constructor can potentially throw the checked exception `FileNotFoundException` (see the Java API documentation), and you have not yet made any provision for this. You can provide for these situations by placing the statements that can throw an exception within a try...catch block, as follows:

```
try {
    FileReader someFile = new FileReader("filename.txt");
} catch (FileNotFoundException ex) {
    System.out.println(ex.getMessage());
}
```

Note the following:

- Inside the `try` block you include the statement(s) which could throw a checked exception.

- If an exception is thrown, any statements following the one that caused the exception will be skipped and execution will pass to the `catch` block.

- The `catch` block specifies the name of the exception class that is being handled (`FileNotFoundException` in the above case), an object of which is assigned to a reference variable (ex in the above case). The code within the `catch` block will be executed.

- If no exception is thrown then the code within the `catch` block is <u>not</u> executed.

If you have a series of statements then it is possible that between them they may throw more than one type of exception. In this case you can either catch them individually (if you need to do something different for each exception should it occur) or catch them all inside a single catch handler:

Continuing the earlier example, after instantiating a `FileReader` object you invoke its `read()` method to return a character from the file. This method can throw a `IOException`:

```
try {
    FileReader someFile = new FileReader("filename.txt");
    int c = someFile.read();
} catch (FileNotFoundException ex) {
    System.out.println(ex.getMessage());
} catch (IOException ex) {
    System.out.println(ex.getMessage());
}
```

The above shows how you can have a separate catch block for each exception. If you look at the Java API for `FileNotFoundException` you will see that it inherits from `IOException`. When this is the case you need to catch the more specialised exception (which in this case is FileNotFoundException) before the more generalised exception (which in this case is IOException). The compiler will not allow you to catch IOException first since it could then never reach the FileNotFoundException block.

What you can do, however, is combine the inherited exceptions into a single catch block when you are performing the same handling code in all cases, as is the case in the above example. You could therefore change the above to the following:

```
try {
    FileReader someFile = new FileReader("filename.txt");
    int c = someFile.read();
} catch(IOException ex) {
    System.out.println(ex.getMessage());
}
```

The above approach works because FileNotFoundException "is a" (i.e. inherits from) IOException, so it will be caught by the latter's catch clause.

With the try...catch mechanism you can optionally add a finally block containing code which will always be executed, whether or not an exception is thrown:

```
FileReader someFile = null;
try {
    someFile = new FileReader("filename.txt");
    int c = someFile.read();
} catch(IOException ex) {
    System.out.println(ex.getMessage());
} finally {
    if (someFile != null) {
        try {
            someFile.close();
        } catch (IOException ex) {
            System.out.println(ex.getMessage());
        }
```

```
        }
    }
```

The `finally` block is frequently used to close opened resources, such as files and network connections. Note in the above example that the `FileReader` object `someFile` needed to be declared prior to the `try` block in order for it to still be in scope inside the `finally` block. Note also that the `close()` method can itself throw an exception, so that needs to be caught too.

It is important that opened resources such as files are closed when you have finished with them in order to ensure that the file is properly updated.

Enhancements in Java 7

If you are using Java 7 you can get the resources that require closing to be automatically taken care of, using a modification to the `try...catch` block. For example, the above example could instead be written as follows:

```
try (FileReader someFile = new FileReader("filename.txt")) {
    int c = someFile.read();
} catch(IOException ex) {
    System.out.println(ex.getMessage());
}
```

If you need multiple files to be automatically closed you can place each of them inside the same brackets of the try statement, where each is separated by a semi-colon.

Another enhancement in Java 7 is the ability to catch multiple exceptions in the same block, which is useful if you want to take the identical action in each case. Here is an example from an earlier part of this chapter:

```
try {
    FileReader someFile = new FileReader("filename.txt");
    int c = someFile.read();
} catch (FileNotFoundException ex) {
    System.out.println(ex.getMessage());
```

```
} catch (IOException ex) {
    System.out.println(ex.getMessage());
}
```

In Java 7 you can use a single catch block with each exception separated by a vertical bar:

```
try {
    FileReader someFile = new FileReader("filename.txt");
    int c = someFile.read();
} catch (FileNotFoundException | IOException ex) {
    System.out.println(ex.getMessage());
}
```

Throwing Exceptions

Instead of catching an exception and handling it in the current method, you could choose to `throw` it back to the client object. You would do this if different clients might need to handle the situation in different ways. If you throw an exception you need to decide whether to throw a checked or an unchecked exception:

> Throw a ***checked*** exception for situations from which the client object or the user can recover from.
>
> Throw an ***unchecked*** exception for programming errors.

If you look at the `Animal` class it currently includes the following method to update the animal's age:

```
public void setAge(int age) {
    this.age = age;
}
```

The method ought to validate the argument value to prevent nonsensical age values from being set, such as a negative or large number. Because the programmer can prevent an invalid value from being passed to the method it would be appropriate to throw an unchecked exception, and the Java supplied `IllegalArgumentException` is ready made for this purpose:

```java
// Change the animal's age
public void setAge(int age) {
    // Ensure new age is between 0 and 50
    if ((age >= 0) && (age <= 50)) {
        this.age = age;
    } else {
        throw new IllegalArgumentException("Age must be 0 - 50");
    }
}
```

- All exceptions allow you to pass a string which can be used to provide helpful information to the client object. In the case of unchecked exceptions, as above, this is useful when debugging the program.

You can see the exception being thrown if you use the following sample code:

```java
Animal leo = new Lion("Leo", Gender.MALE, 5);
leo.setAge(-12);
```

It is also possible for constructors to throw an exception, and noticing that the animal's age is set in the constructor you first might be tempted to invoke the `setAge()` method rather than directly assign the argument value, as follows:

```java
public Animal(String name, Gender gender, int age) {
    this.name = name;
    this.gender = gender;
    setAge(age); // DON'T DO THIS
    dateAdmitted = new Date(); // today's date is assumed

    // Add this animal's age to the combined age total
    combinedAge += this.age;
}
```

You will notice, however, that NetBeans indicates a warning glyph on the `setAge()` statement which if you hover over warns you that you are invoking an overridable method from within a constructor. The reason for this warning is that should any subclass of `Animal` override the `setAge()` method it is possible that there will be uninitialised instance variables. To illustrate this, suppose you define a class called `Dog` where you want the age to be set in "human years" as defined by a multiplier:

```
package virtualzoo.core;

public class Dog extends Animal {

    private int ageMultiplier;

    public Dog(String myName, Gender myGender, int myAge,
                                        int ageMultiplier) {
        super(myName, myGender, myAge);
        this.ageMultiplier = ageMultiplier;
    }

    @Override
    public boolean isEndangered() {
        return true;
    }

    @Override
    public String favouriteFood() {
        return "bone";
    }

    @Override
    public void setAge(int age) {
        super.setAge(age);
        System.out.println("In human years = " +
                            (age * ageMultiplier));
    }

}
```

- The `Dog` class introduces a new instance variable called `ageMultiplier`, which is specified as an additional argument inside the constructor, and assigned within it;

- The `setAge()` method is overridden to output the given age by the multiplier.

Try the following code:

```
Animal fido = new Dog("Fido", Gender.MALE, 2, 7);
System.out.println(fido.getAge());
```

Your intention would be that the output would be 14 (the result of multiplying 2 by 7) but in fact you will receive zero. This is because the superclass constructor of `Dog`, being `Animal`, will be run before the `Dog` constructor, and therefore the `ageMultiplier` instance variable will not be initialised in time.

> The Dog class will not form part of the application in this book and may be deleted from the project if you wish.

Given that the `setAge()` method now performs validation on the age argument, and you have seen that it is inappropriate to invoke an overridable method from the constructor, your next thought might be to duplicate the age validation code inside the constructor. But code duplication is to be avoided wherever possible, so a better approach would be to define a private helper method to perform it:

```
private void validateAge(int age) {
    // Ensure new age is between 0 and 50
    if ((age < 0) || (age > 50)) {
        throw new IllegalArgumentException("Age must be 0 - 50");
    }
}
```

Now you can modify the `setAge()` method to invoke the helper method:

```
public void setAge(int age) {
```

```
    validateAge(age);
    this.age = age;
}
```

Likewise, you can invoke the helper method from the constructor, too:

```
public Animal(String name, Gender gender, int age) {
    validateAge(age);

    this.name = name;
    this.gender = gender;
    this.age = age;
    dateAdmitted = new Date(); // today's date is assumed

    // Add this animal's age to the combined age total
    combinedAge += this.age;
}
```

Creating your own exception classes

It is possible to create an exception class of your own, if you can't find an appropriate Java supplied one to use. As an example, in a later chapter you will develop a user interface where the user can make entries onto various forms. If the user makes an invalid entry you could throw an exception in order to trigger an error message, informing the user of the error so that it can be corrected. You can create your own exception classes simply by inheriting from one of the base Java supplied classes, as follows:

- For a checked exception type, extend Exception or one of its checked[1] subclasses;

- For an unchecked exception type, extend RuntimeException or one of its subclasses.

---

1   Note that RuntimeException is a subclass of Exception so you should not extend that or any of RuntimeExceptions' sub-classes if you want your exception class to be checked.

Because validation is a user recoverable situation you will create a new checked exception class. In package `virtualzoo.core` create a new Java class called `ValidationException` with the following code:

```
package virtualzoo.core;

public class ValidationException extends Exception {

    public ValidationException(String message) {
        super(message);
    }

}
```

- The constructor defined above requires a `String` message to be supplied which will contain the text of the validation error.

You will make use of the `ValidationException` class in a later chapter.

8. Refactoring and Utility Classes

Refactoring refers to the process of improving how you application is internally structured. Utility classes can be defined to provide commonly used services for multiple applications.

In this chapter you will learn:

- *Some basic refactoring techniques;*

- *How to define a utility class.*

Refactoring

To **refactor** a software system means modifying the structure or the code of your classes but without changing any of the functionality, in order to make the system better designed and easier to maintain. This is a natural part of the iterative process of development that is a recurrent theme in this book as you gradually build and improve the zoo application.

If you consider the classes `ZooKeeper` and `Visitor` you will notice that in the real world they are both types of *people*, and thus share certain characteristics. This is borne out just by looking at the attributes in these two classes; they each have an attribute called `name` together with methods `setName()` and `getName()`. Just as you placed the attributes common to different types of animal into an `Animal` class, so it makes sense to define a `Person` class along similar lines. As you will see, however, there will be some subtle differences coming to light.

Utility Classes

When developing any application it makes sense to reuse classes which have already been developed, assuming you can find something suitable, of course. This will save you the time of having to specify, code and test something from scratch, in other words from "reinventing the wheel". By the same token, if you don't find anything readily to hand it is always worth considering whether any of the classes you need to write could themselves be used in future, totally unrelated, applications.

The `Person` class mentioned in the previous section is a perfect candidate for such a case; it is easy to envisage many different types of application, nothing to do with zoos, that could make use of a class that models a person, provided its attributes remain generic. There are potentially several attributes that could form a general-purpose `Person` class, but for simplicity you will define these:

- A `String` object to store the person's name, together with methods `setName()` and `getName()`;

- A `String` object to store the person's address, together with methods `setAddress()` and `getAddress()`;

- A `Gender` object to store the person's gender, together with methods `setGender()`, `getGender()`, `isMale()` and `isFemale()`. For this you can reuse the `Gender` enum you have already developed.

A general-purpose class, such as `Person`, is known as a **utility class**. In fact, `Gender` is also a utility class (enum) since it too could readily be used in many different types of applications. Something that needs to be determined before proceeding though is what package to place utility classes into? While they could be placed into `virtualzoo.core` that would mean that other applications would need to access your entire zoo project when it only requires its utilities. A better approach is to place utility classes not only into an entirely separate package but also into a separate project in its own right. You will begin this process now, firstly by transferring the `Gender` enum out of `virtualzoo.core` and into a new project. After that, you will build the `Person` class, also in the new project.

In NetBeans select **File | New Project...**, ensure **Java** is selected in the **Categories** list and **Java Class Library** is selected in the **Projects** list. Click **Next >**.

For the **Project Name** enter `Utilities` and then click **Finish**. The new project will appear in the **Projects** window, above `VirtualZoo` if you still have that open. You can have multiple projects open in NetBeans concurrently, so if you don't have `VirtualZoo` open then you should open it now.

Right-click on the `Source Packages` node under the `Utilities` project and select **New | Java Package...**, entering `com.example.util` as the **Package Name**, and click **Finish**.

There is a convention when naming packages which could potentially be used in many applications, or whose name is likely to clash with other similar packages, to begin with your domain name in reverse.

If your domain is `example.com` then packages for your organisation should begin `com.example`, which are then suffixed by some other name that describes the system or application being developed. Here, you have used `util` as the suffix as a commonly used abbreviation of "utilities". Hence the full package name is `com.example.util`

If some other vendor of Java classes were to have a package of utilities and which you also needed to use, you should now be able to without a name clash, since the domain prefix should be different.

You now need to move `Gender` into the new project, so right-click on `Gender.java` under the `virtualzoo.core` package of `VirtualZoo` and select **Cut**. Now right-click on the `com.example.util` package node of `Utilities` and select **Paste | Refactor Move...**, upon which a **Move Class** dialog will appear. After your click **Refactor** a warning dialog will appear telling you that there are references in `VirtualZoo` to moved files. You will address this in a moment so click **Refactor** again to perform the move.

If you expand the `com.example.util` package node you will see that `Gender.java` has moved there and has disappeared from `virtualzoo.core`. If you open `Gender.java` you will see that NetBeans has automatically modified the `package` statement to reflect the new package it exists within:

```
package com.example.util;

public enum Gender {

    MALE, FEMALE;

}
```

You will, however, also notice some small red glyphs appearing next to a number of source files under `virtualzoo.core`, since these are the classes that have a reference to `Gender` which can no longer be found. This has occurred even though NetBeans has also automatically updated the `import` statement to reflect the fact that `Gender` has moved package. For example, if you open the `Animal` class you will see the correct `import` statement:

```
import com.example.util.Gender;
```

Had `Gender` been moved to a different package within the same project then all would have been well – the class would have been found. But because it is now in an entirely separate project (so that it can be plugged into multiple applications) you need to attach it to `VirtualZoo`.

Under the `VirtualZoo` project node, scroll to the end where you should see a node called `Libraries`. Click the "plus" icon to expand it, and notice there is currently one entry for `JDK 1.6 (Default)`[1], representing the

---

1   If you are using Java 7 then you will instead see `JDK 1.7 (Default)`.

Java Development Kit that all projects need. Right-click the `Libraries` node and select **Add Project...**, then locate and select the `Utilities` project and click **Add Project Jar Files**. A new entry will appear under the `Libraries` node called `Utilities - dist/Utilities.jar`.

> A JAR file is a "Java Archive". It is a type of ZIP file which consists of all classes that make up a Java project.

You should now notice that the error glyphs next to the various classes in `virtualzoo.core` have disappeared, since the package is now available to your application.

The Person class

Now that you have a separate `Utilities` project containing the `Gender` enum, you can create the class called `Person` in the `com.example.util` package:

```java
package com.example.util;

public class Person {

    // Instance variables
    private String name;
    private String address;
    private Gender gender;

    // Constructors
    public Person(String name) {
        this(name, null);
    }

    public Person(String name, String address) {
        this(name, address, null);
    }
```

```java
public Person(String name, String address, Gender gender) {
    this.name = name;
    this.address = address;
    this.gender = gender;
}

// Copy constructor
public Person(Person person) {
    this.name = person.getName();
    this.address = person.getAddress();
    this.gender = person.getGender();
}

// Instance methods
public String getName() {
    return name;
}

public void setName(String name) {
    this.name = name;
}

public String getAddress() {
    return address;
}

public void setAddress(String address) {
    this.address = address;
}

public Gender getGender() {
    return gender;
}

public void setGender(Gender gender) {
    this.gender = gender;
}

public boolean isMale() {
    return gender.equals(Gender.MALE);
}
```

```
public boolean isFemale() {
    return gender.equals(Gender.FEMALE);
}

@Override
public String toString() {
    return name + ", " + gender + ", " + address;
}
}
```

- Note that in addition to the normal constructors this class has defined a **copy** constructor that takes a `Person` object as its argument. This is useful since `Person` is a mutable class (that is, contains setter methods), and you will see how this is used later in this chapter.

- The `equals()` method, as used within the `isMale()` and `isFemale()` methods, is used to check whether the argument has the same value as the object upon which it is invoked, returning a `boolean`.

With the `Person` class in place, you may naturally assume that you should modify the `ZooKeeper` and `Visitor` classes to each inherit from it, since they are both kinds of `Person`. This is a valid approach, of course, but there is an alternative way of utilising `Person` that you should also consider where instead of using inheritance you use **composition**.

Object composition simply means that one object is "composed of" another object, of a particular type. You have already used this approach several times, in fact. For example, the `Person` class is composed of two `String` objects and a `Gender` object, through its instance variables. Whereas inheritance describes an "is a" (or "is a type of") relationship, composition describes a "has a" (or "comprises") relationship.

You will now see how the two approaches, inheritance and composition, compare when applied to the ZooKeeper class.

> For each option, you need to import the com.example.util package. Before making any changes however, it is suggested that you just read the following sections to understand the relative advantages and disadvantages of the two approaches.

Option 1 – Inheritance

To change ZooKeeper to inherit from Person you have to use the extends keyword on the class header:

```
public class ZooKeeper extends Person implements
                         Emailable, Comparable<ZooKeeper> {
```

You would then need to remove the instance variables for name and address, and their associated methods setName(), getName(), setAddress() and getAddress().

You would then need to change the constructor to pass the name and address arguments to the superclass constructor:

```
public ZooKeeper(String name, String address, String email,
                                    BigDecimal salary){
    super(name, address);
    this.email = email;
    this.salary = salary;
}
```

- Note that because you are inheriting from Person but don't actually need the gender attribute, client objects will be able to invoke the `setGender()` and `getGender()` methods, even though they are not appropriate for zoo keepers.

This illustrates a particular disadvantage of inheritance – you are stuck with the attributes and methods you are inheriting. You could, of course, override the unwanted methods, but what should they do instead? Also, you may have other classes which use `Person` objects and rely on the value of the gender. Consider also the `Visitor` class: as well as not needing to inherit gender it also doesn't need to inherit address.

The main advantage of inheritance is that you don't have to duplicate the instance variables and methods in the subclass, so it does generally result in a smaller, cleaner class.

Option 2 – Composition

To change `ZooKeeper` to use `Person` through composition rather than inheritance you instead define an instance variable for `Person` which can replace the attributes for `name` and `address`:

```
public class ZooKeeper implements Emailable, Comparable<ZooKeeper> {

    private Person person;
    private String email;
    private BigDecimal salary;
```

The constructor needs to replace the two `String` arguments for `name` and `address` with a `Person` object argument:

```
public ZooKeeper(Person person, String email, BigDecimal salary){
    this.person = new Person(person);
    this.email = email;
    this.salary = salary;
}
```

- Note that the copy constructor of `Person` is used to take a defensive copy of the argument, since `Person` objects are mutable. You will recall from Chapter 4 that if you were to directly use a reference to a mutable object it results in a privacy leak.

You would also need to change any client object that instantiates `ZooKeeper` objects to pass a single `Person` object rather than two `String` objects to the constructor.

You need a getter and setter method for the `person` attribute:

```
public Person getPerson() {
    return new Person(person);
}

public void setPerson(Person person) {
    this.person = new Person(person);
}
```

- Both the `getPerson()` and `setPerson()` methods make use of the copy constructor of `Person` rather than directly using a reference to the person object.

You should now remove the `setName()` and `setAddress()` methods since these ar now modifiable through the `setPerson()` method. While you could remove the `getName()` and `getAddress()` retaining them would serve as a convenience for client objects. You would, however, need to modify them to forward to the `person` object, as follows:

```
public String getName() {
    return person.getName();
}

// DELETE setName()
```

```
public String getAddress() {
    return person.getAddress();
}

// DELETE setAddress()
```

The advantage of composition is that you can totally ignore any attributes that aren't needed, such as `gender` in the above case. The method `setGender()` and `getGender()` are simply not available to be invoked. The main disadvantage is that you have to write some forwarding methods to the composed of object for the attributes you do want, although as you can see they are typically very simple.

> It may initially seem counter-intuitive to think of `ZooKeeper` as "having" a `Person` rather than "being" a type of `Person`, but another way to think about it is that is that of a `Person` "taking on the role" of a `ZooKeeper`. Likewise if you use composition in the `Visitor` class, the `Person` is taking on the role of being a `Visitor`.

The discussion in the note-box above leads to a further advantage of composition over inheritance, in that if you declare that `ZooKeeper` and `Visitor` each inherit from `Person` then it is not possible for a particular `Visitor` to ever become a `ZooKeeper`, or for a `ZooKeeper` to ever be a `Visitor`. You would need to instantiate two separate objects (one `ZooKeeper` and one `Visitor`) to model this scenario even though they should be referring to the same person. This limitation does not occur with composition since you can instantiate a single `Person` object and assign it to both a `ZooKeeper` object and to a `Visitor` object. In other words the `Person` is taking on two roles concurrently, that of being both a `ZooKeeper` and a `Visitor`.

Conclusion

Having discussed the two options, a decision needs to be made as to whether to use inheritance or composition. In view of the relative advantages and disadvantage this book takes the view that composition is a slightly preferred approach, and you should now modify the `ZooKeeper` as detailed above and then the `Visitor` class along identical lines.

The modified `ZooKeeper` class should look like this:

```java
package virtualzoo.core;

import java.math.*;
import com.example.util.*;

public class ZooKeeper implements Emailable {

    private Person person;
    private String email;
    private BigDecimal salary;

    public ZooKeeper(Person person, String email, BigDecimal salary){
        this.person = new Person(person); // uses copy constructor
        this.email = email;
        this.salary = salary;
    }

    public Person getPerson() {
        return new Person(person); // uses copy constructor
    }

    public void setPerson(Person person) {
        this.person = new Person(person); // uses copy constructor
    }

    public String getName() {
        return person.getName();
    }

    public String getAddress() {
        return person.getAddress();
```

```
    }

    @Override
    public String getEmail() {
        return email;
    }

    void setEmail(String email) {
        this.email = email;
    }

    public BigDecimal getSalary() {
        return salary;
    }

    void setSalary(BigDecimal salary) {
        validateSalary(salary);
        this.salary = salary;
    }

    @Override
    public String toString() {
        return getName();
    }

    @Override
    public int compareTo(ZooKeeper otherZooKeeper) {
        // Sort alphabetically by name
        int result = getName().compareTo(otherZooKeeper.getName());
        if (result != 0) return result;

        // Names are the same, so sort by email
        result = getEmail().compareTo(otherZooKeeper.getEmail());
        if (result != 0) return result;

        /* If reached here name and email are the same.
         * So that method is consistent with equals() will now
         * sort on hash code.
         */
        return hashCode() - otherZooKeeper.hashCode();
    }

}
```

The modified `Visitor` class should look like this:

```
package virtualzoo.core;

import com.example.util.*;

public class Visitor implements Emailable {

    // Instance variables
    private Person person;
    private String email;
    private Animal sponsoredAnimal;


    // Create a Visitor object without a sponsored animal
    public Visitor(Person person, String email) {
        this(person, email, null);
    }

    // Create a Visitor object with a sponsored animal
    public Visitor(Person person, String email,
                                Animal sponsoredAnimal) {
        this.person = new Person(person);
        this.email = email;
        this.sponsoredAnimal = sponsoredAnimal;
    }

    public void setPerson(Person person) {
        this.person = new Person(person);
    }

    public Person getPerson() {
        return new Person(person);
    }

    public String getName() {
        return person.getName();
    }

    @Override
    public String getEmail() {
```

```
            return email;
        }

        void setEmail(String email) {
            this.email = email;
        }

        public Animal getSponsoredAnimal() {
            return sponsoredAnimal;
        }

        void setSponsoredAnimal(Animal sponsoredAnimal) {
            this.sponsoredAnimal = sponsoredAnimal;
        }

        public boolean hasSponsoredAnimal() {
            return (sponsoredAnimal != null);
        }

        @Override
        public String toString() {
            return getName();
        }

    }
```

In `ZooAdministrator` **you will need to import** `com.example.util` **and modify the methods** `createExampleZooKeepers()` **and** `createExampleVisitors():`

```
    private void createExampleZooKeepers() {
        alice = new ZooKeeper(new Person("Alice Smith", "Some City"),
                    "alice@example.com", new BigDecimal("20000"));
        bob = new ZooKeeper(new Person("Bob Jones", "2 The Road"),
                    "bob@example.com", new BigDecimal(22000));
        charles = new ZooKeeper(new Person("Charles Green", "3 The
                Avenue"), "charles@example.com",
                    new BigDecimal(18000));
    }


    private void createExampleVisitors() {
```

```
mary = new Visitor(new Person("Mary Smith"), "mary@example.com");
peter = new Visitor(new Person("Peter Harris"),
            "peter@example.com");
richard = new Visitor(new Person("Richard York"),
                "richard@example.com");
tanya = new Visitor(new Person("Tanya West"),
            "tanya@example.com");
}
```

9. Immutable Classes and the Object Class

Immutable classes are those which don't enable their state to change after they have been constructed. The `Object` class provides a core set of functionality inherited by every Java class, including those you define yourself.

In this chapter you will learn:

- *How to develop an immutable class;*

- *The recommended overrides from the `Object` class.*

Developing an immutable class

The `ZooKeeper` and `Visitor` classes each currently define an `email` attribute of type `String` to store an email address. Because emails need to be in a prescribed format, and are applicable to many applications, it would make sense to define another utility class to model this rather than a using plain `String` object directly. You will therefore write a class called `Email` in `com.example.util` with the following features:

- The constructor will accept a `String` argument representing the email address. This will be validated to ensure that it is in an acceptable format:

  ○ There must be no spaces in any part of the entire email address;

  ○ There must be exactly one @ symbol in the entire email address.

  ○ It should consist of a **local-part** before the @ symbol and a **domain-part** after it;

  ○ The local-part must contain at least one character;

  ○ The domain-part must contain at least one dot, either side of which is at least one character;

- There will be getter methods to return the entire email address, the local-part only, and the domain-part only;

- The `toString()` method will return the entire email address;

- The class will have a natural ordering of alphabetical by the entire email address.

> This is not intended to be a full implementation of a class to model an email. In particular, the validation described above does not detect all possible incorrect email formats.

You may have noticed that no setter methods were specified – only getters. This is known as an immutable class – once the state of an object has been set through its constructor then it cannot be changed. Immutable classes offer several advantages over mutable ones, and if you see an opportunity to make a class immutable then you should seriously consider doing so. As mentioned previously, the ubiquitous `String` class is immutable, as are several other Java supplied classes.

The natural question to ask, therefore, is how to handle the inevitable time when a person's email address changes? The answer is straightforward: simply create a brand new `Email` object and discard the old one. This applies even to simple changes such as correcting a spelling mistake, and is a reasonable approach since modifications to email address are relatively uncommon.

In `com.example.util` define a new class called `Email`:

```
package com.example.util;

public class Email {

    private String email;

    public Email(String email) {
```

```
        this.email = email;
    }

    public String getEmail() {
        return email;
    }

}
```

You need a method to return the local-part (i.e. the part before the @ symbol):

```
public String getLocalPart() {
    int atIndex = email.indexOf('@');
    return email.substring(0, atIndex);
}
```

- The `indexOf()` method of the `String` class returns the index of the first occurrence of the `char` or `String` specified in the argument. In this case it looks for @ in the email attribute. If it is not found then `-1` will be returned;

  o For example, if `email` contains `fred@example.com` then `atIndex` will become 4, since the @ character is in the fifth position[1].

- The `substring()` method of the `String` class returns a `String` consisting of the characters which lie between the first argument index position (which here is 0) and the second argument index position <u>less one</u> (which here is `atIndex`).

  o For example, if `email` contains `fred@example.com` then the characters from index 0 to 3 will be returned as a `String`, which will be "fred".

You need a similar method to return the domain-part:

---

[1]   Remember, strings are indexed starting from zero.

```java
public String getDomainPart() {
    int atIndex = email.indexOf('@');
    return email.substring(atIndex + 1);
}
```

- You can see above that the `substring()` method is overloaded to accept a single argument. In this case, it returns the characters from the argument index until the end of the string;
  - For example, if `email` contains `fred@example.com` then characters from index position 5 onwards will be returned, in this case "example.com".

You can override the `toString()` method to return the full email address:

```java
@Override
public String toString() {
    return getEmail();
}
```

For the natural ordering you need to implement the `Comparable` interface:

```java
public class Email implements Comparable<Email> {
```

And provide the code for the interface's `compareTo()` method:

```java
@Override
public int compareTo(Email otherEmail) {
    return email.compareTo(otherEmail.email);
}
```

- The method delegates to the `compareTo()` method of the `String` attribute `email`.

You now need to write a helper method to validate the email address. If it is invalid an exception will be thrown. Define a private `validate()`

method, initially only validating that the email contains no spaces anywhere within:

```
private void validate() {
    // Ensure there are no spaces
    if (email.indexOf(' ') >= 0) {
        throw new IllegalArgumentException
                ("Email must not contain a space character");
    }

    // OTHER VALIDATIONS WILL GO HERE ...
}
```

- The above code uses the indexOf() method of String which you saw previously, this time to search for a space character. If its returned value is zero or more then a space was found, in which case an IllegalArgumentException is thrown with some explanatory text.

Now include another section inside the method to ensure that there is exactly one @ character:

```
// Ensure there is exactly one @ character
int countAts = 0;
for (char c : email.toCharArray()) {
    if (c == '@') countAts++;
}
if (countAts != 1) {
    throw new IllegalArgumentException
            ("Email must contain exactly one @ character");
}
```

- The toCharArray() method of String returns an array of char primitives, where each element of the array is a single character. This is then looped over, and each time the @ character is found the variable countAts is incremented.

- When the loop has completed `countAts` is tested to ensure it is exactly 1.

The next section needs to ensure the local-part is not empty:

```java
// Ensure local-part is not empty
if (getLocalPart().isEmpty()) {
    throw new IllegalArgumentException
            ("Email local-part must contain at least one character");
}
```

- The `isEmpty()` method of `String` returns `true` if the string is empty and `false` otherwise. Note that "empty" is not the same as `null`; an empty string is one which exists but has no characters in it.

The domain-part needs to contain at least one dot:

```java
// Ensure domain-part contains at least one dot
int countDots = 0;
for (char c : getDomainPart().toCharArray()) {
    if (c == '.') countDots++;
}
if (countDots < 1) {
    throw new IllegalArgumentException
            ("Email domain-part must contain at least one dot");
}
```

Finally, each `String` either side of any dot character must not be empty:

```java
// Ensure each part of domain-part is not empty
int fromIndex = 0;
for (int i = 0; i < countDots; i++) {
    int dotIndex = getDomainPart().indexOf('.', fromIndex);
    String part = getDomainPart().substring(fromIndex, dotIndex);
    if (part.isEmpty()) {
        throw new IllegalArgumentException
                ("Email domain-part is not valid");
```

```
        }
        fromIndex = dotIndex + 1;
    }
    // check the part after the last dot
    String part = getDomainPart().substring(fromIndex);
    if (part.isEmpty()) {
        throw new IllegalArgumentException
                ("Email domain-part is not valid");
    }
```

- The above is the most complex of the validation sections, although it uses techniques you have already learned about. Essentially, it loops through the domain-part for each `String` before a dot character, and ensures it is not empty. After the loop completes, the `String` after the final (or only) dot character is tested to ensure it is not empty. Note the use of a second argument passed to the `indexOf()` method which tells it the starting index to search from.

> Some of the code in the `validate()` method could be simplified through the use of the `String` method called `split()`, which returns an array of `String` objects either side of the argument to `split()`. However, the argument needs to be a **regular expression** which is beyond the scope of this book.

With the validation method completed you need to call it from inside the constructor:

```
public Email(String email) {
    this.email = email;
    validate();
}
```

Preventing the compromisation of immutable classes

Whenever you decide to create an immutable class you need to take steps to ensure the immutability is not compromised, since you may have coded the rest of the application on the strict assumption that the attribute values cannot change. At the moment the immutability of Email could be compromised by creating a subclass which adds a mutable attribute and overrides one of the getter methods:

```
package com.example.util;

public class CompromisedEmail extends Email {

    private String spamAddress;

    public CompromisedEmail(String email) {
        super(email);
    }

    public void setSpamAddress(String spamAddress) {
        this.spamAddress = spamAddress;
    }

    @Override
    public String getEmail() {
        return spamEmail;
    }

}
```

The CompromisedEmail class breaks the immutability of Email in two separate ways:

1. By declaring an additional attribute which has a setter method; and

2. By overriding the getEmail() method to return the spam email address instead of the original one.

In short, you need to prevent this from happening, and the easiest way to do so is to declare the `Email` class as `final`:

```
public final class Email implements Comparable<Email> {
```

The `final` keyword, when applied to the class declaration, means that this class can no longer be sub-classed. If you entered the `CompromisedEmail` class above then you will find it no longer compiles, and you should delete it[1].

The `final` keyword can also be used to prevent specific methods from being overridden:

```
public final String getEmail() {
    // etc.
```

However, if you mark the class as **final** there is no need to mark the methods as **final** since they automatically cannot be overridden since the class cannot be sub-classed in the first place.

You may recall from Chapter 4 that you defined an interface called `Emailable`. Because this is another good candidate for a utility you should move it to the `Utilities` project and then change it to specify that its `getEmail()` method returns type `Email` instead of `String`:

```
package com.example.util;

public interface Emailable {

    public Email getEmail();      // recipient's email address

}
```

---

1   In NetBeans, right-click on the `CompromisedEmail.java` node and select **Delete**.

Now that you have an `Email` utility class in place you can use that as the type instead of `String` in the `ZooKeeper` and `Visitor` classes.

> For `ZooKeeper`, you will need to change the type from `String` to `Email` on the instance variable named `email`, the second argument to the constructor, the argument to the `setEmail()` method and the return type on the `getEmail()` method.
>
> For `Visitor`, you will need to change the type from `String` to `Email` on the instance variable named `email`, the second argument to both constructors, the argument to the `setEmail()` method and the return type on the `getEmail()` method.
>
> You may need to fix your import statements when applying the above changes.

You will also need to change the `createExampleZooKeepers()` and `createExampleVisitors()` methods in `ZooAdministrator` to instantiate an `Email` object which wraps the `String`:

```java
private void createExampleZooKeepers() {
    alice = new ZooKeeper(new Person("Alice Smith", "Some City"),
                new Email("alice@example.com"),
                new BigDecimal("20000"));
    bob = new ZooKeeper(new Person("Bob Jones", "2 The Road"),
                new Email("bob@example.com"),
                new BigDecimal(22000));
    charles = new ZooKeeper(new Person("Charles Green", "3 The
                Avenue"), new Email("charles@example.com"),
                new BigDecimal(18000));
}


private void createExampleVisitors() {
    mary = new Visitor(new Person("Mary Smith"),
                    new Email("mary@example.com"));
    peter = new Visitor(new Person("Peter Harris"),
                new Email(peter@example.com"));
    richard = new Visitor(new Person("Richard York"),
                new Email("richard@example.com"));
    tanya = new Visitor(new Person("Tanya West"),
```

```
                    new Email("tanya@example.com"));
    }
```

Recommended overrides from class Object

You will recall that every class (both those supplied by Java and those you write yourself) inherits from the Java supplied class called `Object`. So far, the only method from `Object` that you have overridden in your classes has been `toString()`, to return a textual representation of your object's state, and it is recommended that you override this method for virtually all classes that you write.

There are two further methods from `Object` that you should consider overriding within your classes, although this time you need to decide whether it is appropriate and meaningful to do so, or whether the default processing that you automatically inherit should be retained.

The two methods are `equals()` and `hashCode()`, and they work hand-in-hand.

Overriding equals() and hashCode()

You have previously seen the double equals operator being used to compare two primitive values, for example:

```
int a = 3;
int b = 3;
int c = 4;

boolean x = a == b;
boolean y = a == c;

System.out.println("x=" + x);
System.out.println("y=" + y);
```

Above, three `int` primitives called a, b and **c** are assigned the values 3, 3 and 4 respectively. Then, a is compared to b (with the result stored in `boolean` primitive x), and a is compared to c (with the result stored in `boolean` primitive y). Hopefully you can see that this will result in x containing `true` and y containing `false` (the comparisons are performed first, and then the assignment is performed using the result of the comparison).

What happens if you use the double equals comparison operator on object references? You may recall that each primitive type has an object "wrapper" class, and the wrapper for `int` is the class `Integer`. To see what happens, create three `Integer` objects and two comparisons:

```
Integer integerA = new Integer(3);
Integer integerB = new Integer(3);
Integer integerC = new Integer(4);

boolean x = integerA == integerB;
boolean y = integerA == integerC;

System.out.println("x=" + x);
System.out.println("y=" + y);
```

You will find that both x and y result in `false`. While the result for y should not surprise you, that for x might since `integerA` and `integerB` were set to the same value. The reason that they are considered to be different is because when comparing object references using `==` it is their identity which is compared, and not their contents. By identity is meant their independent existence in memory – the references `integerA` and `integerB` point to two separate objects, and the fact that their attribute values are the same is irrelevant to the `==` operator.

Often, however, when you compare object references you want it to be comparing their attribute values since they can be considered "logically" equal even if they exist in separate objects in memory. This is the purpose of the `equals()` method provided within the `Object` class.

Change the two comparison statements above to the following:

```
boolean x = integerA.equals(integerB);
```

```
boolean y = integerA.equals(integerC);
```

You will now find that while `y` is still `false`, `x` now results in `true` since it is the attribute content (i.e. the actual numeric value) of the objects which are being compared.

This is not the end of the story, however. Try entering the following statements which use your recently defined `Email` class instead of `Integer`:

```
Email emailA = new Email("fred@example.com");
Email emailB = new Email("fred@example.com");
Email emailC = new Email("barney@example.com");

boolean x = emailA.equals(emailB);
boolean y = emailA.equals(emailC);

System.out.println("x = " + x);
System.out.println("y = " + y);
```

Now `x` results in `false`, even though the attribute value of `emailA` and `emailB` are identical. The reason is that the default implementation of `equals()` in class `Object` merely does the following:

```
public boolean equals(Object other) {
    return this == other;
}
```

The designers of Java overrode the implementation of the `equals()` method in the `Integer` class to compare the actual value rather than the perform the simple identity comparison. Your `Email` class, however, has not overridden the `equals()` method so when you invoke `equals()` on `Email` objects it performs the default identity comparison, inherited from `Object`.

Therefore, you should override the `equals()` method when your class can have instances that have **logical equality**. This is typically the case for **value classes**; that is, classes that have some intrinsic state that represents a value. As well as `Integer` and the other primitive wrapper classes, Java also overrides it in the `String` class (among others), enabling sensible text comparisons:

```
String stringA = "abc";
String stringB = "abc";
String stringC = "def";

boolean x = stringA.equals(stringB);
boolean y = stringA.equals(stringC);

System.out.println("x=" + x); // will output true
System.out.println("y=" + y); // will output false
```

Having determined that two separate `Email` objects which have the same attribute value (i.e. the same email string) ought to be considered as logically equal, the next step is to override the `equals()` method inside the `Email` class. Enter the following statements:

```
@Override
public boolean equals(Object other) {
    if (! (other instanceof Email)) return false;    // 1
    Email otherEmail = (Email) other;                // 2
    return email.equals(otherEmail.email);           // 3
}
```

- The method signature accepts an argument which can be any `Object` (which also means it can accept any subclass of `Object`, such as `Email`);

- Statement 1 uses the `instanceof` operator to see whether the argument reference (called `other`) is an instance of the `Email` class. The **!** Operator applies the "not" condition, so the statement can be read as "*if* `other` *is not an instance of* `Email`, *return* `false`";

- Statement 2 performs a cast on `other` to convert it back to an `Email` object. This is needed so as to enable you to access its members;

- Statement 3 compares the `email` `String` attribute value of the current object and the argument `Email` object. Because the `email` attribute is a `String`, the `equals()` invoked on this statement is the one overridden by the `String` class. The result of the comparison is a `boolean`, and is returned;

Now you can re-run the email comparison and receive a more sensible outcome:

```
Email emailA = new Email("fred@example.com");
Email emailB = new Email("fred@example.com");
Email emailC = new Email("barney@example.com");

boolean x = emailA.equals(emailB);
boolean y = emailA.equals(emailC);

System.out.println("x = " + x); // will now output true
System.out.println("y = " + y); // will still output false
```

The `hashCode()` method returns an `int`, and it works hand-in-hand with the `equals()` method. Its purpose is to return a numeric identifier for any object, so that objects of a particular type can be efficiently stored in **collections**. A collection is a grouping of multiple objects and will be explored in Chapter 11. If two objects are equal according to the `equals()` method then their hash codes should both have the same value. Many Java supplied classes, including `String`, override their version of `hashCode()` and you can take advantage of this for the `Email` class. Define the following method:

```
@Override
public int hashCode() {
    return email.hashCode();
}
```

The formula for generating a hash code is not always as straightforward as above. You can use NetBeans to generate it for you by right-clicking where you would start to enter the next method and selecting **Insert Code...** followed by hashCode(). NetBeans can also generate the equals() method for you, or even both equals() and hashCode() at the same time.

To complete this section, a natural question to ask is whether the other classes you have developed so far should also have implementations to override the equals() and hashCode() methods. A short explanation for each of these follows:

- For Emailable, interface types cannot provide implementations of any method, only the method signatures. Since all classes automatically inherit equals() and hashCode() anyway (through Object) there is also no need to ever specify them in any interface;

- For Gender, enum types specify the equals() and hashCode() methods as final, meaning you cannot override them even if you wanted to. The Java provided implementation correctly treats each constant in an enum as unique;

- For the Person class the attributes are name, address and gender. Suppose you create the following two objects:

```
Person p1 = new Person("Fred", "London", Gender.MALE);
Person p2 = new Person("Fred", "London", Gender.MALE);
```

The question is, does this refer to two separate people who just happen to have the same name, address and gender, or should they be treated as if they refer to the same person? This book takes the view that if separate Person objects are created with the same attribute values then they are still independent entities. Therefore, comparison though object identity is the correct approach, and equals() and hashCode() should not be overridden.

- This book will also not override `equals()` and `hashCode()` for `Animal`, `ZooKeeper`, `ZooAdministrator` or `Visitor` for similar reasons.

There is in fact another reason to be cautious about overriding the methods in the above classes, including `Person`, and that is that the classes are mutable. The methods `equals()` and `hashCode()` are used when placing objects inside collections, but if their attribute values are changed while inside a collection then unpredictable results can occur. This is not to suggest you should never override these methods for mutable classes; but it is only safe to do so if the attributes being used in the overridden methods are not themselves mutable. This can sometimes require creating an additional attribute (such as a unique id number), but this book takes the simpler approach of treating each mutable object by its identity.

10. Documentation, Testing and Debugging

Java provides a built-in tool to help you document your classes. NetBeans incorporates the JUnit testing tool and a debugging tool.

In this chapter you will learn:

- *How to document your classes and packages;*

- *How to test your classes and application;*

- *How to debug your classes.*

Class & package documentation

In an earlier chapter you saw the web based documentation of the Java APIs, known as Javadoc. This was generated using a Java supplied tool of the same name, and which you can use to generate documentation for your own classes, too.

To see this in action, you will return to the `Email` utility class created previously. You need to insert multi-line comments in a particular format which the Javadoc tool looks for, where these comments immediately precede the class header, constructor or method being documented.

Insert the following lines just before the class header:

```
package com.example.util;

/**
 * The Email class represents an immutable email address
 * in the format <code>local-part@domain-part</code>.
 */
public final class Email implements Comparable<Email> {
```

- Note that there are two asterisks after the slash character on the first line, which indicates to Javadoc that this is a documentation comment block;

- You can embed HTML formatting tags, such as `<code></code>` above.

You should document the constructor:

```java
package com.example.util;

/**
 * The Email class represents an immutable email address
 * in the format <code>local-part@domain-part</code>.
 */
public final class Email implements Comparable<Email> {

    private String email;

    /**
     * Constructs an <code>Email</code> object with the specified
                        address.
     * @param email the full email address
     * @throws <code>IllegalArgumentException</code> if the argument
                        is not a valid email.
     * @throws <code>NullPointerException</code> if the argument is
                        <code>null</code>
     */
    public Email(String email) {
```

- The @param annotation is used for each argument (also known as parameter), made up of three parts separated by spaces:

  ◦ @param – the annotation code;

  ◦ email – the argument variable name;

  ◦ An explanation of the argument.

- The @throws annotation is used for each exception which could be thrown, also made up of three parts. Because the constructor invokes the `validate()` method which throws `IllegalArgumentException` you should document this here. A `NullPointerException` could also be thrown from the `validate()` method if the email value is `null` when it attempts to invoke a method upon it.

Here is the documentation for the `getEmail()` method:

```
/**
 * Returns the full email address.
 * @return the email address
 */
public String getEmail() {
```

- The `@return` annotation describes the value which will be returned from this method.

The `getLocalPart()` method could be as follows:

```
/**
 * Returns the local-part of the email address,
 * that is, the part before the @ character.
 * @return the email local-part
 */
public String getLocalPart() {
```

The `getDomainPart()` method would be very similar:

```
/**
 * Returns the domain-part of the email address,
 * that is, the part after the @ character.
 * @return the email domain-part
 */
public String getDomainPart() {
```

As would the `toString()` method:

```
/**
 * Returns the full email address.
 * @return the email address
 */
@Override
public String toString() {
```

For the `equals()` method:

```
/**
 * Compares this email to the specified object.
 * Returns <code>true> if the argument is not <code>null</code>
 * and is an <code>Email</code> object with the same email address.
 * @param other the object to compare this <code>Email</code>against.
 * @return <code>true</code> if the given object represents
 * an <code>Email</code> with the same address, <code>false</code>
                                              otherwise.
 */
@Override
public boolean equals(Object other) {
```

For the `hashCode()` method:

```
/**
 * Returns the hash code for this <code>Email</code> object.
 * The returned hash code will be the hash code of the email address
                                              string
 * @return a hash code value for this object.
 */
@Override
public int hashCode() {
```

For the `compareTo()` method:

```
/**
 * Compares this <code>Email</code> to the argument,
 * alphabetically by the email address string.
 * @param otherEmail the <code>Email</code> to compare against.
 * @return the value zero if the email address strings are the same,
 * a value less than zero if this email is alphabetically
 * before the argument, and a value greater than zero if this email
```

```
 * is alphabetically after the argument.
 */
@Override
public int compareTo(Email otherEmail) {
```

Because the `validate()` method is `private`, the Javadoc tool will ignore any comments you supply. This is because the purpose of Javadoc is to tell you which constructors and methods are able to be invoked from client objects, and private members are by definition not available externally to the class in which they are defined. However, it can still be useful for other programmers reading your source code so a Javadoc will still be written:

```
/**
 * Validate that the email:
 * 1. Has no spaces;
 * 2. Has exactly one @ character;
 * 3. Local-part is not empty;
 * 4. Domain-part contains at least one dot;
 * 5. Domain-part sections are not empty.
 * @throws <code>IllegalArgumentException</code> if the argument is
                                 not a valid email.
 * @throws <code>NullPointerException</code> if the argument is
                                 <code>null</code>
 */
private void validate() {
```

With the Javadoc comments in place, right-click the `Utilities` node in the `Projects` window and select `Generate Javadoc`. A browser window should appear, as follows:

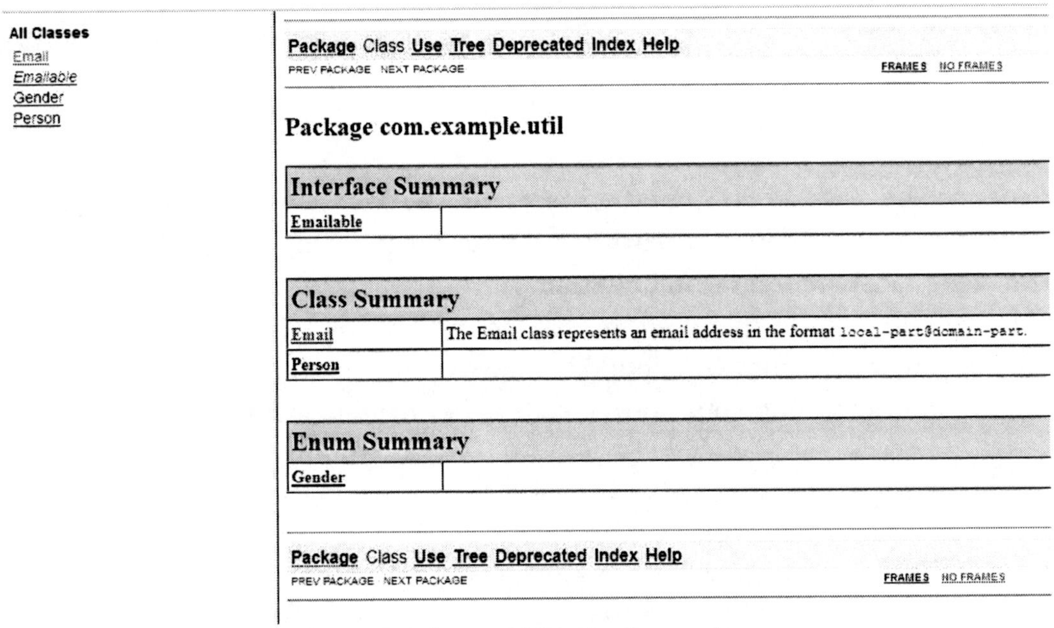

All Classes

Email
Emailable
Gender
Person

Package Class **Use** **Tree** **Deprecated** **Index** **Help**
PREV PACKAGE   NEXT PACKAGE   FRAMES   NO FRAMES

Package com.example.util

Interface Summary	
Emailable	

Class Summary	
Email	The Email class represents an email address in the format `local-part@domain-part`.
Person	

Enum Summary	
Gender	

Package Class **Use** **Tree** **Deprecated** **Index** **Help**
PREV PACKAGE   NEXT PACKAGE   FRAMES   NO FRAMES

Figure 10.1: Generated Javadoc for a package

You can see the comment line next to the `Email` class. Click on its hyperlink to see the full documentation for the class:

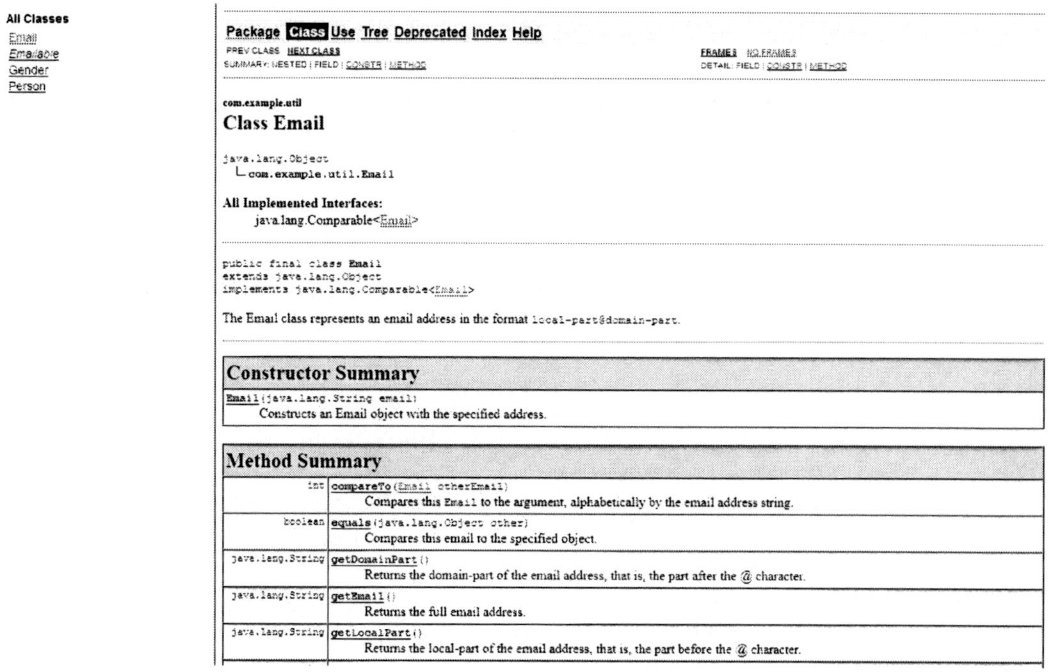

Figure 10.2: Generated Javadoc for a class

You can scroll down to see the detailed documentation for the constructor and methods.

You can provide an overview of the classes in an entire package by creating an HTML file in the package called `package.html`, which needs to be in standard HTML format. Right-click the `com.example.util` package node and select `New Other`, then select **Other** from the **Categories** list and **HTML File** from the **File Types** list. Click **Next>** and then enter `package` as the **File Name** and click **Finish**. A template is built for you and you only need to provide the <body> text:

```
<!--
To change this template, choose Tools | Templates
and open the template in the editor.
-->
<!DOCTYPE html>
<html>
    <head>
        <title></title>
```

```
        <meta http-equiv="Content-Type" content="text/html;
                                  charset=UTF-8">
    </head>
    <body>
        <div>The <code>com.example.util</code> package contains
                      general utility classes.</div>
    </body>
</html>
```

Regenerate the Javadoc to see the package description appear on the initial page.

More detail about Javadoc can be found at the following link:

```
http://www.oracle.com/technetwork/java/javase/documentation/index-jsp-
135444.html
```

Purely for reasons of space, no further Javadoc comments will appear in this book.

How to test a class

Testing that your classes do what they are supposed to is an essential part of software development. In practical terms, it is impossible to ensure that software is totally bug-free; however, with good testing you can be reasonably sure that your application will be sufficiently reliable for use in the real world. While testing can often be seen as a tedious, though necessary, chore, it is possible to create special Java classes that can help to automate the process of testing and re-testing your system. To do this you will make use of the **JUnit** testing tool which is installed as part of NetBeans. Again, you will use the `Email` utility class as an example.

Right-click the `Email.java` node in the **Projects** window and select **Tools | Create JUnit Tests**. The first time you do this you will be asked what version of JUnit to use, so you should select **JUnit 4.x**.

In the **Create Tests** dialog, make sure you deselect the check-box for **Default Method Bodies**:

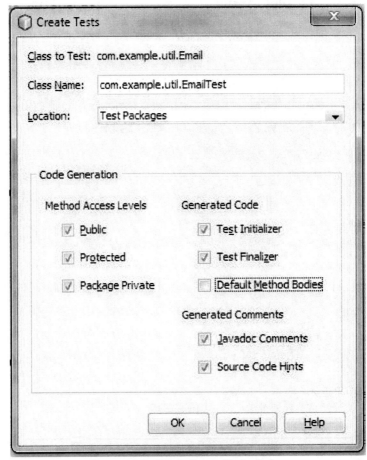

Figure 10.3: JUnit Create Tests dialog

Click **OK.**

A new Java class is automatically created called `EmailTest`. It is in a separate area under `Test Packages` in the **Projects** window, which mirrors the package structure of the class it is testing. Expand this node until you can see `EmailTest.java`. Locate the `testGetEmail()` method inside this class, which is initially empty:

```
@Test
public void testGetEmail() {
}
```

- The `@Test` annotation is used by JUnit to indicate that this is a testing method that it should call;

- The method name begins with `test`, and is followed by the name of the actual method to be tested.

Inside the method you need to create the state of the object(s) that are relevant to the test (which is known as its **fixture**), and then perform the test by invoking the appropriate method. Finally, you make an **assertion** that something should be the case:

```
@Test
public void testGetEmail() {
    // Setup the fixture
    Email fredEmail = new Email("fred@example.com");

    // Run the method being tested
    String result = fredEmail.getEmail();

    // Make the assertion
    assert result.equals("fred@example.com") : "email not correct";
}
```

- The fixture is set-up by instantiating an `Email` object with some sample data;

- The method being tested is invoked, which in this case returns a `String`;

- The Java `assert` statement checks whether the returned value matches what you expect it to be. It is made up of two parts separated by a colon character:

  ○ The first part is an expression which returns a `boolean` value – here it is the `equals()` method of `String`;

  ○ The second part is a message that informs the programmer if the assertion failed, that is, the actual value did not match the expected value, to help in the location of the problem.

To run the test, right-click on the `EmailTest.java` node in the **Projects** window, and select **Run File**[1]. The test should succeed, leading to the following shown on the **Output** window:

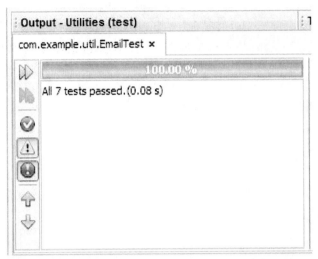

Figure 10.4: NetBeans JUnit Output successful results

The reason it states that seven tests have passed is that there are seven test methods inside `EmailTest.java`, although you have only coded one, the other six being currently empty.

Here is some test code for `testGetLocalPart()`:

```
@Test
public void testGetLocalPart() {
    // Setup the fixture
    Email fredEmail = new Email("fred@example.com");

    // Run the method being tested
    String result = fredEmail.getLocalPart();

    // Make the assertion
    assert result.equals("fred") : "email local-part not correct";
}
```

---

1   Alternatively, you can right-click the `Email.java` node under `Source Packages` and select **Test File**.

You may have noticed that the code for the fixture is identical to that in `testGetEmail()`. This is a common occurrence when testing, and to reduce the amount of code duplication you can move shared fixture code so that the `Email` object becomes an instance variable which is instantiated in the `setUp()` method which appears above the test methods in the source file. You will now refactor the `EmailTest` class to do this:

Define an instance variable:

```
private Email fredEmail;
```

Instantiate it in the `setUp()` method:

```
@Before
public void setUp() {
    fredEmail = new Email("fred@example.com");
}
```

You now need to remove the fixture set-up lines from the `testGetEmail()` and `testGetLocalPart()` methods so they read as follows:

```
@Test
public void testGetEmail() {
    // Run the method being tested
    String result = fredEmail.getEmail();

    // Make the assertion
    assert result.equals("fred@example.com") : "email not correct";
}

@Test
public void testGetLocalPart() {
    // Run the method being tested
    String result = fredEmail.getLocalPart();

    // Make the assertion
    assert result.equals("fred") : "email local-part not correct";
}
```

Run the test to verify that all seven tests are still successful.

> It is important to note that when JUnit runs your test, the `setUp()` method is automatically invoked just before each individual test method. This means that if any of your test methods change the state of an object in the fixture it will be reset before the next test method is run. Because the `Email` class is immutable this is not an issue here, but is something you need to be aware of when testing mutable classes.
>
> Do not confuse `setUp()` with `setUpClass()`. The former is invoked before each individual test method but the latter only once before the very first test.
>
> The `tearDown()` and `tearDownClass()` methods are only needed if you need to close objects like file resources. They are not needed here.

It will be helpful to see what happens if an assertion fails, so you should now introduce a temporary bug that the testing will catch. In the `Email` class change the `getEmail()` method to wrongly return `email` as a `String` constant rather than as a variable reference, to simulate a programmer mistake:

```java
public String getEmail() {
    return "email";
}
```

Run the test and note the results in the **Output** window:

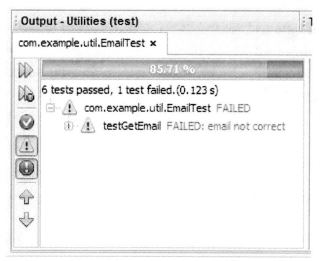

Figure 10.5: NetBeans JUnit Output failure results

From the above you can see the method which failed its test. This can help you pinpoint where the error is by tracing the lines of code which lead up to it. Change the getEmail() method back to correct the bug.

The testGetDomainPart() method will be similar to testGetLocalPart():

```
@Test
public void testGetDomainPart() {
    String result = fredEmail.getDomainPart();
    assert result.equals("example.com") : "email domain-part not
                                           correct";
}
```

The testToString() method:

```
@Test
public void testToString() {
    String result = fredEmail.toString();
    assert result.equals("fred@example.com") : "email not correct";
}
```

In order to test the `equals()` method you need two separate tests; one where the method should return `true` and the other where it should return `false`. While you could accomplish this inside a single test method it is also possible to split them into separate methods. Rename the `testEquals()` method to `test1Equals()`, and then include the following statements:

```
@Test
public void test1Equals() {
    Email otherEmail = new Email("fred@example.com");
    assert fredEmail.equals(otherEmail) : "equals() should be true";
}
```

Now define a `test2Equals()` method that tests for when the `equals()` method should return `false`:

```
@Test
public void test2Equals() {
    Email otherEmail = new Email("barney@example.com");
    assert ! fredEmail.equals(otherEmail) : "equals() should be
                                              false";
}
```

- Note the ! operator to negate the test.

Because `hashCode()` should work in harmony with `equals()` you can also split this into two test methods:

```
@Test
public void test1HashCode() {
    Email otherEmail = new Email("fred@example.com");
    assert fredEmail.hashCode() == otherEmail.hashCode()
            : "hash codes should be same";
}

@Test
public void test2HashCode() {
    Email otherEmail = new Email("barney@example.com");
    assert fredEmail.hashCode() != otherEmail.hashCode()
```

```
                : "hash codes should be different";
}
```

> While the hash code should be the same when two objects are equal according to the `equals()` method, technically the hash codes don't have to be different for unequal objects. It is, however, the ideal to strive for and is therefore a useful test to include in case it pinpoints a problem with your `hashCode()` algorithm.

The testing of `compareTo()` needs to account for three situations:

1. Where the objects being compared are equal;

2. Where the first object "comes after" the second object;

3. Where the first object "comes before" the second object.

Here are three corresponding test methods:

```
@Test
public void test1CompareTo() {
    Email otherEmail = new Email("fred@example.com");
    assert fredEmail.compareTo(otherEmail) == 0
            : "compareTo() should be zero";
}

@Test
public void test2CompareTo() {
    Email otherEmail = new Email("barney@example.com");
    assert fredEmail.compareTo(otherEmail) > 0
            : "compareTo() should be positive";
}

@Test
public void test3CompareTo() {
    Email otherEmail = new Email("zebedee@example.com");
    assert fredEmail.compareTo(otherEmail) < 0
            : "compareTo() should be negative";
}
```

You may have noticed that no test method shell was generated for the validate() method of Email. This is because validate() was defined as private and therefore not directly accessible to the test class. It still needs to be tested somehow, though, and since it is invoked through Email's constructor you can define new test methods to do so.

The first check made by validate() is that the email string contains no spaces, so define this test method:

```
@Test
public void test1aValidate() {
    try {
        // space at start
        Email otherEmail = new Email(" fred@example.com");
        assert false : "exception should be thrown, space in email";
    } catch (IllegalArgumentException ex) {
        // test passed
    }
}
```

- Note that there is a space at the start of the email address, and therefore the test succeeds when an exception is thrown, hence the try...catch statements and empty catch block. If the expected exception is not thrown then the statement following the instantiation of otherEmail will be executed, so you can force notification by using assert false.

The previous method tested for a space at the beginning of the email string, so you also need to test for a space at the end and in the middle:

```
@Test
public void test1bValidate() {
    try {
        // space at end
        Email otherEmail = new Email("fred@example.com ");
        assert false : "exception should be thrown, space in email";
    } catch (IllegalArgumentException ex) {
        // test passed
```

```
        }
    }

    @Test
    public void test1cValidate() {
        try {
            // space in middle
            Email otherEmail = new Email("fred@ex ample.com");
            assert false : "exception should be thrown, space in email";
        } catch (IllegalArgumentException ex) {
            // test passed
        }
    }
```

The second check made in `validate()` is that there is exactly one @ character, so you should test where there are none, one, and more than one:

```
    @Test
    public void test2aValidate() {
        try {
            // no @ character
            Email otherEmail = new Email("fredexample.com");
            assert false : "exception should be thrown, no @ found";
        } catch (IllegalArgumentException ex) {
            // test passed
        }
    }

    @Test
    public void test2bValidate() {
        try {
            // one @ character
            Email otherEmail = new Email("fred@example.com");
        } catch (IllegalArgumentException ex) {
            assert false : "exception should not be thrown as one @
                                          found";
        }
    }

    @Test
    public void test2cValidate() {
```

```
        try {
            // two @ characters
            Email otherEmail = new Email("fred@example@.com");
            assert false : "exception should be thrown, two @s found";
        } catch (IllegalArgumentException ex) {
            // test passed
        }
    }
```

The third check made in `validate()` is that the local-part is not empty:

```
@Test
public void test3Validate() {
    try {
        // empty local-part
        Email otherEmail = new Email("@example.com");
        assert false : "exception should be thrown, empty local-
                                                part";
    } catch (IllegalArgumentException ex) {
        // test passed
    }
}
```

The fourth check made in `validate()` is that the domain-part contains at least one dot:

```
@Test
public void test4aValidate() {
    try {
        // no dot in domain-part
        Email otherEmail = new Email("fred@examplecom");
        assert false : "exception should be thrown, no dot in domain-
                                                part";
    } catch (IllegalArgumentException ex) {
        // test passed
    }
}

@Test
public void test4bValidate() {
    try {
        // two dots in domain-part
```

```
            Email otherEmail = new Email("fred@example.co.m");
        } catch (IllegalArgumentException ex) {
            assert false : "exception should not be thrown, two dots in
                                                domain-part";
        }
    }
}
```

The fifth and final check made in `validate()` is that each sub-part of the
domain-part is not empty:

```
@Test
public void test5aValidate() {
    try {
        // empty first sub-part of domain-part
        Email otherEmail = new Email("fred@.com");
        assert false : "exception should be thrown, empty first sub-
                                        part in domain-part";
    } catch (IllegalArgumentException ex) {
        // test passed
    }
}


@Test
public void test5bValidate() {
    try {
        // empty second sub-part of domain-part
        Email otherEmail = new Email("fred@example.");
        assert false : "exception should be thrown, empty second sub-
                                        part in domain-part";
    } catch (IllegalArgumentException ex) {
        // test passed
    }
}


@Test
public void test5cValidate() {
    try {
        // empty third sub-part of domain-part
        Email otherEmail = new Email("fred@example.com.");
        assert false : "exception should be thrown, empty third sub-
                                        part in domain-part";
    } catch (IllegalArgumentException ex) {
        // test passed
```

```
        }
    }
```

Make sure all of the tests succeed before continuing. If you are seeing testing failures then it is most likely that you have mistyped something in either the `EmailText.java` or `Email.java`.

When you created the `EmailTest.java` class you did so as an individual case, but in practice you will need to test all of your classes. JUnit allows you to define a **test-suite** which will automatically run the tests on all of your classes. In NetBeans, right-click on the `Source Packages` node of the `Utilities` project in the **Projects** window and select **Tools | Create JUnit Tests**. You will note in the **Create Tests** dialog that there are some additional options available, including one called **Generate Test Suites**. You should ensure this is checked and then click **OK**.

NetBeans will generate test classes for all classes in your project, although it won't overwrite the tests you have already defined in the `EmailTest.java` class[1]. It will also generate an additional class called `UtilSuite.java` (the prefix `Util` is taken from the last part of the package name), and because your package name consists of three parts (`com`, `example` & `util`) will also generate a suite class in each.

Open `UtilSuite.java` to see the following just before the class header:

```
@RunWith(Suite.class)
@Suite.SuiteClasses({com.example.util.PersonTest.class,
com.example.util.EmailableTest.class, com.example.util.GenderTest.class,
com.example.util.EmailTest.class})
public class UtilSuite {
```

The `@Suite.SuiteClasses` annotation is used to tell JUnit which classes should be tested, and as you can see it has automatically included all of the individual classes in the package. You don't need to make any changes to this file, but bear in mind that if you create a completely new class in

---

1   Although it will re-generate the `testEquals()`, `testHashCode()` and `testCompareTo()` methods because you renamed them. These can be ignored.

the future together with a test class then you will need to add an entry for it to the list in `UtilSuite.java`.

Under the `Test Packages` node open the `<default package>` node, and then open the `RootSuite.java` source file. This is the class it is recommend to run whenever you want to test the entire project, since it runs all the other suites and their referenced classes for you. If you run it now all should pass, since you haven't written the individual test methods for any class other than `EmailTest.java`.

Purely for reasons of space, this book will not document any further test classes.

How to debug a class

Finding where you have a bug in your classes can sometimes be a time-consuming process. To help you, NetBeans incorporates a debugging tool that lets you set one or more breakpoints at any point in your code. A **breakpoint** is a statement at which code execution will pause, allowing you to step through the subsequent statements one at a time, viewing the state of the variables as you go.

You will now introduce a bug into the `validate()` method of `Email.java`. In the section that ensures that there is exactly one @ character, change the following line from:

```
if (countAts != 1) {
```

To this:

```
if (countAts != 2) {
```

This would cause an error to be flagged when testing. Put the following code in the `main()` method of `Experiments.java` (in the `VirtualZoo` project):

```
public static void main(String[] args) {
    Email e = new Email("fred@example@.com");
    System.out.println(e);
}
```

The above email contains two @ characters, so run `Experiments.java` to ensure that no exception is being thrown.

Now, in the `Email.java` source file locate the first line of code inside the `validate()` method, and click inside the grey numbered margin at the left of the statement. The statement should turn red, indicating that you have set a breakpoint at that line:

```
111   private void validate() {
112       // Ensure there are no spaces
      if (email.indexOf( ) >= 0) {
114       throw new IllegalArgumentException
115           ("Email must not contain a space character");
116   }
117
118       // Ensure there is exactly one @ character
119   int countAts = 0;
120   for (char c : email.toCharArray()) {
121       if (c == '@') countAts++;
122   }
123   if (countAts != 2) {
124       throw new IllegalArgumentException
125           ("Email must contain exactly one @ character");
126   }
```

Figure 10.6: Breakpoint set on statement 113

On the `Experiments.java` node, right-click and select **Debug File**. This will tell NetBeans to run the program only as far as the first breakpoint it finds and then pause. The code will be displayed in the main window with the line which has its breakpoint set coloured green. In the **Output** window you can see the state of the object:

Output		Tasks	Variables		Breakpoints	Test Results
	Name		Type			Value
	<Enter new watch>					
	this		Email			=50

Figure 10.7: NetBeans JUnit debugging mode

The `this` entry under the **Name** column refers to the current object. Click the small plus icon next to it to view the instance variables. You should see `email` appear, of type `String` and with a value of "`fred@example.com`".

Above the source code you will see a bank of icons:

Figure 10.8: Debug mode controls

Click the fourth of these (whose hover help is **Step Over**) and the statement will be executed, causing the green line to move and stop at the next statement. It jumps over the line which throws the exception since the condition was not met, hence it should now be on the line that declares `countAts`:

```
111     private void validate() {
112         // Ensure there are no spaces
            if (email.indexOf(' ') >= 0) {
114             throw new IllegalArgumentException
115                 ("Email must not contain a space character");
116         }
117
118         // Ensure there is exactly one @ character
⇨           int countAts = 0;
120         for (char c : email.toCharArray()) {
121             if (c == '@') countAts++;
122         }
123         if (countAts != 2) {
124             throw new IllegalArgumentException
125                 ("Email must contain exactly one @ character");
126         }
```

Figure 10.9: Debugging mode currently paused at statement 119

Step over to the next line and verify that the value of `countAts` is zero. Keep stepping over to loop through the check of each character until the green line reaches the following statements:

```
if (countAts != 2) {
```

At this point, the **Output** window should show that `countAts` has value **2**, and that the comparison should be against **1**. As you now know the problem, you can stop execution completely by clicking the first icon in Figure 10.8 (whose hover help is **Finish Debugger Session**).

In `Email.java`, change the comparison statement back to compare not equal to 1 rather than 2. Now click in the grey numbered margin next to the red line to turn off the breakpoint. Each time you click the margin the statement will toggle between being set and unset. You should now be able to run `Experiments.java` with a correct outcome, i.e. an exception is correctly being thrown.

If while you are single-stepping a debugging session the next statement is a method call, you have a choice of either stepping over it or inside of it. Stepping over is useful if you are sure the method itself is not the problem, because its code is still executed but you don't have to waste time stepping through each line. However, if you are unsure where the fault lies then using the **Step Into** icon takes you into the called method, even if it is in a completely different class that has no breakpoints of its own. This is very useful for tracing the cause of an error.

11. Collections & Maps

The Java Collections Framework provides a set of classes and interfaces that let you manage groups of related objects in a more powerful way than arrays.

In this chapter you will learn:

- *How the collections framework is structured;*

- *How to use lists for ordered groups of objects;*

- *How to use sets for unordered groups of objects;*

- *How to use maps for keyed-pair groups of objects.*

The collections framework

In Chapter 6 you created the `Pen` class that defined an array to store a group of `Animal` objects. While arrays are efficient, you saw a particular downside in that after you have declared the number of elements the array will contain you cannot change that amount thereafter. The capacity of ten chosen for each pen in the zoo was completely arbitrary. While it may be sufficient to store the number of lions the penguin pen is likely to need to be able to store several dozen.

Rather than having to guess a likely maximum and then have many `null` elements, a far more flexible approach is to make use of Java's **collections framework**. This incorporates several related classes and interfaces that enable you to store groups of objects and which can dynamically expand or contract in size as required.

The root of the framework is an interface called `Collection`. If you look at the API for this interface you will see a number of methods, the most frequently used being:

- `add()` - adds an object to the collection;

- `remove()` - removes an object from the collection;

- `size()` - returns the number of objects currently in the collection.

The collection framework can be shown diagrammatically as in the following figure. Note that all of the items shown are Java interfaces, and there are corresponding classes that implement the interfaces and which you actually use to hold the collection data:

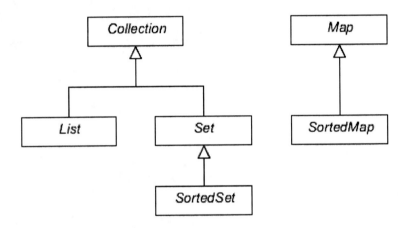

Figure 11.1: Collections framework class hierarchy

The main restriction of the collection classes is that they can only contain object references – primitives are not allowed. There is a simple workaround for this, however, since you can use the wrapper objects (`Integer` instead of `int`, for example), as described in Chapter 2.

> The collections framwork classes and interfaces are in the `java.util` package, so you will need to import this into the classes which make use of them.

Lists

The type of collection which most closely resembles an array is `List`, which contains a number of objects in the order in which they were added to the list. `List` is in fact another interface; the most commonly used class that implements it is `ArrayList`. Here is an example of using `ArrayList`:

```java
// Create an empty list of words
Collection<String> words = new ArrayList<String>(); // statement 1

// Add some words to the list
words.add("To");                              // statement 2
words.add("be");                              // statement 3
words.add("or");                              // statement 4
words.add("not");                             // statement 5
words.add("to");                              // statement 6
words.add("be");                              // statement 7
words.add("that");                            // statement 8
words.add("is");                              // statement 9
words.add("the");                             // statement 10
words.add("question");                        // statement 11

// Output the words
for (String s : words) {                      // statement 12
    System.out.println(s);                    // statement 13
}

System.out.println("The list contains " +     // statement 14
                words.size() + " words");
```

- Statement 1 declares a `Collection` of `String` objects called `words`, and then instantiates an `ArrayList` of `String` objects (the `ArrayList` class implements the `List` interface, which in turn extends the `Collection` interface). Note that the syntax includes both the formal type parameter in angle-brackets and then empty round brackets to indicate a call to the constructor of `ArrayList`;

- Statements 2 through 11 add a series of `String` objects to the list;

- Statement 12 initiates a for-each loop over the words;

- Statement 13 sends the current word in the loop to output;

- Statement 14 reports how many words are in the list.

You should see the following output:

```
To
be
or
not
to
be
that
is
the
question
The list contains 10 words
```

You will notice that lists store the objects in the order they were added, and that they can contain duplicate items, for example the word "be".

If you need to access a specific object in a list by its position, you can use the get() method passing the required index position. However, get() is defined in the List interface so you would need to modify the declaration as follows:

```
List<String> words = new ArrayList<String>();
```

You will now be able to invoke the get() method:

```
String firstWord = words.get(0);
String secondWord = words.get(1);
String lastWord = words.get(words.size() - 1);
```

- Like arrays, lists are indexed such that the first element has index zero, the second element has index 1, etc.;

- The index number of the last element can be calculated by subtracting one from the number of elements in the list.

Sets

A `Set` differs from a `List` in the following ways:

- Sets do not allow duplicate objects to be added. An object is considered to be a duplicate if its `equals()` method returns `true` for any object already in the set;

- The order in which objects are added to the set is not maintained unless you use a sorted set:

  - This means there is no `get()` method available to sets.

  - The `HashSet` class maintains a set of objects in no particular order;

  - The `TreeSet` class maintains a set of objects sorted into their natural order, as defined by the `compareTo()` method. Alternatively, you can specify an different ordering using a `Comparator` object.

Replace the following statement:

```
List<String> words = new ArrayList<String>();
```

With this:

```
Collection<String> words = new HashSet<String>();
```

The remainder of the code does not need to change. Your output may look like this:

```
to
not
that
is
or
```

```
To
question
the
be
The list contains 9 words
```

- It is possible that your words will be listed in a different order to that shown above, and even that you may get a different order if you run it again;

- There are only nine words in the set since the word "be" was duplicated and so was not added twice.

If you want to ensure the objects are iterated using their natural ordering, specify a `TreeSet` rather than a `HashSet`. Because the set contains `String` objects, the natural ordering will be alphabetically:

```
Collection<String> words = new TreeSet<String>();
```

The output should now be as follows:

```
To
be
is
not
or
question
that
the
to
The list contains 9 words
```

- Note that upper-case characters are sorted before lower-case, hence "To" is listed before "be".

Be aware that the `HashSet` class has better performance that `TreeSet` since it does not need to take steps to keep the objects in a particular order, so it is recommended that you only use `TreeSet` when you actually require the objects to be sorted.

Converting the Pen class to use a collection

You have seen that the collection classes offer greater flexibility than arrays when needing to store groups of objects. In terms of the `Pen` class that currently uses an array that can hold up to ten animals, the first decision that needs to be made is whether to use instead a `List` or a `Set`. To help answer this you can address the following questions:

1. Does it make sense for the same animal to exist in the collection more than once?

2. Does the sequence in which animals are added into the pen have any significance?

3. Does it matter what sequence animals are retrieved from the pen?

It seems clear that that the answer to question 1 is that each individual animal can only exist once inside a pen. For question 2, there is no obvious significance to the order in which animals will be placed inside the pen, and likewise for question 3, there is no particular need to have to store them in any particular order. The conclusion, therefore, is that `Set` would be more appropriate than `List`, and that the `Set` does not need to be sorted. The best implementation class to achieve this would be `HashSet`. You are therefore now ready to start modifying the `Pen` class.

Because collections do not have an upper size limit you no longer need to specify an arbitrary capacity[1]. Remove the the following statement from `Pen`:

```
public static final int CAPACITY = 10;
```

---

1   In a real pen there would, of course, be a maximum capacity based upon the physical dimensions of the pen and the animals it would contain. For simplicty this will not be considered here.

The instance variable `animals` is currently declared to be an array of `Animal` objects, but it should now be a `Collection` of `Animal` objects. Change the declaration statement so it reads as follows:

```
private Collection<Animal> animals;
```

You no longer need the instance variable to hold the next element index since collections will manage this internally. Remove the following declaration:

```
private int nextElementIndex;
```

Change the constructor to instantiate the animals collection as a new unsorted set:

```
public Pen(String name) {
    this.name = name;
    animals = new HashSet<Animal>();
}
```

The `add()` method now simply needs to forward to the `add()` method of the collection:

```
public void add(Animal animal) {
    animals.add(animal);
}
```

It is generally a good idea when providing an `add()` method to also provide a `remove()` method. Insert the new method below so that an animal object can be removed from the pen:

```
public void remove(Animal animal) {
    animals.remove(animal);
}
```

The `getAnimals()` method currently returns an array, but it should instead return a collection. Change the method signature and the body to return the whole collection:

```
public Collection<Animal> getAnimals() {
    return animals;
}
```

The `getCount()` method needs to be changed to return the size of the collection (i.e. the number of objects it currently contains):

```
public int getCount() {
    return animals.size();
}
```

It will prove useful later on for each animal to "know" what pen it is in. Add the following instance variable inside the `Animal` class:

```
private Pen pen;
```

Define a getter and setter method for the `pen` field:

```
public Pen getPen() {
    return pen;
}

public void setPen(Pen pen) {
    this.pen = pen;
}
```

It will be useful for the natural ordering of `Pen` object to be alphabetically by the pen's name, so implement the `Comparable` interface:

```
public class Pen implements Comparable<Pen> {
```

And provide the required `compareTo()` method code:

```
@Override
public int compareTo(Pen otherPen) {
```

```
    // Sort alphabetically by name
    int result = getName().compareTo(otherPen.getName());
    if (result != 0) return result;

    /*
     * If reached here names are the same.
     * So that method is consistent with equals() will now
     * sort on hash code.
     */
    return hashCode() - otherPen.hashCode();
}
```

Making use of the Pen class in ZooAdministrator

The zoo administrator will keep a record of each pen in the zoo, being one
for each of the animal types. In the ZooAdministrator class define these
Pen instance variables:

```
private Pen lionPen, monkeyPen, penguinPen;
```

You will now define a private helper method that "acquires" an animal into
a pen:

```
private void acquireAnimal(Animal animal, Pen pen) {
    pen.add(animal);
    animal.setPen(pen);
}
```

Whenever you have a method that adds to a collection (as above) it is often
a good idea to provide a way of reversing the process:

```
private void relinquishAnimal(Animal animal) {
    Pen currentPen = animal.getPen();
    currentPen.remove(animal);
    animal.setPen(null);
}
```

You will now define a private helper method that simulates the acquisition of a number of lions by placing them in the lion's pen:

```
private void acquireLions() {
    acquireAnimal(new Lion("Leo", Gender.MALE, 2), lionPen);
    acquireAnimal(new Lion("Mr Fuzz", Gender.MALE, 2), lionPen);
    acquireAnimal(new Lion("Bazooka", Gender.FEMALE, 5), lionPen);
}
```

You can now define two similar methods for the other pens:

```
private void acquireMonkeys() {
    acquireAnimal(new Monkey("Bonzo", Gender.MALE, 5), monkeyPen);
    acquireAnimal(new Monkey("Norti", Gender.FEMALE, 5), monkeyPen);
    acquireAnimal(new Monkey("Hairball", Gender.MALE, 4), monkeyPen);
}

private void acquirePenguins() {
    acquireAnimal(new Penguin("Sammy", Gender.FEMALE, 1), penguinPen);
    acquireAnimal(new Penguin("Oswald", Gender.MALE, 2), penguinPen);
    acquireAnimal(new Penguin("Percy", Gender.MALE), penguinPen);
    acquireAnimal(new Penguin("Petra", Gender.FEMALE, 2), penguinPen);
}
```

Now define a `createExamplePens()` method which instantiates the three Pen instance variables and assigns the relevant animals to them:

```
private void createExamplePens() {
    lionPen = new Pen("Lion Lane");
    acquireLions();

    monkeyPen = new Pen("Monkey Mews");
    acquireMonkeys();

    penguinPen = new Pen("Penguin Parade");
    acquirePenguins();
}
```

You can now invoke the `createExamplePens()` method at the end of the constructor:

```
public ZooAdministrator() {
    createExampleZooKeepers();
    createExampleVisitors();
    createExamplePens();
}
```

You will now define a `public` method to simulate feeding time at the zoo. This could be written to iterate over each collection separately, but instead you will combine the three collections into one and then iterate over that:

```
public void feedingTime() {
    // Collect all the animals
    Collection<Animal> animals = new HashSet<Animal>();
    animals.addAll(lionPen.getAnimals());
    animals.addAll(monkeyPen.getAnimals());
    animals.addAll(penguinPen.getAnimals());

    // Feed them one at a time
    for (Animal anAnimal : animals) {
        System.out.println(anAnimal.getName() +
                " is eating a " + anAnimal.favouriteFood());
    }
}
```

- In the method body, a new empty collection called `animals` is created;

- The `addAll()` method is invoked on `animals` to add the objects within each of the pens;

- The `animals` collection is then iterated over. Note that because the `animals` collection is unsorted you cannot predict the sequence in which the objects will be processed.

To see the results of the `feedingTime()` method you can now invoke it upon the `admin` object inside the `main()` method of `Experiments`:

```
ZooAdministrator admin = new ZooAdministrator();
```

```
// methods to be invoked on admin will go here...
admin.feedingTime();
```

If you want the animals to be sorted into their natural order then you can pass the collection into a new `TreeSet` (which will be sorted). In `feedingTime()` insert the following statement after the last `addAll()` statement and before the for-each loop:

```
Collection<Animal> sortedAnimals =
            new TreeSet<Animal>(animals);
```

- Previously when instantiating a collection class you have used empty brackets so that an empty collection is created. Above, however, you can see that it is possible to pass another collection inside the brackets so that the new collection will contain all of the objects in the passed collection. This technique enables you to pass in an unsorted collection and turn it into a sorted collection.

To see the sorted results ensure you change the for-each loop to use `sortedAnimals` instead of `animals`:

```
for (Animal anAnimal : sortedAnimals) {
```

To sort in a different sequence than the natural ordering you can utilise the same `Comparator` object that was used when sorting arrays, although for a collection it is a two-step process.

Firstly, you need to instantiate an <u>empty</u> `TreeSet` passing the `Comparator` object as its argument. This tells the `TreeSet` how it should sequence any objects subsequently added into it:

```
Collection<Animal> sortedAnimals =
            new TreeSet<Animal>(new Animal.SortByAgeName());
```

Secondly, you can add all of the objects within the unsorted collection into the new sorted collection in one go though its addAll() method:

```
sortedAnimals.addAll(animals);
```

You can now iterate over sortedAnimals and they will be sorted into the order specified by the Comparator object, which in this case is age and name.

There is one final consideration that needs to be addressed. You will recall the discussion of privacy leaks in Chapter 4, and the Pen class currently leaks the collection of animals through the getAnimals() method. You can see this if you insert the following statements in, for example, the constructor of ZooAdministrator:

```
Collection<Animal> monkeys = monkeyPen.getAnimals();
monkeys.add(new Monkey("Invader", Gender.MALE, 9));
```

You have now managed to modify the internal contents of the Pen object without going through Pen's add() method, which is supposed to be the only way animals should be added to a pen. You saw in Chapter 8 the **copy constructor** technique when returning an instance variable, and that would be a valid way of preventing the privacy leak. You could change the getAnimals() method in Pen as follows to return a new collection which contains the objects of the current collection:

```
public Collection<Animal> getAnimals() {
    return new HashSet<Animal>(animals);
}
```

Now, if the client object adds or removed objects from the returned collection it will not affect the collection inside the Pen object. There is an alternative technique you can use with collections which will also prevent client objects from adding or removing at all. This uses a static utility method of the Collections class (note the plural name) called unmodifiableCollection(), which returns a read-only version of the collection specified in its argument. Change the getAnimals() method again:

```
public Collection<Animal> getAnimals() {
    return Collections.unmodifiableCollection(animals);
}
```

You will now find that if a client object (such as ZooAdministrator) tries to add or remove objects from the collection returned from getAnimals() then although the program will compile you will receive an UnsupportedOperationException at run-time. If you added the statements to the end of the constructor to see the effects of the privacy leak then please delete them.

Maps

You can think of a Map as being like a dictionary – you can look up a word to find its definition. But maps in Java are much more flexible than that since you can use them to look up any object in order to find another object which is associated to it. The object you search for is known as the **key**, and the object that is associated with it is known as the **value**. Because a map can contain many items you can think of it as being a **collection of pairs** of keys and their associated values.

So you can see a simple example to start with, here is a map which you can use to translate English words into French:

```
// Create a Map: key is English word, value is French word
Map<String, String> dictionary = new HashMap<String, String>();

// Add some words to the dictionary
dictionary.put("yes", "oui");
dictionary.put("no", "non");
dictionary.put("hello", "bonjour");
dictionary.put("goodbye", "au revoir");
```

- You declare a Map by specifying the formal type parameters of the key and value inside angle-brackets[1], which in this case is String for both (the first String relates to the type for the key and the second String relates to the type for the associated value);

- Map is an interface, so you need to instantiate a class which implements it. There are two main choices: HashMap (which is unsorted) and TreeMap (which is sorted by the key). Because there is no current need to sort the items you will use HashMap;

- The put() method is used to place a pair of items into the map, where the first argument is the key and the second argument is the associated value. If you use put() using a key that is already in the map then it will replace the existing entry. There is a corresponding remove() method which removes an entry pair where you specify the key.

To retrieve an item from a map you use the get() method passing a key:

```
// What is the French for hello?
System.out.println("The French for hello is " +
                          dictionary.get("hello"));
```

If you want to iterate over a map you can use a for-each loop, but you need to specify whether you want to iterate over the keys or the values. Iterating over the keys is more common, since you can then use the get() method inside the loop to get each associated value:

```
// Output the dictionary
for (String englishWord : dictionary.keySet()) {
    String frenchWord = dictionary.get(englishWord);
    System.out.println("The English word " + englishWord +
              " is " + frenchWord + " in French.");
}
```

---

1   Like the other collections you saw previously, specifying the formal type parameters is optional but strongly recommended.

- The `keySet()` method is used to tell the loop to use the keys to iterate over;

- Inside the loop, the `get()` method retrieves the value associated with the current key.

To iterate over the values, specify `values()` in place of `keySet()`:

```
// Output the French words
for (String frenchWord : dictionary.values()) {
    System.out.println(frenchWord);
}
```

If you want the map to be sorted on its keys you can simply change the instantiation of the dictionary map from `HashMap` to `TreeMap`:

```
Map<String, String> dictionary = new TreeMap<String, String>();
```

It is also possible to convert an unsorted map into a sorted map by passing the unsorted map as an argument to a new map object, similar to how you converted an unsorted set. Therefore, instead of changing dictionary to `TreeMap` as above, you could keep it as a `HashMap` and then do this:

```
Map<String, String> sortedDictionary =
                new TreeMap<String, String>(dictionary);
```

If you need to sort the values as opposed to the keys, then you can use the `values()` method to return a `Collection` and then pass that collection into a `TreeSet`:

```
Collection<String> sortedFrenchWords =
                new TreeSet<String>(dictionary.values());
```

A more advanced use of a map is where the associated value can be a collection; that is, each key can be associated with any number of values. You declare such a map as follows:

```
Map<String, Collection<Integer>> lotterySyndicate =
                   new HashMap<String, Collection<Integer>>();
```

- Note the second formal type parameter is a `Collection` of `Integer`[1] objects. Take care to include both ending angle-brackets.

You use the normal `put()` method to place a key and value into the map, but need to create a collection capable of being the value associated with the key:

```
// John's lottery numbers
Collection<Integer> numbersForJohn = new TreeSet<Integer>();
numbersForJohn.add(4);
numbersForJohn.add(16);
numbersForJohn.add(23);
numbersForJohn.add(29);
numbersForJohn.add(36);
numbersForJohn.add(42);
lotterySyndicate.put("John", numbersForJohn);

// Sue's lottery numbers
Collection<Integer> numbersForSue = new TreeSet<Integer>();
numbersForSue.add(9);
numbersForSue.add(11);
numbersForSue.add(19);
numbersForSue.add(25);
numbersForSue.add(36);
numbersForSue.add(37);
lotterySyndicate.put("Sue", numbersForSue);

// Output the lottery numbers
System.out.println(lotterySyndicate);
```

---

1   Using the `Integer` wrapper class since primitives are not allowed in collections.

Using a Map for zoo keepers' responsibilities

At the zoo each zoo keeper is responsible for certain pens, as listed below:

- Alice looks after the monkeys and penguins;

- Bob looks after the lions, monkeys and penguins;

- Charles only looks after the penguins.

This can be modelled using a map by taking the view that each zoo keeper will be the "key" and each will require an associated value of a collection of pens.

In the `ZooAdministrator` class declare a new instance variable called `responsibilities` that will be a `Map`, keyed by `ZooKeeper` objects and with the associated value being a collection of `Pen` objects:

```
private Map<ZooKeeper, Collection<Pen>> responsibilities;
```

Define a new method `createExampleResponsibilities()` which will instantiate the map as a `HashMap` and then assign the appropriate pens into the map, for each zoo keeper:

```
private void createExampleResponsibilities() {
    responsibilities = new HashMap<ZooKeeper, Collection<Pen>>();

    // Alice
    Collection<Pen> alicePens = new HashSet<Pen>();
    alicePens.add(monkeyPen);
    alicePens.add(penguinPen);
    responsibilities.put(alice, alicePens);

    // Bob
    Collection<Pen> bobPens = new HashSet<Pen>();
    bobPens.add(lionPen);
    bobPens.add(penguinPen);
    bobPens.add(monkeyPen);
    responsibilities.put(bob, bobPens);
```

```
    // Charles
    Collection<Pen> charlesPens = new HashSet<Pen>();
    charlesPens.add(penguinPen);
    responsibilities.put(charles, charlesPens);
}
```

- Note how for each zoo keeper, a HashSet is used to group the relevant pens, and this is used as the value argument when being placed into the map, which is keyed on the ZooKeeper object.

You can now invoke the method at the end of the constructor:

```
public ZooAdministrator() {
    createExampleZooKeepers();
    createExampleVisitors();
    createExamplePens();
    createExampleResponsibilities();
}
```

It will be useful to output each zoo keeper's responsibilities, so define a new method in ZooAdministrator called showZooKeeperResponsibilities(). This will contain some nested loops:

- The outer loop will iterate over each zoo keeper in turn;

- For each zoo keeper, a second loop will iterate over each pen the zoo keeper is responsible for in turn;

- For each pen, a third loop will iterate over each of the animals that exist in that pen in turn, sending the animal's state to output.

Here is the method:

```
public void showZooKeeperResponsibilities() {
    System.out.println("Zoo keeper responsibilities");
    System.out.println("===========================");
```

```java
// For each zoo keeper in turn...
for (ZooKeeper aZooKeeper : responsibilities.keySet()) {
    System.out.println(aZooKeeper.getName() +" looks after:");

    // Get current zoo keeper's pens
    Collection<Pen> pens = responsibilities.get(aZooKeeper);

    // For each pen in turn...
    for (Pen aPen : pens) {

        // Get the animals in the current pen
        Collection<Animal> animals = aPen.getAnimals();

        // For each animal in turn...
        for (Animal anAnimal : animals) {
            System.out.println("-> " + anAnimal);
        }
    }

    // That's it for this zoo keeper
    System.out.println("--------------------------");
  }
}
```

- You will see each nested loop indented inside the one outside of it.

In the `main()` method of `Experiments` you can now invoke the above method:

```java
ZooAdministrator admin = new ZooAdministrator();
admin.showZooKeeperResponsibilities();
```

Enhancements in Java 7

If you are using Java 7 you only need to specify the generic types on the variable declaration and not its instantiation. Taking an example from earlier in this chapter, contrast the two statements below:

```java
// Pre-Java 7 style...
```

```
Map<String, String> dictionary = new HashMap<String, String>();

// In Java 7 you can do this...
Map<String, String> dictionary = new HashMap();
```

12. Multi-threading

Threads allow your application to perform more than one process concurrently.

In this chapter you will learn:

- *The principles of multi-threading;*

- *Extending the* Thread *class;*

- *Implementing the* Runnable *interface;*

- *Using* wait() *and* notifyAll() *to coordinate dependent threads.*

The principles of multi-threading

You will probably be familiar with the idea of **multi-tasking**, whereby one computer is able to run more than one application at the same time. For example, on a desktop system you might have a word processor, a browser and an email application open and operating concurrently. Even if the desktop system in question only has a single physical processor as part of its hardware, it is still able to give the appearance of multi-tasking by rapidly and automatically switching between them under the control of the operating system.

Multi-threading is a similar concept except that it refers to a single application being able to run multiple processes concurrently, or at least give the appearance of doing so. This can be a very useful feature for certain types of application:

- A "space invaders" style game needs to move aliens across the screen and at the same time be able to respond to your keyboard and mouse clicks to fire ammunition at the aliens;

- A browser needs to be able to download a movie file while still letting you browse to other sites on a different tab;

- A bank needs to be able to serve its ATM machines around the country.

In all of the above cases, and many more, each of the activities that needs to run independently is defined in the software as a separate **thread**. A thread is therefore a single line of execution that can run concurrently with one or more other threads. In the case of Java it is the JVM that takes care of the switching between separate threads. It does so by giving each thread a small amount of time to do some processing before pausing it and then giving time to some other thread. The Garbage Collector, mentioned in Chapter 4, runs in its own thread.

It is worth bearing in mind that all Java applications run in at least one thread automatically. When you code your own threaded classes you are adding additional threads to it.

An example multi-threaded scenario

Suppose the zoo requires a facility to allow entry tickets to be booked in advance, and that there could be multiple persons trying to make bookings at the same time , such as through an online booking system. You would therefore have a single object of type `BookingCounter` (to be created shortly) and multiple objects of type `Booker` (also to be created shortly) each of which is an individual thread.

Here is the `BookingCounter` class, which simply keeps a count of the number of bookings made. Create this class in the `virtualzoo.core` package:

```
package virtualzoo.core;

public class BookingCounter {

    private int count;
```

```java
    public BookingCounter() {
        count = 0;
    }

    public int getCount() {
        return count;
    }

    public void makeBooking() {
        // Get copy of the current count
        int copyCount = count;

        // Add one to the count copy
        copyCount++;

        // Sleep for 1 millisecond to allow another thread to run
        try {
            Thread.sleep(1);
        } catch (InterruptedException ex) {
            System.out.println(ex.getMessage());
        }

        // Update the actual count from the copy
        count = copyCount;
    }

}
```

- The class contains a single instance variable called `count` to keep a count of how many bookings have been made. The constructor initialises this to zero;

- The `getCount()` method just returns the current value of `count`;

- The `makeBooking()` method increments the count by one. The code to do so has been made more complex than it needs to be in order to demonstrate a problem that can and will occur with multi-threaded code. The `Thread.sleep()` method call causes the current thread to sleep for the number of milliseconds specified in the argument.

This has been used here to effectively force the JVM to give time to a different thread, if there are any.

You now need to define a multi-threaded class to represent persons making a booking. There are two ways in which you can make objects of a class capable of being executed concurrently: by extending the the Thread class or by implementing the Runnable interface[1].

Extending the Thread class

The first way of defining a multi-threaded class is to extend the Thread class and override its run() method. Here is the Booker class which does just that:

```
package virtualzoo.core;

public class Booker extends Thread {

    private BookingCounter booking;

    public Booker(BookingCounter booking) {
        this.booking = booking;
    }

    @Override
    public void run() {
        booking.makeBooking();
    }

}
```

- Each object of type Booker needs a reference to the BookingCounter object, which it gets in its constructor;

- The run() method defined in Thread does nothing, so you need to override it to do something useful. Here, you simply invoke the makeBooking() method of the referenced BookingCounter object.

---

1   Both the Thread class and the Runnable interface are in package java.lang so you don't need any import statement for them.

Here is the code needed to simulate 100 separate persons (each of whom will be a threaded object of the `Booker` class) each making one booking. You could enter this in the `Experiments` class in order to run it:

```
// Create a single BookingCounter
BookingCounter booking = new BookingCounter();

// Create 100 Booker threads using same BookingCounter
for (int i = 0; i < 100; i++) {
    Booker b = new Booker(booking);
    b.start();
}

// Allow time for all threads to complete
try {
    Thread.sleep(1000); // 1000 milliseconds = 1 second
} catch (InterruptedException ex) {
    System.out.println(ex.getMessage());
}
System.out.println("Number of bookings made: " + booking.getCount());
```

- An instance of `BookingCounter` is created;

- Then, 100 separate `Booker` objects are created in a `for` loop. Note the call to a method called `start()` (which is inherited from `Thread`). It is the `start()` method which sets up the object in its own thread and which invokes the `run()` method for you, which you overrode in the `Booker` class. If you were to call `run()` yourself instead of calling `start()` then while your code would execute it would not do so in its own thread;

- The current thread is put to sleep for 1000 milliseconds (which is 1 second) in order to give all of the threads time to complete;

- Finally, the total number of bookings made is sent to the **Output** window.

The number of `bookings` output should of course be 100, since that was how many `Booker` objects made a single booking each. But if you run the above code you will almost certainly find it outputs a number smaller than 100, possibly much smaller. It is also possible that you will get different results each time you run it. So what is causing this to happen? To answer this question it will be helpful to see diagrammatically how a thread transitions between its various states:

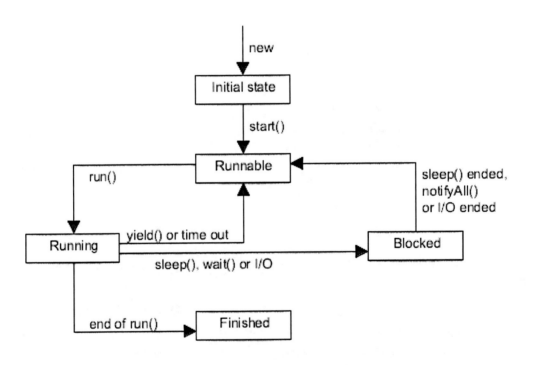

Figure 12.1: Transitions between thread states

The above diagram looks a little daunting at first, but here is a descriptive summary:

- The `new` keyword is used to instantiate a thread (just as it is used to instantiate any object). This puts the thread into the **initial** state, which means it just exists;

- When the `start()` method is invoked it moves into the **runnable** state. This means it is eligible to begin executing but is not currently doing so. It will wait until the JVM scheduler gives it some time;

- When the scheduler decides to give it some time, it goes into your `run()` method and the thread goes into the **running** state, meaning it is actually doing something;

- Because the scheduler tries to share time across multiple threads it may decide to pause part way inside the `run()` method of the running thread (which is in effect a "time-out"). It will then move the thread back into the **runnable** state while the other thread or threads are given time. If instead of a time-out the running thread invokes a `sleep()`, `wait()` or input/output process it will move into the **blocked** state before going back into the runnable state;

- At some point the scheduler will give time back to the thread where it will resume where it left off. The thread may need to switch between **running** and **runnable** (or **blocked**) many times before it finally completes;

- When the `run()` method ends the thread moves into the **finished** state.

Now look again at the pertinent code inside the `makeBooking()` method of `BookingCounter`:

```
int copyCount = count;    // 1
copyCount++;              // 2
count = copyCount;        // 3
```

Suppose there are only two separate `Booker` threads that each need to execute the above code. When the first thread moves into the **running** state it needs to execute statements 1, 2 and 3 above but it is possible that it might only complete statement 1 before the scheduler decides to pause it, giving control to the second thread. At this stage, the `count` variable has not had a chance to be incremented so will be at its initial value of zero.

Now the second thread starts and when it executes statement 1 finds that `count` is still zero. Suppose it then goes on to complete statements 2 and three, leaving `count` with the value of 1.

Now the scheduler passes control back to the first thread where it will carry on from where it left off, but its object `copyCount` is still zero so it when it completes statements 2 and 3 `count` ends up being 1 again, instead of 2 which it should be.

You might think that replacing the above three statements with the one below would solve the problem:

```
count++;
```

However, a single Java statement could still require multiple machine code instructions to do its work, and the scheduler might pause it before they complete. Taking the incrementation above, the machine code still needs three processes to achieve this:

1. Read the current value from memory;

2. Update the value;

3. Write the new value back to memory.

You may find that using `count++` as the only statement inside `makeBooking()` appears to work – but you cannot guarantee that it always will.

The solution is to **lock** the object such that other threads won't be allowed to gain access until it completes. To do this you need to specify the `synchronized` keyword as part of the method definition:

```
public synchronized int getCount() {
    return count;
}

public synchronized void makeBooking() {
    // Get copy of the current count
    int copyCount = count;
```

```
    // Add one to the count copy
    copyCount++;

    // Sleep for 1 millisecond to "force" another thread to run
    try {
        Thread.sleep(1);
    } catch (InterruptedException ex) {
        System.out.println(ex.getMessage());
    }

    // Update the actual count from the copy
    count = copyCount;
}
```

Once the first thread gains access to a `synchronized` method it puts a lock on the object the method belongs to, such that no other thread can access any `synchronized` method in that object until the first thread completes. In this way, you know the `count` variable will be updated properly for each thread, and you should now find that executing the code results in the correct output of 100.

To summarise, any method which returns or changes an instance variable and which could be invoked by multiple threads, should be marked as `synchronized`. This ensures that a lock is placed upon the object by the invoking thread and the lock only gets released when that thread completes all of the code within the method. This means that no other thread will be able to access either that or any other `synchronized` method until the lock is released. Methods which aren't marked as `synchronized` will still be available to other threads.

> Use of synchronisation does have a performance impact, so you should avoid using the `synchronized` keyword if you know it can never be invoked by multiple threads.
>
> It is also possible to synchronize blocks of code within a method rather than an

> entire method.

Implementing the Runnable interface

You have seen that you can extend the `Thread` class to define a class which can run concurrently with other threads, but what if the class you want to make multi-threaded already extends some other class? The answer is to instead implement the `Runnable` interface.

Suppose you want `Visitor`[1] objects to be multi-threaded, so you decide to create a new class `VisitorBooker`:

```
package virtualzoo.core;

import com.example.util.*;

public class VisitorBooker extends Visitor implements Runnable {

    private BookingCounter booking;

    public VisitorBooker(Person person, Email email,
                                    BookingCounter booking) {
        super(person, email);
        this.booking = booking;
    }

    @Override
    public void run() {
        booking.makeBooking();
    }

}
```

- The `VisitorBooker` class extends `Visitor` so it can't also extend `Thread`. Therefore, it has been declared as implementing the `Runnable` interface;

---

1   You defined the `Visitor` class in Chapter 4.

- The `Runnable` interface has a `run()` method which you need to write code for, being the same as for the `Booker` class;

- Note that the `Visitor` class needs a `Person` and `Email` object so these are obtained via the constructor.

You only need a couple of minor changes in the `Experiments` class to use `VisitorBooker` instead of `Booker`:

```
// Create a single booking counter
BookingCounter booking = new BookingCounter();

// Create a Person and an Email
Person p = new Person("Fred");
Email e = new Email("fred@example.com");

// Create 100 VisitorBooker threads using same BookingCounter
for (int i = 0; i < 100; i++) {
    VisitorBooker vb = new VisitorBooker(p, e, booking);
    Thread t = new Thread(vb);
    t.start();
}

// Allow time for all threads to complete
try {
    Thread.sleep(1000);
} catch (InterruptedException ex) {
    System.out.println(ex.getMessage());
}
System.out.println("Number of bookings made: " + booking.getCount());
```

- You will need to import `com.example.util`;

- A `Person` object and an `Email` object are created because they are required by the `Visitor` class;

- One hundred `VisitorBooker` objects are created (each of which is `Runnable`);

- A `Thread` object is created, passing the `Runnable` to it (in this case, each `VistorBooker`);

- The `start()` method is invoked on the `Thread` object.

Essentially, implementing the `Runnable` interface resulted in one additional line of code to make use of it: instantiating a `Thread` object passing the `Runnable` object as its argument.

Thread waiting and notification

For some types of multi-threaded application using the `synchronized` keyword alone is not enough on its own. Imagine that at the zoo the penguins are fed fish from a barrel in the following manner:

- The barrel has a capacity of 15 fish in total. Fish have to be placed into the barrel one at a time, and each fish can only be taken from the barrel one at a time;

- A zoo keeper has a total of 35 fish that can be put in the barrel;

- Each penguin can compete with other penguins for the fish, but each one can only eat a maximum of 10 fish.

Create a `FishBarrel` class follows:

```java
package virtualzoo.core;

public class FishBarrel {

    public static final int CAPACITY = 15;

    private int fishCount;

    public FishBarrel() {
        fishCount = 0;
    }
```

```
public synchronized int getCount() {
    return fishCount;
}

public synchronized boolean isEmpty() {
    return fishCount == 0;
}

public synchronized boolean isFull() {
    return fishCount == CAPACITY;
}

public synchronized void addFish() {
    // To be completed...
}

public synchronized void takeFish() {
    // To be completed...
}

}
```

- The above class includes the instance variable `fishCount` to hold the number of fish currently inside the barrel. Methods are included to return that count, and whether the barrel is empty or full;

- The `addFish()` method will be invoked by a zoo keeper thread, and provided the barrel is not already full a new fish will be added to it;

- The `takeFish()` method will be invoked by a penguin thread, and provided the barrel is not empty a fish will be removed from it;

- All of the methods are `sychronized` because they all access the `fishCount` instance variable which is to be shared among multiple threads.

You now need to provide the code for the `addFish()` and `takeFish()` methods. Looking first at `addFish()`, here is what it needs to do:

1. Check whether the barrel is already full. If so, wait until it isn't;

2. Provided the barrel is not full then add one fish to it;

3. Notify other threads which might be waiting for the barrel to contain some fish that at least one fish now exists in the barrel. This might be the case if a particular penguin thread found an empty barrel, so this notification will allow the thread to try again.

Here is the code to achieve the above steps:

```
public synchronized void addFish() {
    // Check whether barrel is already full
    while (isFull()) {
        // Barrel is full so wait
        try {
            wait();
        } catch (InterruptedException ex) {
            System.out.println(ex.getMessage());
        }
    }

    // If reached here barrel is not full so add a fish
    fishCount++;

    // Notify other waiting threads that state of barrel has changed
    notifyAll();
}
```

*   The wait() method is defined in Object and is therefore available to every class through inheritance. It causes the lock on the object to be released to give a chance for a different thread to run. In this case you are waiting for a different thread to take a fish from the barrel so it is no longer full;

*   Note that the following about the wait() method:

- It can throw an `InterruptedException` so this needs to be caught, although this won't occur in this simple application as no other thread will cause an interrupt;

- It is nested inside a `while` loop. It is very important that you use a `while` loop rather than just an `if` condition because when this thread gets control back it needs to recheck whether the condition (`isFull()` in this case) has actually changed.

- After the fish count has been incremented a call is made to `notifyAll()`. This is another method inherited through `Object`, and it serves to notify all other waiting threads that are themselves waiting that they can try and continue.

> There is also a `notify()` method which notifies a single thread, but it is up to the scheduler which one is notified (and is effectively random). If you have more than one waiting thread this means that the one that gets notified might not be the one that does what you are waiting for. Because of this drawback, unless you know for certain that there is only one other thread then it is strongly recommended that you use `notifyAll()` rather than `notify()`.

The code for the `takeFish()` method follows a very similar pattern:

```
public synchronized void takeFish() {
    // Check whether barrel is currently empty
    while (isEmpty()) {
        // Wait until barrel no longer empty
        try {
            wait();
        } catch (InterruptedException ex) {
            System.out.println(ex.getMessage());
        }
    }

    // If reached here barrel is not empty so remove a fish
    fishCount--;
```

```
    // Notify other waiting threads that state of barrel has changed
    notifyAll();
}
```

Here is the code for a threaded zoo keeper[1] class:

```
package virtualzoo.core;

public class FishKeeper implements Runnable {

    public static final int TOTAL_FISH = 35;

    private FishBarrel barrel;
    private int fishRemaining;

    public FishKeeper(FishBarrel barrel) {
        this.barrel = barrel;
        fishRemaining = TOTAL_FISH;
    }

    public int getFishRemaining() {
        return fishRemaining;
    }

    @Override
    public void run() {
        while (fishRemaining > 0) {
            barrel.addFish();
            fishRemaining--;
        }
    }

}
```

- The constructor takes a reference to a `FishBarrel` object, and the `run()` method adds the fish to the barrel one at a time.

---

1   For simplicity this class does not extend `ZooKeeper` since it is not relevant to the example.

Here is the code for a threaded penguin[2]:

```
package virtualzoo.core;

public class HungryPenguin implements Runnable {

    public static final int FISH_LIMIT = 10;

    private String name;
    private FishBarrel barrel;
    private int fishEaten;

    public HungryPenguin(String name, FishBarrel barrel) {
        this.name = name;
        this.barrel = barrel;
        fishEaten = 0;
    }

    public int getEatenCount() {
        return fishEaten;
    }

    @Override
    public void run() {
        while (fishEaten < FISH_LIMIT) {
            barrel.takeFish();
            fishEaten++;
            System.out.println(name + " has eaten fish " +fishEaten);
        }
    }

}
```

- The constructor takes a reference to a `FishBarrel` object, and the `run()` method keeps taking a fish from the barrel until it has eaten its quota.

2   For simplicity this class does not extend Penguin since it is not relevant to the example.

In the `Experiments` class you can enter the following statements to simulate a barrel, a single threaded zoo keeper and three threaded hungry penguins:

```java
FishBarrel barrel = new FishBarrel();

FishKeeper keeper = new FishKeeper(barrel);

HungryPenguin penguin1 = new HungryPenguin("penguin1", barrel);
HungryPenguin penguin2 = new HungryPenguin("penguin2", barrel);
HungryPenguin penguin3 = new HungryPenguin("penguin3", barrel);

new Thread(keeper).start();
new Thread(penguin1).start();
new Thread(penguin2).start();
new Thread(penguin3).start();

// Allow time for all threads to complete
try {
    Thread.sleep(1000);
} catch (InterruptedException ex) {
    System.out.println(ex.getMessage());
}
System.out.println("--- TOTALS ---");
System.out.println("penguin1 eaten: " + penguin1.getEatenCount());
System.out.println("penguin2 eaten: " + penguin2.getEatenCount());
System.out.println("penguin3 eaten: " + penguin3.getEatenCount());
System.out.println("keeper has left: " + keeper.getFishRemaining());
System.out.println("fish left in barrel: " + barrel.getCount());
```

If you run the above you should see in the **Output** window that the order in which the penguins eat each fish is mixed, although they all end up eating their fill. Each time you run the code you could get a different order.

Writing multi-threaded applications can get considerably more complex than the relatively simple examples in this chapter.

13. Introduction to Graphical User Interfaces

A Graphical User Interface provides the primary means by which users of your application interact with it.

In this chapter you will learn:

- *The structure of graphical programs;*

- *Some common layouts;*

- *Using containers to organise graphical components;*

- *Handling events such as button clicks;*

- *Using inner classes.*

Graphical programs

The original releases of Java included graphical component classes that utilise the native graphical facilities of the running machine. These classes are collectively known as the **Abstract Windowing Toolkit** (**AWT**) and are in package java.awt and its sub-packages.

Later, a complete new set of platform independent graphical classes were released known as **Swing** – these are in package javax.swing and its sub-packages (note the 'x' after 'java'). Swing classes are more complete and advanced, and solve the problems that AWT components sometimes had with components displaying and functioning slightly differently on different platforms.

Graphical layouts

Whenever you create a graphical Java class you need some way of placing the various components you need (buttons, labels, text entry fields, etc.) in a consistent and orderly fashion. In Chapter 16 you will learn how to use the graphical builder that comes with NetBeans, but for now you will learn the fundamentals of laying out graphical component objects using the components directly.

There are two main concepts you need to know:

1. A graphical application is made up of one or more **containers**, where each container may contain individual components or other containers. It is therefore possible to nest containers inside other containers, as deep as you like. You make use of this through the `Container` class, and more usually through one of its subclasses;

2. Each container is associated with a **layout manager** which determines how the components inside that container will be arranged. Each container may have a different layout manager. You make use of this through the `LayoutManager` interface, generally through one of its implementing classes.

> The `Container` class and the `LayoutManager` interface are in the `java.awt` package. However, since the graphical components you will develop will use the Swing classes you will mostly need to import `javax.swing`.

An example layout

All of the graphical classes you will develop in this book will be placed in package `virtualzoo.ui`, which you should have created earlier in this book. Right-click on the `virtualzoo.ui` package node and select **New | Java Class...**, entering a class name of `ExampleFrame`. In the source code, specify a wild-card import for the `javax.swing` package and make the class inherit from `JFrame`. Your source should look like this:

```
package virtualzoo.ui;

import javax.swing.*;

public class ExampleFrame extends JFrame {

}
```

The JFrame class provides a simple means of generating a desktop application window, with a built-in title bar and buttons to minimise, maximise and close the window. The JFrame class itself inherits from Container.

Even though the frame is currently empty, you can get it displayed on your desktop by instantiating it and telling it to become visible. Enter this into Experiments, **ensuring you import** virtualzoo.ui:

```
ExampleFrame frame = new ExampleFrame();
frame.setVisible(true);
```

You should see a tiny application window in the top-left corner of your screen that looks similar to this:

Figure 13.1: Empty frame

You can click the  button to close the window, but note that this does not actually end the application itself. To do this you need to tell NetBeans to end the application, which you can do by clicking the small close button that appears on the right-hand side of the bottom of the NetBeans window:

VirtualZoo (run)   running...   ⊠

Figure 13.2: NetBeans application process window

The first change you will make will be to cause the application to end itself whenever the window's close button is clicked, so define a constructor with the following code:

```
public ExampleFrame() {
    setDefaultCloseOperation(DISPOSE_ON_CLOSE);
}
```

- The `setDefaultCloseOperation()` (which is inherited from `JFrame`) tells the frame that the application should exit when the window's close button is clicked. If you are wondering why this is not automatically performed, it is because it allows you to control the exiting of your application, for example by displaying a confirmation prompt or saving any data;

- `DISPOSE_ON_CLOSE` is a constant inherited through `JFrame` which is the option to dispose of the resources associated with the window.

You can also set the size of the frame in pixels and a give it a title:

```
public ExampleFrame() {
    setDefaultCloseOperation(JFrame.DISPOSE_ON_CLOSE);
    setSize(300, 200);
    setTitle("My Application");
}
```

The frame should now look as follows:

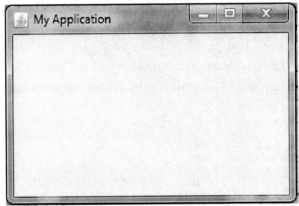

Figure 13.3: A sized frame

Now close the frame. You should also remember to close the frame after running each set of changes that follow, otherwise you will end up with multiple open windows.

You will recall that every constructor invokes a superclass constructor, and when this is not explicitly coded (as here) then it invokes the no-argument constructor. Therefore, the above is the equivalent of saying:

```
public ExampleFrame() {
    super();
    setDefaultCloseOperation(JFrame.DISPOSE_ON_CLOSE);
    setSize(300, 200);
    setTitle("My Application");
}
```

If you look at the Java API for `JFrame` you will see that there is another constructor that accepts a `String` argument to serve as the frame's title. You can therefore modify the constructor to take advantage of this and thereby remove the `setTitle()` method call:

```
public ExampleFrame() {
    super("My Application");
    setDefaultCloseOperation(JFrame.DISPOSE_ON_CLOSE);
    setSize(300, 200);
}
```

FlowLayout

To see how to place graphical components onto a container (such as a frame) you will initially use the one of the simplest layouts, the `FlowLayout`. This lays out components in a similar manner to how words are placed in a paragraph: each component is placed to the right of the previous component until the right-hand margin is reached, after which it is placed underneath.

You use the `setLayout()` method to specify that you want to use a `FlowLayout` as follows (place at the end of the constructor):

```
setLayout(new FlowLayout());
```

- Note that you need to import package `java.awt` to find the `FlowLayout` class.

The above instantiates a new FlowLayout object and assigns it to the frame. After the above statement write the following to instantiate a button and place it on the frame:

```
JButton myButton = new JButton("Click Me");
add(myButton);
```

The JButton class constructor lets you specify the text that will appear on the button. After myButton is created it is added to the frame, which should now look like this:

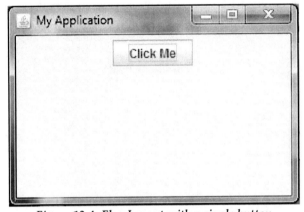

Figure 13.4: FlowLayout with a single button

You can click the button but nothing will happen at this stage. Later, you will learn how to attach an **event** to a button so that it performs an action of some kind when clicked.

Now add four more buttons:

```
JButton myButton2 = new JButton("Click Me 2");
add(myButton2);
JButton myButton3 = new JButton("Click Me 3");
add(myButton3);
JButton myButton4 = new JButton("Click Me 4");
add(myButton4);
JButton myButton5 = new JButton("Click Me 5");
add(myButton5);
```

Your screen should now look like this, which shows how subsequent components flow inside a `FlowLayout`:

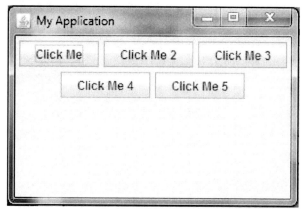

Figure 13.5: FlowLayout with five buttons

Try adjusting the width of the frame to see how the buttons adjust their placement.

If you prefer the placements to be left-aligned rather than centred, as is the above default, you pass an argument to the `FlowLayout` constructor:

```
setLayout(new FlowLayout(FlowLayout.LEFT));
```

- You may alternatively specify `FlowLayout.RIGHT` to get right-alignment, or `FlowLayout.CENTER` for centre alignment, although as mentioned, the latter is the default for the `FlowLayout` class.

The GridLayout

The `GridLayout` arranges components in a grid like fashion, where you specify the number of rows and columns that form the grid. Each "cell" in the grid will be of the same size. Change the `setLayout()` call as follows:

```
// Replace this line…
setLayout(new FlowLayout(FlowLayout.LEFT));

// with this…
setLayout(new GridLayout(3, 2)); // 3 rows, 2 columns
```

- The two int arguments supply the number of rows and the number of columns that are to make up the grid:

  o If you specify zero for the number of rows then it will build however many rows are needed for the specified number of columns;

  o If you specify zero for the number of columns then it will build however many columns are needed for the specified number of rows;

The code above should result in the following frame:

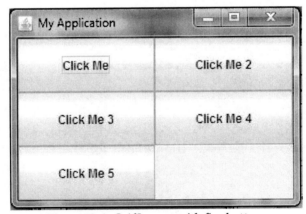

Figure 13.6: GridLayout with five buttons

Now change the number of rows to 2 and the number of columns to 3 and see how it changes the display.

You can specify a horizontal and vertical gap between the cells by passing two additional `int` arguments to the `GridLayout` constructor:

```
// 2 rows, 3 columns, 20 pixel gap
setLayout(new GridLayout(2, 3, 20, 20);
```

Note how if you resize the window all of the components adjust to fill the new size.

The BorderLayout

The `BorderLayout` is divided into five areas, representing the four points of the compass (north, south, east and west) together with a central area. You need to place your components in one of these five areas, although if you don't use a particular area then that area uses no space and the rest of the layout adjusts itself accordingly.

To see this more clearly, as well as changing the `setLayout()` method you can also change the button texts:

```
setLayout(new BorderLayout());

JButton myButton = new JButton("North");
add(myButton, BorderLayout.NORTH);

JButton myButton2 = new JButton("South");
add(myButton2, BorderLayout.SOUTH);

JButton myButton3 = new JButton("East");
add(myButton3, BorderLayout.EAST);

JButton myButton4 = new JButton("West");
add(myButton4, BorderLayout.WEST);

JButton myButton5 = new JButton("Center");
add(myButton5, BorderLayout.CENTER);
```

Note the following:

- The add() method has been passed an optional second argument representing the **constraint**; in this case BorderLayout uses it to place the component in the specified area. As you saw, FlowLayout and GridLayout did not require the constraint (had you specified one it would have been ignored);

- If you do not specify the constraint argument when using a BorderLayout then Java will assume you want to place the component in the centre area[1];

- There can be no more than one component in each area; if you place a component in an area where one exists already it will replace the existing one;

- The north and south areas stretch all the way across the screen;

- The centre area takes up whatever space remains after the other areas have been rendered.

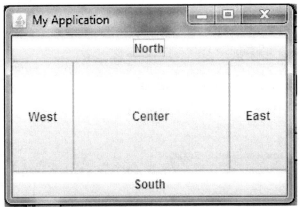

Figure 13.7: BorderLayout with five buttons

Try commenting out one or more of the placement statements to see how the layout adjusts itself when not all areas have been used.

---

1   Note the American spelling of the constant CENTER.

> `BorderLayout` is the default layout for `JFrame` if you don't specifically set one.

Using containers and the JPanel class to organise layouts

Because the `Container` object is capable of containing other components, including other containers, it is possible to create some very sophisticated layouts. Rather than place your components directly onto a frame, as shown in the previous examples, it is good practice to place them instead onto a `JPanel`, and then place the `JPanel` onto the frame. You can think of a `JPanel` as being a blank canvas onto which you can place your components (including other `JPanel` objects), and using this approach can facilitate reuse since the `JPanel` can be included in multiple frames or even inside a browser window.

You will now modify the constructor code to create a panel, add each of the buttons to the panel, and then add the panel to the frame.

```java
public ExampleFrame() {
    super("My Application");
    setDefaultCloseOperation(JFrame.DISPOSE_ON_CLOSE);
    setSize(300, 200);

    setLayout(new BorderLayout());

    // Create a panel to hold the components
    JPanel panel = new JPanel(new BorderLayout());

    // Create the components and add to the panel
    JButton myButton = new JButton("North");
    panel.add(myButton, BorderLayout.NORTH);

    JButton myButton2 = new JButton("South");
    panel.add(myButton2, BorderLayout.SOUTH);
```

```
        JButton myButton3 = new JButton("East");
        panel.add(myButton3, BorderLayout.EAST);

        JButton myButton4 = new JButton("West");
        panel.add(myButton4, BorderLayout.WEST);

        JButton myButton5 = new JButton("Center");
        panel.add(myButton5, BorderLayout.CENTER);

        // Add the panel to the frame
        add(panel); // defaults to BorderLayout.CENTER
    }
```

Note the following:

- The default layout for `JPanel` is a centred `FlowLayout`, and you therefore changed it to use `BorderLayout`.

- The `JButton` objects are added to the panel instead of directly onto the frame.

- Finally, the `JPanel` is added to the centre area of the frame.

To show you how a panel can contain other panels, you will no longer place a button in the "north" area but instead create another panel to contain a label and a text entry field:

```
// Replace these lines...
JButton myButton = new JButton("North");
panel.add(myButton, BorderLayout.NORTH);

// With these...
JPanel nameEntryPanel = new JPanel(); // defaults to FlowLayout

JLabel nameLabel = new JLabel("Enter your name:");
JTextField nameField = new JTextField(15);

nameEntryPanel.add(nameLabel);
nameEntryPanel.add(nameField);

panel.add(nameEntryPanel, BorderLayout.NORTH);
```

- A `JPanel` called `nameEntryPanel` is instantiated and which will use a `FlowLayout` (which is the default for `JPanel` if you don't specify a layout);

- The `JLabel` class creates a read-only label you can display on a screen;

- The `JTextField` class creates a text entry box. The argument is the width of the box in characters;

- The created label and text field are added to `nameEntryPanel` and then the latter is added to the north area of the containing panel.

The frame should now look like this:

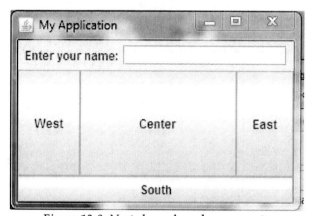

Figure 13.8: Nested panels and components

You will learn more about `JLabel`, `JTextField`, and many other graphical components in the next chapter.

The last change you will make in this section will be to let Java work out a sensible size for your frame rather than set it explicitly. Remove the following statement:

```
setSize(300, 200);
```

Now, at the end of the constructor insert this statement:

```
pack();
```

- The `pack()` method analyses each panel and component to work out their "preferred" size and adjusts the size of the panel accordingly.

The frame should now look as follows:

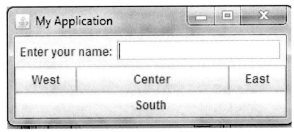

Figure 13.9: Result of pack() on a frame

Handling events

So far you have displayed some `JButton` objects on the screen but nothing happens when they are clicked because you have not yet defined any code to do so.

Java handles actions (such as button clicks, mouse movements, key presses, etc.) by notifying each **event** to all of its **listeners**. Like most other things in Java, events and listeners are just objects, and you therefore need to define an object which can listen to the event that Java will **fire**, since otherwise its action will be lost.

You will initially listen out for clicks to the **Center** button such that whenever it is clicked then whatever text value was typed in `nameField` (the `JTextField` object) will be sent to the **Output** window. This will entail telling this button object that you are interested in listening to its events, so look at the statements for this button that are currently defined:

```
JButton myButton5 = new JButton("Center");
panel.add(myButton5, BorderLayout.CENTER);
```

You have a reference object called `myButton5` that points to the `JButton` object. To make this button respond to a click you need to do two things:

1. Define a listener object that listens for a click and does something as a result; and

2. Assign the `myButton5` button object to the listener object.

An object to respond to a button click

You can define the `ExampleFrame` class itself to be the object that responds to button clicks. You do this by implementing the `ActionListener` interface:

```
public class ExampleFrame extends JFrame implements ActionListener {
```

At this stage the `ExampleFrame` class will no longer compile for the following two reasons:

1. The `ActionListener` interface is in package `java.awt.event` that you have not yet imported.

2. The `ActionListener` interface requires implementing classes to define a method called `actionPerformed()`.

To rectify these issues, firstly add the following import statement to the class:

```
import java.awt.event.*;
```

Secondly, define the `actionPerformed()` method somewhere in your class:

```
@Override
public void actionPerformed(ActionEvent event) {
    System.out.println("A button was clicked");
}
```

Assigning the listener to the button

At this point your frame should compile but it will still not do anything when a button is clicked because you have not yet told the button object that you want to listen to its events. Insert the following statement (marked in bold) between the two existing statements:

```
JButton myButton5 = new JButton("Center");
myButton5.addActionListener(this);
panel.add(myButton5, BorderLayout.CENTER);
```

The `addActionListener()` method tells the button object referenced by `myButton5` that the `ActionListener` object referenced by `this` wants to listen to its events. The `this` keyword refers to the current instance of the `ExampleFrame` class, which is allowed to be passed as an argument because the `ExampleFrame` class now implements the `ActionListener` interface.

You will now see the message **"A button was clicked"** whenever you click the **Center** button (the message will appear in the NetBeans **Output** window). At the moment this is the only button that responds to any clicks.

To see which button was clicked, change the `actionPerformed()` method as follows:

```
@Override
```

```
public void actionPerformed(ActionEvent event) {
    JButton source = (JButton) event.getSource();
    System.out.println("A button was clicked: " + source.getText());
}
```

The getSource() method of the ActionEvent class returns a reference to the object that caused the event to be fired, in other words the particular button that was clicked. Because the method returns it as type Object, and because you know it must actually be a JButton, you can cast it in order to invoke button specific methods. The getText() method returns the text label that appears on the button.

However, the purpose of the button was to output the name typed into the text field and not the button, so modify the actionPerformed() method:

```
@Override
public void actionPerformed(ActionEvent event) {
    // Get entered name
    String enteredName = nameField.getText();

    // Output the entered name
    System.out.println("Hello " + enteredName);
}
```

The code will not currently compile because it is unable to locate the nameField reference. This is because it is declared within the constructor and therefore local to the constructor only. The solution is to make nameField an instance variable:

```
private JTextField nameField;
```

Now you need to modify the constructor to use the instance variable instead of defining it locally:

```
// Replace this statement...
JTextField nameField = new JTextField(15);

// With this...
nameField = new JTextField(15);
```

Run the application again and enter a name into the name field box. After clicking the centre button you should now see the entered name displayed.

Suppose now you want to output the entered name in upper-case if the **West** button is clicked. You therefore need to listen to the west button:

```
JButton myButton4 = new JButton("West");
myButton4.addActionListener(this);
panel.add(myButton4, BorderLayout.WEST);
```

And you need to modify the `actionPerformed()` method to see which button was clicked, since the center button should still output the name unchanged. While you could read the button text label, as shown earlier, a better way would be to compare the objects themselves (in case you change the label text at a later time). In order to get access to the button objects you will need to make them instance variables and change the constructor so as not to declare them locally:

```
package virtualzoo.ui;

import java.awt.*;
import java.awt.event.*;
import javax.swing.*;

public class ExampleFrame extends JFrame implements ActionListener {

    private JTextField nameField;
    private JButton myButton2, myButton3, myButton4, myButton5;


    public ExampleFrame() {
        super("My Application");
        setDefaultCloseOperation(DISPOSE_ON_CLOSE);

        setLayout(new BorderLayout());

        // Create a panel to hold the components
        JPanel panel = new JPanel(new BorderLayout());
```

```java
        // Create the components and add to the panel
        JPanel nameEntryPanel = new JPanel();

        JLabel nameLabel = new JLabel("Enter your name:");
        nameField = new JTextField(15);

        nameEntryPanel.add(nameLabel);
        nameEntryPanel.add(nameField);

        panel.add(nameEntryPanel, BorderLayout.NORTH);

        myButton2 = new JButton("South");
        panel.add(myButton2, BorderLayout.SOUTH);

        myButton3 = new JButton("East");
        panel.add(myButton3, BorderLayout.EAST);

        myButton4 = new JButton("West");
        myButton4.addActionListener(this);
        panel.add(myButton4, BorderLayout.WEST);

        myButton5 = new JButton("Center");
        myButton5.addActionListener(this);
        panel.add(myButton5, BorderLayout.CENTER);

        // Add the panel to the frame
        add(panel); // defaults to BorderLayout.CENTER

        // Pack the components
        pack();
    }


    @Override
    public void actionPerformed(ActionEvent event) {
        // Get entered name
        String enteredName = nameField.getText();

        // Output the entered name
        System.out.println("Hello " + enteredName);
    }


}
```

You can now modify the `actionPerformed()` method to check for specific buttons being clicked using object identity:

```
@Override
public void actionPerformed(ActionEvent event) {
    // Get entered name
    String enteredName = nameField.getText();

    // Which button was clicked?
    Object source = event.getSource();
    if (source == myButton4) {
        // Convert name to uppercase
        System.out.println("Hello " + enteredName.toUpperCase());
    } else if (source == myButton5) {
        // Output the entered name as-is
        System.out.println("Hello " + enteredName);
    }
}
```

You could take a similar approach to handle the other two buttons, but there is an alternative way that enables you to avoid having lots of `if...else` blocks by defining separate objects to listen for each button, and making use of **inner classes**.

Using inner classes

The majority of classes you write are **top-level** classes, that is, independent classes in its own right and in their own class file. It is often useful to create **inner classes**, being classes that exist inside of another class. You would create an inner class when the outer class (i.e. the top-level class that contains it) requires a service that is specific to the outer class only. This is frequently the case when coding event listeners.

Inner classes are often declared `private`, though they don't have to be. You will now modify `ExampleFrame` to use an inner class as the listener for the centre button object, instead of the frame (the outer class) being the direct listener.

Step 1

Surround the `actionPerformed()` method with the inner class declaration *(this should be indented the same as if it were another method, and therefore the `actionPerformed()` method should be indented one level further in that it is currently)*:

```
private class ButtonListener implements ActionListener {

    @Override
    public void actionPerformed(ActionEvent event) {
        // Get entered name
        String enteredName = nameField.getText();

        // Which button was clicked?
        Object source = event.getSource();
        if (source == myButton4) {
            // Convert name to uppercase
            System.out.println("Hello " + enteredName.toUpperCase());
        } else if (source == myButton5) {
            // Output the entered name as-is
            System.out.println("Hello " + enteredName);
        }
    }

}
```

Step 2

remove the `implements ActionListener` section from the outer class declaration so that it reads as follows:

```
public class ExampleFrame extends JFrame {
```

Step 3

change the constructor to read as follows:

```
public ExampleFrame() {
    super("My Application");
    setDefaultCloseOperation(DISPOSE_ON_CLOSE);
```

```
        setLayout(new BorderLayout());

        // Create a panel to hold the components
        JPanel panel = new JPanel(new BorderLayout());

        // Create a ButtonListener (i.e inner class)
        ButtonListener buttonListener = new ButtonListener();

        // Create the components and add to the panel
        JPanel nameEntryPanel = new JPanel();

        JLabel nameLabel = new JLabel("Enter your name:");
        nameField = new JTextField(15);

        nameEntryPanel.add(nameLabel);
        nameEntryPanel.add(nameField);

        panel.add(nameEntryPanel, BorderLayout.NORTH);

        myButton2 = new JButton("South");
        panel.add(myButton2, BorderLayout.SOUTH);

        myButton3 = new JButton("East");
        panel.add(myButton3, BorderLayout.EAST);

        myButton4 = new JButton("West");
        myButton4.addActionListener(buttonListener);
        panel.add(myButton4, BorderLayout.WEST);

        myButton5 = new JButton("Center");
        myButton5.addActionListener(buttonListener);
        panel.add(myButton5, BorderLayout.CENTER);

        // Add the panel to the frame
        add(panel); // defaults to BorderLayout.CENTER

        // Pack the components
        pack();
    }
```

Verify that the frame correctly responds to the West and Center buttons.

Using separate listeners for each event

As programs become more complex it can be helpful to define a separate listener class for each individual event rather than use just one listener to serve all.

Step 1

Rename `ButtonListener` to `CenterButtonListener`. The most effective way to do this is by right-clicking on the `ButtonListener` text on the inner class declaration and selecting **Refactor | Rename**. Then enter `CenterButtonHandler` in the **New Name** box and click **Refactor**. As well as renaming the inner class, NetBeans will automatically locate and find everywhere it is referenced and update those as well.

Step 2

Simplify the `actionPerformed()` method inside `CenterButtonHandler` to just output the text entered into `nameField`:

```
private class CenterButtonHandler implements ActionListener {

    @Override
    public void actionPerformed(ActionEvent e) {
        System.out.println("Hello " + nameField.getText());
    }

}
```

Step 3

Modify the call to `addActionListener()` against `myButton5` to instantiate a new `CenterButtonHandler` object instead of specifying `buttonListener`:

```
myButton5.addActionListener(new CenterButtonHandler());
```

Step 4

At the end of the source code enter another inner class to handle the west button:

```
private class WestButtonHandler implements ActionListener {

    @Override
    public void actionPerformed(ActionEvent e) {
        System.out.println("Hello " +
                            nameField.getText().toUpperCase());
    }

}
```

Step 5

Modify the call to `addActionListener()` against `myButton4` to instantiate a new `WestButtonHandler` object instead of specifying `this`:

```
myButton4.addActionListener(new WestButtonHandler());
```

Step 6

Remove the following statements from the constructor as they are no longer needed:

```
// Create a ButtonListener (i.e inner class)
ButtonListener buttonListener = new ButtonListener();
```

Step 7

Verify that the application works as before.

The complete source code for `ExampleFrame` should look as follows:

```
package virtualzoo.ui;
```

```java
import java.awt.*;
import java.awt.event.*;
import javax.swing.*;

public class ExampleFrame extends JFrame {

    private JTextField nameField;
    private JButton myButton2, myButton3, myButton4, myButton5;


    public ExampleFrame() {
        super("My Application");
        setDefaultCloseOperation(DISPOSE_ON_CLOSE);

        setLayout(new BorderLayout());

        // Create a panel to hold the components
        JPanel panel = new JPanel(new BorderLayout());

        // Create the components and add to the panel
        JPanel nameEntryPanel = new JPanel();

        JLabel nameLabel = new JLabel("Enter your name:");
        nameField = new JTextField(15);

        nameEntryPanel.add(nameLabel);
        nameEntryPanel.add(nameField);

        panel.add(nameEntryPanel, BorderLayout.NORTH);

        myButton2 = new JButton("South");
        panel.add(myButton2, BorderLayout.SOUTH);

        myButton3 = new JButton("East");
        panel.add(myButton3, BorderLayout.EAST);

        myButton4 = new JButton("West");
        myButton4.addActionListener(new WestButtonHandler());
        panel.add(myButton4, BorderLayout.WEST);

        myButton5 = new JButton("Center");
        myButton5.addActionListener(new CenterButtonHandler());
```

```java
        panel.add(myButton5, BorderLayout.CENTER);

        // Add the panel to the frame
        add(panel); // defaults to BorderLayout.CENTER

        // Pack the components
        pack();
    }

    private class CenterButtonHandler implements ActionListener {

        @Override
        public void actionPerformed(ActionEvent e) {
            System.out.println("Hello " + nameField.getText());
        }

    }

    private class WestButtonHandler implements ActionListener {

        @Override
        public void actionPerformed(ActionEvent e) {
            System.out.println("Hello " +
                    nameField.getText().toUpperCase());
        }

    }

}
```

To handle the other buttons you can follow the same pattern of defining an inner class and instantiating an object of that type to serve as the button's listener.

14. Common GUI components

The `javax.swing` package contains several useful graphical components that you can use in your applications.

In this chapter you will learn:

- How to use `JFrame` to provide a desktop window;

- How to use `JLabel` for a piece of uneditable text;

- How to use `JTextField` and `JTextArea` for editable text;

- How to use `JButton` to create buttons;

- How to use `JCheckBox` and `JRadioButton` to provide user options;

- How to use `JSlider` and `JSpinner` to allow selection of a value from a range;

- How to use `JList` to provide a list of related objects;

- How to use `JTable` to provide a spreadsheet-style list of objects;

- How to use `JTree` to provide a list of objects that are hierarchical;

- How to use `JSplitPane` to divide your screen into moveable sections;

- How to use `JTabbedPane` to divide your screen into tabbed sections;

- How to use `JDialog` and `JOptionPane` to create separate dialogue boxes;

JFrame

In the previous chapter you saw that the `JFrame` class can be used to provide a desktop window for your application. For the purposes of this chapter you will create a new `JFrame` that will show various UI components. Define a class called `DemoUI` in the `virtualzoo.ui` package:

```java
package virtualzoo.ui;

import java.awt.*;
import javax.swing.*;

public class DemoUI extends JFrame {

    public static void main(String[] args) {
        new DemoUI().setVisible(true);
    }

    public DemoUI() {
        super("Demonstrate UI Components");
        setDefaultCloseOperation(DISPOSE_ON_CLOSE);

        add(buildUI(), BorderLayout.CENTER);

        pack();
        setLocationRelativeTo(null);
    }

    private JPanel buildUI() {
        JPanel panel = new JPanel(new BorderLayout());

        // Components will go here...


        // Return the built panel
        return panel;
    }

}
```

- The class contains its own static `main()` method which will allow you to run it independently from the rest of the application. To do this, right-click the `DemoUI.java` node in the **Projects** window and select **Run**;

- The constructor does the following:

  ○ Passes the required title to the superclass constructor;

- ○ Ensures the application is ended when the frame is closed;

- ○ Adds the `JPanel` object returned from the `buildUI()` method to the centre of the frame;

- ○ Packs the components and centres the frame on the screen using `setLocationRelativeTo(null)`.

- The `buildUI()` method returns a `JPanel` which will contain the various UI components shown in this chapter.

JLabel

The `JLabel` class will show a read-only piece of text:

```
private JPanel buildUI() {
    JPanel panel = new JPanel(new BorderLayout());

    // Components will go here...
    JLabel label = new JLabel("This is a text label");
    panel.add(label);

    // Return the built panel
    return panel;
}
```

If you run the frame you should see the following:

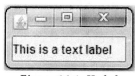

Figure 14.1: JLabel

By default the text is left aligned, but you can optionally supply a second argument to the constructor to specify right or centre alignment:

```
JLabel label = new JLabel("This is a text label", JLabel.RIGHT);
```

If you need to change the text that appears on the label you can invoke the `setText()` method:

```
label.setText("Some different text");
```

There is also a `getText()` method which returns the text to be displayed as a `String`.

If you want to show the label using a different font you can instantiate and assign a suitable `Font` object:

```
Font f = new Font("Serif", Font.BOLD, 22);
label.setFont(f);
```

- The `Font` constructor accepts three argument values:
  - The name of the font you require;
  - Whether the font should be plain, bold or italic (using the constants `Font.PLAIN`, `Font.BOLD` or `Font.ITALIC` respectively. If you want your font to be both bold and italic, you can separate the constants with a vertical bar, i.e. `Font.BOLD|Font.ITALIC`;
  - The point size of the font.

If you want the text to be shown in a particular colour you can assign a suitable `Color` object either through one of its colour constants or a colour combination you specify:

```
// Using a colour constant: available constants are
// BLACK, BLUE, CYAN, DARK_GRAY, GRAY, GREEN, LIGHT_GREY,
// MAGENTA, ORANGE, PINK, RED, WHITE, YELLOW
label.setForeground(Color.RED);

// Using a red, green, blue combination
label.setForeground(new Color(100, 50, 210));
```

- If you use the red, green, blue combination constructor then each value must be between 0 and 255 to indicate the amount of that colour that should be used. This allows you to obtain fine degrees of shading.

JTextField

The `JTextField` class allows the entry by the user of a piece of text in a box consisting of a single line:

```
private JPanel buildUI() {
    JPanel panel = new JPanel(new BorderLayout());

    // Components will go here...
    JTextField field = new JTextField(25);
    panel.add(field);

    // Return the built panel
    return panel;
}
```

- The value in the `JTextField` constructor specifies the number of character spaces for use as the length of the field, although this is for display purposes only, since the user will be able to type any number of characters.

You can make the field show some initial default text by using the two-argument constructor:

```
JTextField field = new JTextField("Default text", 25);
```

Your frame should look like this:

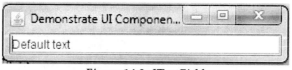

Figure 14.2: JTextField

Like the JLabel class, you can use methods setText() and getText() to change and obtain the text value in the entry box.

The JTextField class is frequently used in combination with the JLabel class in order to give the user an indication of what type of information is expected to be entered. You could add each of these to a left-aligned flow layout, for example:

```
JPanel namePanel = new JPanel(new FlowLayout(FlowLayout.LEFT));
namePanel.add(new JLabel("Enter your name:"));
JTextField field = new JTextField("Default text", 25);
namePanel.add(field);
panel.add(namePanel);
```

The frame should look as follows:

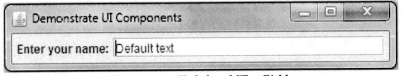

Figure 14.3: JLabel and JTextField

If you want the label above the text field instead of to its left you could place them in a single-column grid:

```
JPanel namePanel = new JPanel(new GridLayout(2, 1));
namePanel.add(new JLabel("Enter your name:"));
JTextField field = new JTextField("Default text", 25);
namePanel.add(field);
panel.add(namePanel);
```

Which will look like this:

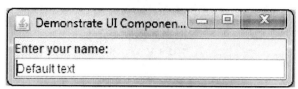

Figure 14.4: JLabel above JTextField

JTextArea

Whereas `JTextField` allows the user to enter text on a single line, the `JTextArea` class allows entry of text in a box consisting of multiple lines, which is useful for entering information such as an address, for example:

```
JTextArea area = new JTextArea(4, 30);
panel.add(area);
```

- The constructor's first argument is the number of rows to display, and the second argument the number of columns to display.

Like `JTextField`, you can supply some default text using a three-argument constructor:

```
JTextArea area = new JTextArea("Default text", 4, 30);
```

The frame should look as follows:

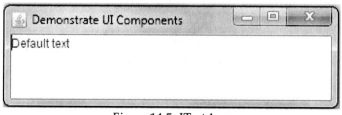

Figure 14.5: JTextArea

In order to handle the possibility of the user typing text which extends beyond the number of rows or columns, it is advisable to nest the

JTextArea object within a JScrollPane. The JScrollPane class will monitor the text within the nested component and automatically display horizontal and/or vertical scroll bars if necessary:

```
JTextArea area = new JTextArea("Default text", 4, 30);
panel.add(new JScrollPane(area));
```

Try entering some text on multiple lines and notice the effect:

Figure 14.6: Scrollable JTextArea

JButton

The JButton class displays a click-able button component with the text you specify:

```
JButton button = new JButton("Please click me");
panel.add(button);
```

The above code result in:

Figure 14.7: JButton

Note that although you can click on the button and it gives the visual feedback of being pressed and released, nothing actually happens until you attach a **listener** object to the button so it knows what action to perform. You saw how to do this in Chapter 13.

JCheckBox

The `JCheckBox` class allows the entry of values which are true or false by enabling the user to click a small rectangular box resulting in a "tick" mark being displayed within:

```
JCheckBox wantFries = new JCheckBox("Do you want fries with that?");
panel.add(wantFries);
```

The screen will look like this:

Figure 14.8: JCheckBox

Each time the user clicks inside the check box it will alternate between being ticked and un-ticked. If you want to make the box ticked in your program, you can use the `setSelected()` method:

```
wantFries.setSelected(true);
```

- The method argument requires a boolean to specify whether the box should be checked.

To see whether or not the check box is checked you can use the `isSelected()` method which returns a `boolean`:

```
boolean b = wantFries.isSelected();
// b will either be true or false
```

JRadioButton

The JRadioButton class allows the selection of one option in a group of mutually exclusive options; that is, where there are two or more possible options but only one option should ever be chosen. To use JRadioButton objects you need to assign them to a ButtonGroup object which manages the mutual exclusion for you:

```java
// Define the options
JRadioButton redOption = new JRadioButton("Red");
JRadioButton greenOption = new JRadioButton("Green");
JRadioButton blueOption = new JRadioButton("Blue");

// Assign the options to a group
ButtonGroup group = new ButtonGroup();
group.add(redOption);
group.add(greenOption);
group.add(blueOption);

// Show the options in a grid
JPanel colourPanel = new JPanel(new GridLayout(0, 1));
colourPanel.add(redOption);
colourPanel.add(greenOption);
colourPanel.add(blueOption);

// Add the grid to the main panel
panel.add(colourPanel);
```

- The first section instantiates three JRadioButton objects, corresponding to the colours red, green and blue;

- The second section adds each of the radio button objects to a ButtonGroup object, which will serve to enforce the fact that only one colour should ever be selected;

- The third section places the radio buttons below each other in a one-column grid[1];

- The fourth section adds the grid to the outer panel.

Running the above should result in this:

Figure 14.9:
JRadioButton objects

If you click in any of the selectable circles then that item will be selected and the previously selected option (if any) will be de-selected. It is generally a good idea, unless it is entirely optional to select any option, to programmatically set one of the options as a default using the `setSelected()` method:

```
blueOption.setSelected(true);
```

You can use `isSelected()` to determine if a radio button is selected:

```
boolean redWanted = redOption.isSelected();
```

There is no straightforward way of determining which radio button within a group has been selected without checking each in turn.

It is important to note the difference between a group of `JRadioButton` objects and a group of `JCheckBox` objects. Whereas radio buttons indicate a mutually exclusive set of options, if you have a series of check boxes then they each operate independently, and any combination of check boxes may be

---

1   The number of rows is set to zero, indicating that any number of rows could be added.

selected or de-selected. You therefore don't require a ButtonGroup object for your check boxes.

As an example, suppose you want the user to select the size and toppings required on a pizza:
The size (small, medium or large) should be selectable with a group of radio buttons because a single pizza can only be one size.
The toppings (chicken, pork, onions, mushrooms, etc.) should be selectable with a group of check boxes because you can have any combination.

JComboBox

The JComboBox class allows the user to select an item using a drop-down list:

```
JComboBox colourCombo = new JComboBox();
colourCombo.addItem("Red");
colourCombo.addItem("Green");
colourCombo.addItem("Blue");
panel.add(colourCombo);
```

It looks like this:

Figure 14.10:
JComboBox

If you click on the small down-pointing arrow to the right of the option then the other options will appear:

Figure 14.11: JComboBox
options

You can select the item required either with the mouse or the keyboard. If there are lots of items then a vertical scrollbar will automatically appear. To obtain which item was selected you can either use `getSelectedItem()` which returns an `Object`, or `getSelectedIndex()` which returns an `int`, being the position in the list of the selected item (where zero is the first item, etc.):

```
String selectedColour = (String) colourCombo.getSelectedItem();
int selectedIndex = colourCombo.getSelectedIndex();
```

- Note that you need to cast the `Object` returned from `getSelectedItem()` back into a `String`, since it was `String` objects which you added to the component.

JSlider

The `JSlider` class allows the user to select a value, from within a range of values, by moving a sliding knob:

```
JSlider slider = new JSlider();
panel.add(slider);
```

- By default, the allowable range of values is from 0 to 100, with the knob pre-selected at 50.

The default slider will look like this:

Figure 14.12: Basic JSlider

You can use your mouse to drag the slider to a new position. To make the slider more useful you can paint tick marks and labels at pre-defined gaps. For example, to place labels every 10 units add the following statements:

```
slider.setMajorTickSpacing(10);
slider.setPaintLabels(true);
slider.setPaintTicks(true);
```

The slider will now look as follows:

Figure 14.13: JSlider with tick marks

If your slider needs a different range and starting value you can use a different constructor:

```
JSlider slider = new JSlider(0, 250, 50);
slider.setMajorTickSpacing(50); // *** NOTE CHANGED TO 50 ***
```

- The first constructor argument is the minimum allowed value;

- The second constructor argument is the maximum allowed value;

- The third constructor argument is the initial value. Note that this argument is optional, and if not supplied then the initial value will be halfway between the minimum and maximum values;

- Note also the the major tick spacing has been changed.

Your slider will now look like this:

Figure 14.14: JSlider with alternate tick marks

You can also specify minor tick spaces to appear between the major tick spaces:

```
slider.setMinorTickSpacing(25);
```

Now the slider will label the major tick spaces every 50 units, as before, but in addition will show minor ticks every 25 units:

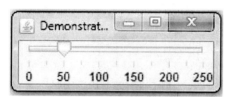

Figure 14.15: JSlider with major and minor tick marks

While the default orientation is horizontal, as shown in the above examples, you can place the slider vertically using the `setOrientation()` method[1]:

```
slider.setOrientation(JSlider.VERTICAL);
```

Which results in this:

---

1   You can also set the orientation using an alternative constructor – see the Javadoc API.

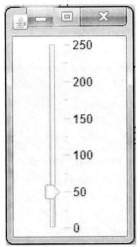

Figure 14.16: Vertical
JSlider

To obtain the selected value use the `getValue()` method:

```
int value = slider.getValue();
```

JSpinner

The `JSpinner` class enables the user to "spin" through a range of items using small up and down arrow buttons:

```
JSpinner spinner = new JSpinner();
panel.add(spinner);
```

- By default the spinner allows the spinning through an unbounded range of integer values, defaulting to zero;

Figure 14.17: JSpinner

You can use the `setValue()` method to change the default value:

```
spinner.setValue(123);
```

The `getValue()` method retrieves the selected value as an `Object`, so if you are using the default integers you need to cast:

```
int v = (Integer) spinner.getValue();
```

> The above statement shows an example of **autoboxing**, in that Java will convert between the object type Integer and the primitive type `int`. Without autoboxing you would have had to use a two-step process:
>
> ```
> Integer temp = (Integer) spinner.getValue();
> int v = temp.intValue();
> ```

If you are wondering why `getValue()` returns `Object` rather than an `int` it is because you can spin any type of object, such as strings or even images. To do this you need to make use of a `SpinnerModel` to supply the range of spinnable objects to the spinner.

Here is an example inner class called `ColourSpinnerModel` which extends the Java supplied `SpinnerListModel` (and which implements `SpinnerModel`):

```
private class ColourSpinnerModel extends SpinnerListModel {

    public ColourSpinnerModel() {
        ArrayList<String> colours = new ArrayList<String>();
```

```
        colours.add("Red");
        colours.add("Green");
        colours.add("Blue");
        setList(colours);
    }

}
```

- You will need to import `java.util.*;`

- The `setList()` method assigns the list of strings to the model.

To use the model you instantiate an object of its type and assign it to the `JSpinner`:

```
ColourSpinnerModel model = new ColourSpinnerModel();
JSpinner spinner = new JSpinner(model);
```

Another convenience class you can use is `SpinnerNumberModel`, which is useful if you need to restrict the range of numbers to spin through:

```
SpinnerNumberModel model = new SpinnerNumberModel(0, 0, 100, 10);
```

- The first argument value indicates the initial default value – here it is zero;

- The second argument value indicates the minimum allowed value – here it is also zero;

- The third argument value indicates the maximum allowed value – here it is one hundred;

- The fourth argument value indicates the step-size, that is, the value by which the selected value is incremented or decremented whenever a spin button is clicked. Normally this will be one, but here it is ten.

JList

The JList class displays a selection of a number of items, from which one or more may be selected. It is possible to pass an array of objects into the JList constructor, and it is usual to nest the list inside a JScrollPane:

```
String[] options = {"Red", "Green", "Blue"};
JList list = new JList(options);
panel.add(new JScrollPane(list));
```

The above should result in the following:

Figure 14.18: JList

By default, the user is allowed to select multiple items in the list. If you want to ensure that only one item can be selected at a time use the setSelectionMode() method:

```
list.setSelectionMode(ListSelectionModel.SINGLE_SELECTION);
```

As you learned in Chapter 6, arrays are of a fixed size and therefore lack the flexibility of being able to dynamically contract or expand with new or removed items. To obtain the additional flexibility you can assign a ListModel object to your JList in order to provide the items to appear in the list[1]. ListModel is an interface which you can implement to provide the list data, although typically an easier way is to extend the Java

---

1   When you passed an array into the JList constructor it used a ListModel behind the scenes.

supplied `DefaultListModel` class (which itself implements `ListModel`). In `DemoUI` define an inner class called `ColourListModel` as follows:

```
private class ColourListModel extends DefaultListModel {

    private ArrayList<String> colours;

    public ColourListModel() {
        colours = new ArrayList<String>();
        colours.add("Red");
        colours.add("Green");
        colours.add("Blue");
    }

    @Override
    public Object getElementAt(int index) {
        return colours.get(index);
    }

    @Override
    public int getSize() {
        return colours.size();
    }

}
```

- `ColourListModel` does not have to be an inner class, although it is common to make it part of the class which defines the `JList`;

- The constructor instantiates an `ArrayList` of `String` objects and adds three strings to it;

- As a minimum, you need to override the following two methods:

  o `getElementAt()` - which requires the index number of the item in the list and returns it as an `Object`;

  o `getSize()` - which returns the total number of items in the list.

You can now instantiate a `ColourListModel` object and pass it as the argument to the `JList` constructor:

```
ListModel model = new ColourListModel();
JList list = new JList(model);
```

If you need to programmatically select one of the items in the list as a default you can use the `setSelectedIndex()` method:

```
list.setSelectedIndex(0); // selects the first item
```

To obtain which item has been selected you can use either the `getSelectedIndex()` or `getSelectedValue()` methods:

```
int i = list.getSelectedIndex();
String s = (String) list.getSelectedValue(); // need to cast
```

JTable

Whereas the `JList` class displayed a list of items in a single column, the `JTable` class is capable of showing items that each have several columns. You need to attach a `TableModel` object (which references the item data) to the `JTable`. The most common way of doing this is to subclass the `AbstractTableModel` class and override three methods that provide the total number of rows, the total number of columns, and the object at a particular row/column intersection, or "cell".

Continuing the simple examples from earlier, where you are using the strings "Red", "Green" and "Blue", assume you want a three-column table where the first column will be the normal text of the colour, the second column the text in upper-case, and the third column the number of characters in the word. Define the following inner class inside `DemoUI`, and note that you need to import package `java.swing.table`:

```
private class ColourTableModel extends AbstractTableModel {

    private ArrayList<String> colours;
```

```java
public ColourTableModel() {
    colours = new ArrayList<String>();
    colours.add("Red");
    colours.add("Green");
    colours.add("Blue");
}

@Override
public int getRowCount() {
    return colours.size();
}

@Override
public int getColumnCount() {
    return 3;
}

@Override
public Object getValueAt(int rowIndex, int columnIndex) {
    // Get the name of the colour at the required row index
    String colourName = colours.get(rowIndex);

    // Which column is required?
    switch (columnIndex) {
        case 0:
            // First column - return name of colour
            return colourName;

        case 1:
            // Second column - return name in upper case
            return colourName.toUpperCase();

        case 2:
            // Third column - return number of characters in name
            return colourName.length();

        default:
            throw new IllegalStateException("columnIndex not
                               valid" + columnIndex);
    }
}
```

}

- Your class `ColourTableModel` extends the Java supplied `AbstractTableModel`;

- The constructor is identical to that used for `ColourListModel` – it adds the three strings to an `ArrayList` object;

- The `getRowCount()` method returns the total number of rows in the table, which will correspond to the total number of items in the `ArrayList` object;

- The `getColumnCount()` method returns the total number of columns in the table, which in this case is three;

- The `getValueAt()` method provides two arguments, being the row index and the column index, where each of them starts from zero. You can think of a table as being like a spreadsheet, where the row and column indexes together point to a particular cell. The method does the following:

  - Retrieves the text from the `ArrayList` object using the specified row index;

  - If the column index is zero then the first column in wanted, so just return the text as-is;

  - If the column index is one then the second column in wanted, so return the text converted to upper-case;

  - If the column index is two then the third column in wanted, so return the number of characters in the text;

  - Because a `switch` statement was used to determine the column index the compiler will check that something is being returned in all cases, including those where `columnIndex` is not 0, 1 or 2. Even though this should never happen (because the `getColumnCount()` method returns 3) the compiler does not know this so you need to specify a default processing for all other cases. In this case you simply throw a unchecked exception.

Now in the `buildUI()` method of the main body of `DemoUI` you can instantiate a `ColourTableModel` object, assign it to a new `JTable` object, put the table in a scroll pane and place it on the panel:

```
TableModel model = new ColourTableModel();
JTable table = new JTable(model);
panel.add(new JScrollPane(table));
```

The `JTable` object takes care of invoking the appropriate `ColourTableModel` methods for you automatically. You should see the following table displayed:

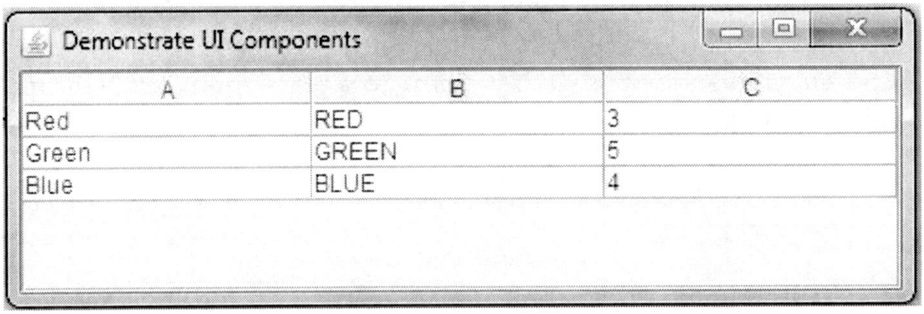

Figure 14.19: JTable

There are a couple of points to note about the table as it stands:

1. Because you have not specifically set the column headings it has defaulted to spreadsheet-style names of A, B, C etc.;

2. All items of data are left-aligned. While this is a sensible default for strings, numbers generally look better when right-aligned.

To set the column headers you can override the `getColumnName()` method inside the `ColourTableModel` inner class:

```
@Override
public String getColumnName(int columnIndex) {
    String[] columnHeaders = {"Colour",
                              "Colour in Uppercase",
                              "Number of Characters"};
    return columnHeaders[columnIndex];
}
```

To make numbers right-aligned you can take advantage of the fact that tables are capable of using default alignments based upon the class of the `Object` which is returned by `getValueAt()`. To do this, override the `getColumnClass()` method inside `ColourTableModel`:

```
@Override
public Class getColumnClass(int columnIndex) {
    return getValueAt(0, columnIndex).getClass();
}
```

- The `getValueAt()` method is called using the specified column index on row zero to determine the object which appears there. The `getClass()` method is then obtained from that object and returned. The table now has the information it needs to render the alignment sensibly.

The table should now look as follows:

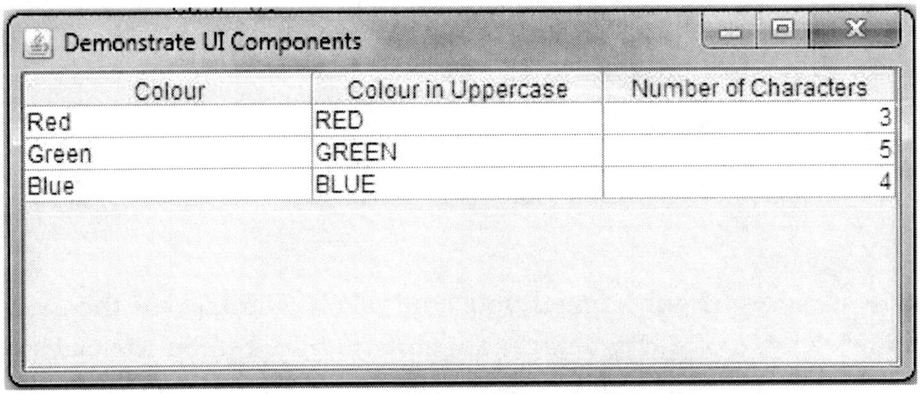

Figure 14.20: JTable with named columns

If you would like users to be able to sort the data on any of the columns, you can add the following statement after you instantiate the JTable object:

```
table.setAutoCreateRowSorter(true);
```

The user can now click on any column header in order to sort the table by that column. Each time a column is clicked it toggles between being sorted in ascending and descending sequence. A small arrow appears in the column heading to indicate the sequencing.

It's possible to enable table cells to be directly edited by the user. Suppose, for example, you want to enable the text of the colour to be edited in the first column. Because the values displayed in columns two and three depend on the text in column one then only column one should be editable. First, you need to override the isCellEditable() method inside ColourTableModel:

```
@Override
public boolean isCellEditable(int rowIndex, int columnIndex) {
    return (columnIndex == 0);
}
```

- The method needs to return `true` if the cell should be editable and false otherwise. Above, `true` will be returned whenever the column index is zero.

If you run the application you can now double-click inside any entry in the first column to make the cell go into edit mode:

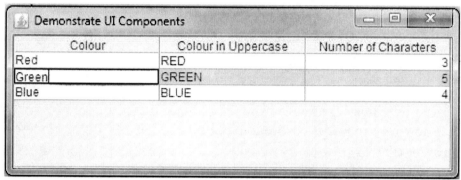

Figure 14.21: Editable JTable

Try changing the text to something else and press **Enter** on your keyboard. You will notice the text revert to what it was previously! To save the edited change you need to override the `setValue()` method as well:

```
@Override
public void setValueAt(Object value, int rowIndex, int columnIndex) {
    colours.remove(rowIndex);
    colours.add(rowIndex, (String) value);
}
```

- Because your model data is being stored in the `ArrayList` object called `colours`, the method firstly removes the old value there at the modified row index and then adds the new value at the same position.

If you run the application again your change is made but you will notice that the upper-case version and number of characters in the second and third columns have not been updated. You can fix this by adding one more statement to the above method to tell the table that the data has been modified so that it can perform a refresh:

```
@Override
public void setValueAt(Object value, int rowIndex, int columnIndex) {
    colours.remove(rowIndex);
    colours.add(rowIndex, (String) value);
    fireTableDataChanged();
}
```

JTree

The JTree class displays items which are structured in a hierarchy. Each item is known as a **node**, and each node can contain other nodes as its "children". Like JList and JTable, the JTree uses an associated model object (a TreeModel) to provide its data. However, in many cases it is easier to make use of the convenience class DefaultMutableTreeNode to represent each node in the tree. Suppose you want to model some of the countries of the five continents and have them displayed in a tree:

(Note – you will need to import package javax.swing.tree)

```
// Create the root node
DefaultMutableTreeNode continents =
                new DefaultMutableTreeNode("Continents");

// Create a node for Africa and add some sample countries
DefaultMutableTreeNode africa =
                new DefaultMutableTreeNode("Africa");
africa.add(new DefaultMutableTreeNode("Kenya"));
africa.add(new DefaultMutableTreeNode("Nigeria"));

// Create a node for America and add some sample countries
DefaultMutableTreeNode america =
                new DefaultMutableTreeNode("America");
america.add(new DefaultMutableTreeNode("Canada"));
america.add(new DefaultMutableTreeNode("USA"));
```

```
// Create a node for Asia and add some sample countries
DefaultMutableTreeNode asia =
                new DefaultMutableTreeNode("Asia");
asia.add(new DefaultMutableTreeNode("China"));
asia.add(new DefaultMutableTreeNode("Japan"));

// Create a node for Australia and add some sample countries
DefaultMutableTreeNode australia =
                new DefaultMutableTreeNode("Australia");
australia.add(new DefaultMutableTreeNode("Australia"));

// Create a node for Europe and add some sample countries
DefaultMutableTreeNode europe =
                new DefaultMutableTreeNode("Europe");
europe.add(new DefaultMutableTreeNode("France"));
europe.add(new DefaultMutableTreeNode("Germany"));
DefaultMutableTreeNode uk =
                new DefaultMutableTreeNode("UK");
uk.add(new DefaultMutableTreeNode("England"));
uk.add(new DefaultMutableTreeNode("Northern Ireland"));
uk.add(new DefaultMutableTreeNode("Scotland"));
uk.add(new DefaultMutableTreeNode("Wales"));
europe.add(uk);

// Add the continents to the root node
continents.add(africa);
continents.add(america);
continents.add(asia);
continents.add(australia);
continents.add(europe);

// Create a JTree with the root node
JTree tree = new JTree(continents);

// Add the tree to the panel
panel.add(new JScrollPane(tree));
```

- Each item in the tree is an instance of `DefaultMutableTreeNode`;

- One of these instances must be the root node, being the one at the top-level that gets assigned to the tree. Here, it is `continents`;

- To each node you can add other nodes as its **children**, and therefore the node that contains one or more children is known as its **parent**;

- The JTree should be nested inside a JScrollPane.

Run the application to see the following display:

Figure 14.22: JTree

You can expand or contract any node by clicking the small "handle" graphic to the left of any parent item. If you expand **Europe** and then **UK** the screen should look as follows:

Figure 14.23: Expanded JTree

- Note that you might get scrollbars appear when you expand the nodes – the above screen shot has adjusted the size of the window so that any scrollbars disappear.

JSplitPane

The JSplitPane class displays two components next to each other with a user moveable dividing bar between them. Usually the components on either side of the divider will be panels, each containing one of more other components:

```
// Panel to go on the left or the top
JPanel panelOne = new JPanel();
panelOne.add(new JLabel("This is panel 1"));

// Panel to go on the right or the bottom
JPanel panelTwo = new JPanel();
```

```
panelTwo.add(new JLabel("This is panel 2"));

// Split the panels
JSplitPane splitter = new JSplitPane(JSplitPane.HORIZONTAL_SPLIT,
                                      panelOne, panelTwo);
panel.add(splitter);
```

The `JSplitPane` constructor needs three arguments:

- Whether the split should be horizontal or vertical;

- The component that should be placed to the left (or top);

- The component that should be placed to the right (or bottom).

Running the above will look as follows:

Figure 14.24: JSplitPane

Notice the dividing bar in the centre of the frame. At the moment it will not move because each of the two panels on either side are at their minimum dimensions and they have not been made scrollable. Enlarge the frame window by dragging the bottom right corner of the frame so it looks as follows:

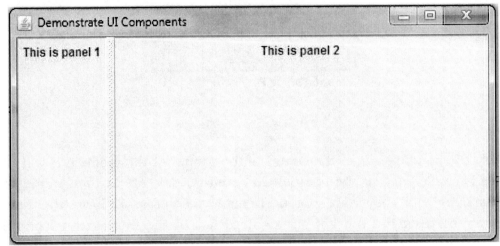

Figure 14.25: JSplitPane enlarged

Now you will be able to drag the centre dividing bar so that it appears in another location:

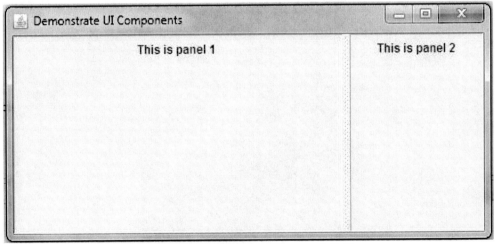

Figure 14.26: JSplitPane with moved divider

You can obtain a vertical split simply by modifying the constructor's first argument value:

```
JSplitPane splitter = new JSplitPane(JSplitPane.VERTICAL_SPLIT,
                panelOne, panelTwo);
```

To result in the following:

*Figure 14.27: Vertical
JSplitPane*

JTabbedPane

The JTabbedPane class displays separate titled "tabs", each of which allows the user to switch between by clicking on a tab:

```
JPanel panelOne = new JPanel();
panelOne.add(new JLabel("This is the first panel"));

JPanel panelTwo = new JPanel();
panelTwo.add(new JLabel("This is the second panel"));

JTabbedPane tabPane = new JTabbedPane();
tabPane.addTab("Tab 1", panelOne);
tabPane.addTab("Tab 2", panelTwo);

panel.add(tabPane);
```

- Two JPanel objects are created, panelOne and panelTwo, each containing a JLabel;

- A JTabbedPane is created to serve as the container for some tabs, and then the addTab() method is invoked upon it to add the panels. The first method argument is the text that should appear in the tab and the second argument is any component, although you would in most cases add instances of JPanel.

This should result in the following being displayed:

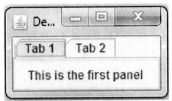

Figure 14.28: JTabbedPane
first tab active

If you click on **Tab 2** the display will switch to the other panel:

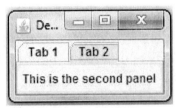

Figure 14.29: JTabbedPane
second tab active

JDialog

The `JDialog` class displays a separate window which is "owned" by an application's frame. You can either add your own components to a dialog or use a simple pre-built one through the `JOptionPane` class. There follows an `ActionListener` inner class that builds and displays a `JDialog` consisting of a label, text field and button (Note: you will need to import `java.awt.event`):

```
private class ShowDialogButtonListener implements ActionListener {

    @Override
    public void actionPerformed(ActionEvent e) {
        JDialog dialog = new JDialog(DemoUI.this, "My Dialog", true);
```

```
dialog.setLayout(new FlowLayout());
dialog.add(new JLabel("Name:"));
dialog.add(new JTextField(20));
dialog.add(new JButton("OK"));
dialog.pack();
dialog.setLocationRelativeTo(DemoUI.this);
dialog.setVisible(true);
    }
}
```

- The JDialog constructor used above has three arguments passed
  into it:

  o The first argument is the owner, which must either be a frame or
    another dialog. Because you need this to be the this instance of
    the outer class (i.e. DemoUI) you need to specify DemoUI.this. If
    you just specify this it would refer to the inner class instance
    instead;

  o The second argument is the text which will appear in the title bar
    of the dialog;

  o The third argument of true means that the dialog will be **modal**.
    A modal dialog is one which will force the user to close it before
    any further action can be taken on the owning frame.

- The dialog is set to use a FlowLayout and then three components
  are added to it. The size of the dialog is packed and its display
  location is set to be relative to the owning frame.

Inside buildUI() create a button that listens for a click by instantiating
the above inner class:

```
JButton showDialogButton = new JButton("Show dialog");
showDialogButton.addActionListener(new ShowDialogButtonListener());
panel.add(showDialogButton);
```

If you run the application you should initially just see the button:

Figure 14.30: Prompt for
dialog

Now click the **Show dialog** button to show the dialog window:

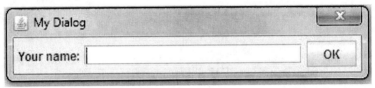

Figure 14.31: JDialog

The dialog does not respond to the OK button in this simple example, but you can close the dialog by clicking the window's close button:

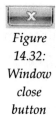

Figure
14.32:
Window
close
button

You are now returned to the frame.

JOptionPane

The JOptionPane class provides a simple way of displaying standard dialogs that show informational, warning or error messages through its static convenience methods. Change the ShowDialogButtonListener inner class as follows:

```
private class ShowDialogButtonListener implements ActionListener {

    @Override
    public void actionPerformed(ActionEvent e) {
        JOptionPane.showMessageDialog(DemoUI.this,
                "This is some message text.", "Dialog Title",
                JOptionPane.INFORMATION_MESSAGE);
    }

}
```

- The method showMessageDialog() is static and hence can be invoked directly on its class JOptionPane;

- Four arguments are passed to the method:

  ○ The first argument is the owning frame. Note how because this is being used from within the inner class ShowDialogButtonListener you need to prefix this with the name of the outer class in order to refer to the frame instance;

  ○ The second argument is the text that will appear in the dialog;

- The third argument is the text of the dialog's title;

- The fourth argument indicates that the message is informational. This is used so that an appropriate icon is displayed inside the dialog.

- You can click **OK** to close the dialog.

You should see the following after clicking the **Show dialog** button:

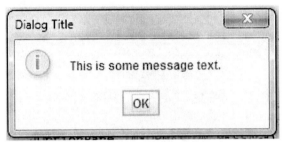

Figure 14.33: Informational JOptionPane

If you change the fourth argument to `JOptionPane.WARNING_MESSAGE` the icon will appear as follows:

Figure 14.34: Warning JOptionPane

Setting it instead to `JOptionPane.ERROR_MESSAGE` will give this icon:

Figure 14.35: Error JOptionPane

If you don't want an icon then specify `JOptionPane.PLAIN_MESSAGE`.

Often it is useful to ask the user a Yes/No question, and for this you can use another `static` method called `showConfirmDialog()`. Change the code inside the button listener to the following:

```
private class ShowDialogButtonListener implements ActionListener {

    @Override
    public void actionPerformed(ActionEvent e) {
        int response = JOptionPane.showConfirmDialog(DemoUI.this,
                "Do you want to exit the program?", "End Program",
                JOptionPane.YES_NO_OPTION);
        if (response == JOptionPane.YES_OPTION) {
            System.exit(0);
        }
    }

}
```

- The first three arguments are the owning frame, the message text and the dialog title, as before;

- The fourth argument specifies that the user should be given the options **Yes** or **No**;

- The `showConfirmDialog()` method returns an `int` when the user chooses either yes or no (or closes the dialog). Above, the returned value is stored in variable `response`;

- The `response` variable is checked to see if the **Yes** option was selected, and if so the program is ended by calling `System.exit(0)`. Otherwise the dialog is closed and returns to the frame.

The dialog looks like this:

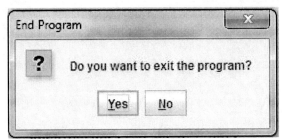

Figure 14.36: Question JOptionPane

In the section on `JDialog` a simple entry box with a label, text field and button was constructed. For simple inputs like this there is another convenience method of `JOptionPane` called `showInputDialog()`:

```
String response = JOptionPane.showInputDialog(DemoUI.this,
                        "Your name", "Name Entry",
                        JOptionPane.QUESTION_MESSAGE);
```

- The method returns a `String`. The dialog will look as follows:

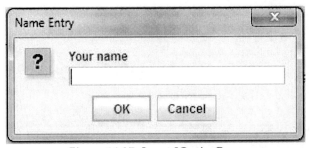

Figure 14.37: Input JOptionPane

15. Access Modifiers & Visibility

Access modifiers enable you to protect and control parts of your application from inappropriate use by other parts or other applications. A "singleton" class is one where no more than one instance of that class can exist.

In this chapter you will learn:

- *An overview of access modifiers;*

- *Using* protected *visibility;*

- *Using "default" visibility;*

- *How to define a "singleton" class.*

Overview of access modifiers

So far in this book you have made use of two different access modifiers, public and private.

When applied to class members (i.e. variables and methods) these modifiers allow different levels of access, summarised as follows:

- public – as well as being accessible inside the class in which it is defined, the member will also be accessible to any other class in any part of the application. If the class that wants to use the public member is in a different package, then it merely needs to import the package that contains the public member;

- private – the member is only available inside the class in which it is defined.

In this book you have developed the core system classes in a package called virtualzoo.core and the user interface classes in a separate package called `virtualzoo.ui`. You have also defined the access modifiers as follows:

- All instance variables as `private`;

- All constructors as `public`;

- Most methods as `public`, except for a few `private` "helper" methods.

While the above approach provides a straightforward starting point it does have the disadvantage of being "all or nothing" - if a class member is `public` then the whole application has access to it while if it's `private` then no other class does. As your application develops it is useful to be able to assign more fine-grained control over member visibility, and Java provides two further levels of visibility modifiers that sit between these two extremes:

- *Default* (or "package") visibility – only other classes within the same package can access these members;

- *Protected* visibility – only other classes within the same package, or subclasses in a different package, can access these members.

The following table summarises all four access modifying options, ordered from the most restrictive to the least restrictive:

Access option	Keyword	Description
Private visibility	`private`	Only the class that declares the member can access the member.
Default (package) visibility	*(none)*	Only the class that declares it, and any other class in the same package, can access the member.
Protected visibility	`protected`	Only the class that declares it, any other class in the same package, and any

Access option	Keyword	Description
		subclass in a different package, can access the member.
Public visibility	`public`	Any class in any package can access the member.

You will notice that for default visibility there is no associated keyword. It is therefore the *absence* of an access modifier keyword that indicates that level of visibility, which is why it is referred to as *default* visibility. From now on this book will refer to default visibility as **package visibility**, since this makes it easier to remember that only classes in the same package can ever access it.

> A good rule-of-thumb is to make your classes, constructors and members as private as reasonably possible.

Using 'protected' visibility

Protected visibility is often used so that a superclass can give subclasses access to its members that are not intended for public use, given that subclasses are often defined in a different package to the superclass from which it inherits. You may recall that the `Animal` class defines a `setAge()` method which invokes a `validateAge()` method, and these are currently defined as follows:

```
public void setAge(int age) {
    validateAge(age);
    this.age = age;
}

private void validateAge(int age) {
    // Ensure new age is between 0 and 50
    if ((age < 0) || (age > 50)) {
        throw new IllegalArgumentException("Age must be 0 - 50");
    }
```

```
}
```

The `validateAge()` method is declared as `private`, which means it is not available to be overridden by any subclass[1]. It is easy to envisage that different species will have different expected age ranges, so it would make sense for `validateAge()` to be overridable, but if you were to make the method `public` it would allow any client object to invoke the method when its purpose is merely internal to `Animal` and its subclasses.

Change the access modifier of `validateAge()` from `private` to `protected`:

```
protected void validateAge(int age) {
    // Ensure new age is between 0 and 50
    if ((age < 0) || (age > 50)) {
        throw new IllegalArgumentException("Age must be 0 - 50");
    }
}
```

In class `Lion` you can now override this method to specify a different age range to validate against:

```
@Override
protected void validateAge(int age) {
    // Ensure new age is between 0 and 20
    if ((age < 0) || (age > 20)) {
        throw new IllegalArgumentException("Age must be 0 - 20");
    }
}
```

> Note that when you override a method its visibility cannot be set to be more private than the superclass visibility of that method.

---

1   It is possible to declare a method with the same signature in a subclass but it won't actually overrride it.

Using package (i.e. default) visibility

You will shortly modify some of the classes so far developed to make use of package visibility instead of public visibility, for certain constructors and methods. Before that, however, you need to understand what is trying to be achieved and the reasons for doing so.

You have developed two main packages, `virtualzoo.core` to hold the classes which form the business domain (i.e. the core system) and `virtualzoo.ui` to hold the classes which form the graphical user interface. These have been separated because it is advantageous to allow each to be developed and modified in the future without the changes impacting upon the other:

- Suppose in the future you want to change the user interface (or develop an alternative user interface) that operates from a web page or from a smartphone. Ideally it should be possible to do this without necessitating any changes to the core system;

- Conversely, suppose in the future you decide to change the core system, perhaps to restructure the existing classes or create new ones. Ideally it should be possible to do this without necessitating any changes to the user interface.

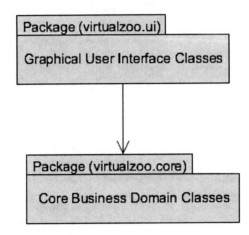

Figure 15.1: Package diagram

The above package diagram illustrates the user interface package depending upon the core system package but not vice versa, as indicated by the arrow pointing in one direction only. This is commonly known as a client-server (or 2-tier) architecture, where the user interface is the client and the core system is the server.

The next question is how should the user interface depend upon the core system? To answer this, think for a moment about the desktop interface of your operating system, whether that be Windows, Macintosh, Linux, or something else. Behind the scenes, inside the operating system there is much complexity regarding such things as how files and folders are physically stored and retrieved, how the devices communicate with each other, etc. And yet all of this complexity is hidden behind a single desktop containing application icons, from which you can achieve any action the operating system allows. When you drag a file to move it from one folder to another, or click an icon to print a document, you don't need to worry about how the internal parts of the computer's software and hardware accomplish those tasks. The operating system, through its desktop interface, enables you to simply make the request and it takes care of the internals for you.

You can think of the desktop as being like a secretary or administrator on a front desk, responsible for taking all incoming requests to perform particular actions or supply certain results. Applying the same principle to the zoo application, because the user interface needs to make requests of the core system then it is the core system that can benefit from its own "front desk" to serve as the middleman between the two packages.

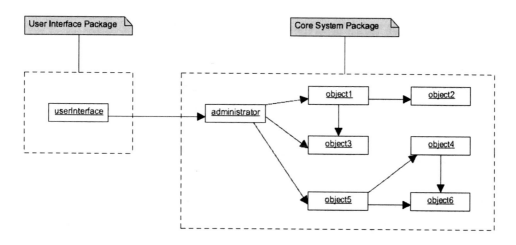

Figure 15.2: Packages and contained objects

The above diagram shows an object in the User Interface Package (which could be the frame, a dialog, or any of the UI panels that make up the user interface) communicating <u>only</u> with an "administrator" object in the Core System Package. The "administrator" object in turn communicates with various other objects that comprise the core system, potentially in complex ways[1]. If the "administrator" object did not exist then the user interface would need to know about the structure of the core system classes and communicate with them directly, which would make it harder to modify either of the packages without it impacting upon the other package.

In the zoo application being developed in the book, the ZooAdministrator class, which is part of the core system package, will take on the role as the

---

1   The objects in the diagram are illustrative only and could be any objects is practice.

"administrator" object. Whenever an object from the user interface package needs the core system to perform an action or provide some data then it will communicate with the core system by invoking a method of a ZooAdministrator object. For example, in the next chapter you will develop a graphical class that enables you to enter details of a new zoo keeper, so this requires the ZooAdministrator class to provide a method called createZooKeeper(), taking as arguments the values entered on the screen. This method will then manage the process of creating a ZooKeeper object on behalf of the core system.

> This approach of having a ZooAdministrator class to coordinate the facilities of the core package is an example application of the **Facade** design pattern. **Design patterns** provide generic approaches to software design problems.

The ZooAdministrator object will also store the data associated with the zoo (in Collection objects); all of the animals, zoo keepers and visitors, and will provide a facility to store this data permanently on disk[2]. Because there should only be one set of data to model the objects in the zoo it would make sense to only ever create one ZooAdministrator object (known as a **singleton**), which all of the the user interface objects will communicate with. You will now start to modify the ZooAdministrator class to make it suitable for the purpose just discussed.

Making ZooAdministrator a "singleton" class

You have previously learned that to instantiate an object of any class you use the new keyword to invoke a class's constructor. For example, to instantiate some animals you may have done this:

```
Animal leo = new Lion("Leo", Gender.MALE, 6);
Animal bob = new Monkey("Bob", Gender.MALE, 5)
```

---

2   This will be covered in Chapter 19.

Given that you only want one instance of `ZooAdministrator`, what is to prevent a class from inadvertently doing this?:

```
ZooAdministrator admin1 = new ZooAdministrator();
ZooAdministrator admin2 = new ZooAdministrator();
```

Above, `admin1` and `admin2` reference two separate `ZooAdministrator` objects, each with their own copy of any contained data. If this data is modified in one of these objects then the other will be out of step. As it stands, any client object can instantiate a `ZooAdministrator` object because its constructor is define as `public`. There are three steps involved to prevent this:

Step 1 – make the ZooAdministrator constructor private

```
// Constructor for ZooAdministrator class
private ZooAdministrator() {
    createExampleZooKeepers();
    createExampleVisitors();
    createExamplePens();
    createExampleResponsibilities();
}
```

With a `private` constructor only the `ZooAdministrator` class itself will be able to instantiate its own objects. You now need to declare a `static` variable to store a reference to one such object.

Step 2 – define a static variable for the singleton

Inside `ZooAdministrator` declare the following `static` variable:

```
private static ZooAdministrator instance;
```

- The variable is `private` because you don't want outside classes to have any direct access to it;

- The variable is `static` because you need to be able to access it without needing a `ZooAdministrator` object to already exist;

- The object type is the same as the class in which it resides, i.e. `ZooAdministrator`;

- The variable is named `instance` because it references the one single instance of this class.

You now need a `static` method to provide the single instance of `ZooAdministrator`.

Step 3 – define a static method for the singleton

Inside `ZooAdministrator` declare the following static method:

```
public static ZooAdministrator getInstance() {
    if (instance == null) {
        instance = new ZooAdministrator();
    }
    return instance;
}
```

- The method is `static` for the same reason the variable `instance` is;

- In the method body, a check is made to see if variable `instance` is `null`, which it will be the very first time this method is invoked. If it is `null`, a new `ZooAdministrator` object is created and assigned to the `instance` reference. If the variable is not `null` it will not create a new one because it will simply return the existing one previously created.

- The variable `instance` is returned. Each time the method is invoked it returns the *same* object.

With the above changes in place the only way for client objects to create a ZooAdministrator object is through the above method:

```
ZooAdministrator admin1 = ZooAdministrator.getInstance();
ZooAdministrator admin2 = ZooAdministrator.getInstance();
```

Above, admin1 and admin2 both refer to the <u>same</u> ZooAdministrator object, so there is therefore only one set of data that needs to be managed.

At this stage you can change the code inside the main() method of VirtualZoo to obtain the ZooAdministrator object in the above way:

```
public static void main(String[] args) {
    ZooAdministrator admin = ZooAdministrator.getInstance();
}
```

Communication between the user interface and the core system

Since the graphical application you will develop will add, change or remove zoo keepers, there needs to be a way of storing a collection of existing ZooKeeper objects and enabling the user interface to communicate with that collection.

Currently in the ZooAdministrator class is defined the following:

- Three ZooKeeper instance variables (alice, bob and charles);

- A createExampleZooKeepers() method which instantiates some sample ZooKeeper objects.

Before developing the user interface you will modify the ZooAdministrator class in the following ways:

1. Use a collection to store any number of ZooKeeper objects;

2. Remove the createExampleZooKeepers() method since by the end of the next chapter you will be able to create zoo keepers using the

user   interface   (you   should   also   remove   method `createExampleResponsibilities()` since it will no longer have access to the sample zoo keepers);

3. Provide a method that will add a new zoo keeper to the collection;

4. Provide a method that will change an existing zoo keeper's details in the collection;

5. Provide a method that will remove an existing zoo keeper from the collection;

6. Provide a method that will return the collection of zoo keepers.

Step 1 – use a collection

In `ZooAdministrator` replace the following instance variable declaration:

```
private ZooKeeper alice, bob, charles;
```

With this:

```
private Collection<ZooKeeper> zooKeepers;
```

Step 2 – don't create the example zoo keepers

Delete the `createExampleZooKeepers()` and `createExampleResponsibilities()` methods and their invocation from within the constructor. You also need to instantiate an empty collection for the zoo keepers (which can be a `HashSet`) and the `responsibilities` map. The constructor should now look as follows:

```
public ZooAdministrator() {
    zooKeepers = new HashSet<ZooKeeper>();
    createExampleVisitors();
    createExamplePens();
    responsibilities = new HashMap<ZooKeeper, Collection<Pen>>();
}
```

Step 3 – define a createZooKeeper() method

Define a `createZooKeeper()` method that requires the appropriate data as its arguments, instantiates a `ZooKeeper` object, adds it to the collection, and returns it:

```
public ZooKeeper createZooKeeper(String name, String address,
                      String email, String salary) {
    ZooKeeper zooKeeper = new ZooKeeper(new Person(name, address),
                          new Email(email),
                          new BigDecimal(salary));
    zooKeepers.add(zooKeeper);
    return zooKeeper;
}
```

Step 4 – define a changeZooKeeper() method

Define a `changeZooKeeper()` method that requires an existing `ZooKeeper` object and its new data as its arguments, modifying the provided object:

```
public void changeZooKeeper(ZooKeeper zooKeeper, String name,
            String address, String email, String salary) {
    zooKeeper.setPerson(new Person(name, address));
    zooKeeper.setEmail(new Email(email));
    zooKeeper.setSalary(new BigDecimal(salary));
}
```

Step 5 – define a removeZooKeeper() method

Define a `removeZooKeeper()` method that requires a `ZooKeeper` object as its argument and removes it from the collection:

```
public void removeZooKeeper(ZooKeeper zooKeeper) {
    zooKeepers.remove(zooKeeper);
}
```

Step 6 – define a getZooKeepers() method

Define a `getZooKeepers()` method that returns the collection of zoo keepers:

```
public Collection<ZooKeeper> getZooKeepers() {
    return Collections.unmodifiableCollection(zooKeepers);
}
```

Modifying the other core system classes

Using the approach given above, it is the intention that the user interface classes only communicate with the core system through the `ZooAdministrator` class. At the moment there is nothing to prevent a user interface class from constructing a `ZooKeeper` object or calling one of its setter methods directly, because currently in `ZooKeeper` the constructor and methods are `public`. While you could take the view that you will simply not use `ZooKeeper` directly it is good practice to code the classes in such a way as it can be enforced.

> In a larger organisation it is possible that there will be separate teams developing the core system and the user interface. By enforcing the way in which they communicate you can protect the integrity of the overall development.

The means of restricting access to the core classes is by taking advantage of package visibility. Starting with the `ZooKeeper` class, remove the `public` modifier on its constructor so it will use package (i.e. default) visibility:

```
public class ZooKeeper implements Emailable {

    private Person person;
    private Email email;
    private BigDecimal salary;

    ZooKeeper(Person person, Email email, BigDecimal salary){
        this.person = person;
        this.email = email;
```

```
        this.salary = salary;
    }

    ... rest of class omitted ...
```

The above change alone will prevent any class outside `virtualzoo.core` from ever instantiating a `ZooKeeper` object. `ZooAdministator` will be able to instantiate `ZooKeeper` objects, of course, since it is within the same package.

`ZooKeeper` objects can still be returned to the user interface, however, through `ZooAdministrator`'s `getZooKeepers()` method. You should also prevent the user interface from changing the state of any `ZooKeeper` object except through `ZooAdministrator`'s `changeZooKeeper()` method. To do this, remove the `public` modifier from all of `ZooKeeper`'s setter methods, although the getter methods can remain `public`:

```
void setPerson(Person person) {
    this.person = new Person(person); // uses copy constructor
}

void setEmail(Email email) {
    this.email = email;
}

void setSalary(BigDecimal salary) {
    this.salary = salary;
}
```

It is safe for the getter methods to remain `public` since except for `getPerson()` they each return immutable objects, and thus the user interface will be unable to modify any of their values. In the case of `getPerson()` a defensive copy is returned. It also means that once the user interface gets a reference to a `ZooKeeper` object it can easily access its attributes.

You should now update the other classes in the core package, as detailed below:

- In the `Animal` class, remove the `public` modifier from the constructor and the methods `setName()`, `setGender()`, `setAge()` and `setPen()`;

- In the `Lion`, `Monkey` and `Penguin` classes remove the `public` modifier from both constructors in each of these three classes;

- In the `Visitor` class, remove the `public` modifier from both of the constructors and from the methods `setPerson()`, `setEmail()` and `setSponsoredAnimal()`;

- In the `Pen` class, remove the `public` modifier from the constructor and from the methods `add()`, `remove()` and `setName()`.

The other classes in `virtualzoo.core` should also have the `public` modifier removed from their constructors and setter methods, and this is left as an optional exercise for the reader.

The classes are `Booker`, `BookingCounter`, `FishBarrel`, `FishKeeper`, `HungryPenguin` and `VisitorBooker`.

16. Developing a User Interface

Now that you have some familiarity with the various graphical components which are available you need to know how to get them to interact with each other to achieve your application's goals.

In this chapter you will learn:

- *How to go about developing interacting components and panels;*

- *How to define a scrollable, selectable list of objects;*

- *How to add objects to a list;*

- *Hot to amend objects in a list;*

- *How to remove objects from a list.*

Developing interacting components and panels

This chapter will demonstrate an approach to developing independent yet interacting panels typical of real-world applications, albeit much simplified in order to focus on the principles involved.

You will return to the `ZooKeeper` class you developed previously and create a desktop application that enables the zoo administrator to create, edit or remove individual zoo keepers.

This part of the application will look like this:

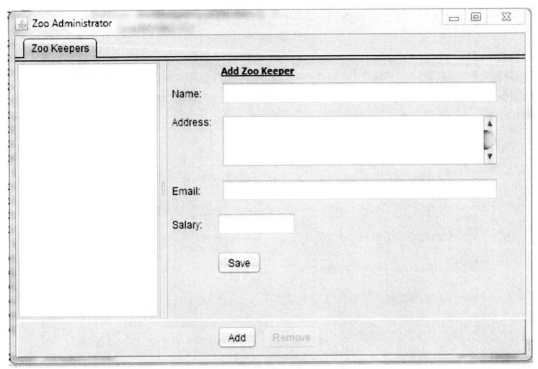

Figure 16.1: Zoo Administrator frame

The tab consists of:

1. A title "Zoo Keepers". Later, you will develop other tabs to contain section for animals and visitors;

2. A selection list of zoo keepers, initially empty;

3. A editor panel where you can add or change a zoo keeper's details by entering them into the entry fields and click the **Save** button;

4. A sliding divider between the zoo keeper list and zoo keeper editor panels;

5. A button bar at the bottom with buttons to allow you to clear the form to add a new zoo keeper, or remove the selected one from the list.

You will also use the NetBeans GUI builder (known as "Matisse") to help build the graphical layouts for the main panels.

Defining a selection list of zoo keepers

The left hand section of the screen will show a scrollable list of all of the zoo keepers working at the zoo, and the natural component to use for this is a `JList` nested inside a `JScrollPane`. The `JList` class is a UI list-box component capable of listing objects, and which allows one or more items to be selected. It gets as its list of items the objects returned from a `ListModel` object (being any class you write that implements the `ListModel` interface). In object-oriented parlance a **model** is a data source, which will generally be a collection of objects, possibly retrieved from a relational database although it can in fact be any source of data you like. Models are deliberately defined as separate objects from the UI components that use them so that each can be developed and modified independently, and the UI component will query the model to obtain the data for its display.

The ZooKeeperList class

Create this class in `virtualzoo.ui` as follows:

```
package virtualzoo.ui;

import virtualzoo.core.*;
import java.util.*;
import javax.swing.*;

public class ZooKeeperList extends JList {

    private ZooKeeperListModel model;

    public ZooKeeperList() {
        setSelectionMode(ListSelectionModel.SINGLE_SELECTION);
        model = new ZooKeeperListModel();
```

```
            setModel(model);
        }


    private class ZooKeeperListModel extends DefaultListModel {

        private ZooAdministrator admin;
        private List<ZooKeeper> zooKeepers;

        public ZooKeeperListModel() {
            admin = ZooAdministrator.getInstance();
            loadModel();
        }

        private void loadModel() {
            zooKeepers =
                    new ArrayList<ZooKeeper>(admin.getZooKeepers());
            Collections.sort(zooKeepers);
            fireContentsChanged(this, 0, zooKeepers.size() - 1);
        }

        @Override
        public Object getElementAt(int index) {
            return zooKeepers.get(index);
        }

        @Override
        public int getSize() {
            return zooKeepers.size();
        }
    }
}
```

- The class extends JList so it can provide a list of objects;

- It defines an inner class called ZooKeeperListModel to serve as the model (i.e. source of data to be shown in the list). This extends the Java supplied DefaultListModel class which provides useful background services, meaning all the inner class needs to do is:

    o Obtain the collection of zoo keepers, which is performed in the loadModel() method. They are placed into an ArrayList so that the items in the collection are indexed by their position, which is required by `getElementAt()`. The items are sorted into their natural ordering, which is by the zoo keeper's name. The `fireContentsChanged()` method, which is inherited from `DefaultListModel`, tells the `JList` component that it needs to refresh its display of the items between the specified indexes;

- o Override the `getElementAt()` method which provides the index as its argument. An index of 0 means the first item in the list, an index of 1 means the second item, etc. The object at the index location in the `ArrayList` is obtained and returned;

- o Override the `getSize()` method which provides the total number of objects in the model, simply obtained via the `size()` method on the collection.

- Note how in the `ZooKeeperList` constructor an instance of the model is created and then assigned to the list using the `setModel()` method. The list is also set to only allow selection of a single item at a time.

An editor panel for a zoo keeper

You will now develop a graphical class called `ZooKeeperEditor` using the NetBeans GUI builder, that will be capable of displaying and enabling the editing of a `ZooKeeper` object's attributes. In NetBeans, right-click on the `virtualzoo.ui` package node and select **New | JPanel Form...**, entering `ZooKeeperEditor` as the **Class Name**. This should result in a blank form being shown on screen:

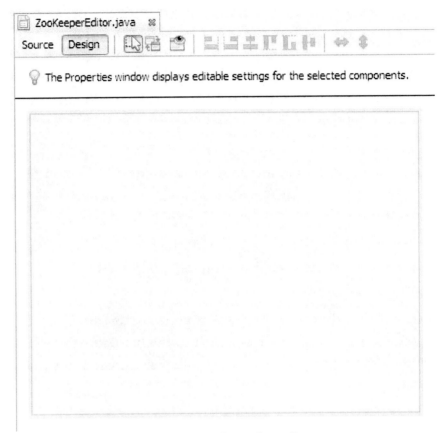

Figure 16.2: NetBeans form editor

By default, NetBeans forms are set to use a NetBeans provided layout called `FreeDesign`, which allows you to place components wherever you like. Above the blank form you will see two tabs called **Source** and **Design**, with the latter currently selected. If you click on the **Source** tab it will show the generated Java source code for the panel. Switch back into **Design** mode and notice the **Palette** window that appears on the right of the screen:

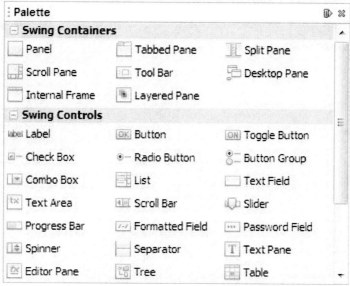

Figure 16.3: NetBeans palette window

You can use the palette to select your required components. Under the **Swing Controls** section click and drag **Label** (which is an instance of JLabel) to the blank panel so that it looks as follows:

Figure 16.4: JLabel placed on a form

Now drag a **Text Field** across to appear to the right of the label, and then use the handles that appear around the component to stretch it to the right so that your screen looks like this:

jLabel1   jTextField1

Figure 16.5: JTextField placed next to JLabel

Right-click on the `jLabel1` component and select **Edit Text**. Use the in-place editor to change it to **Name:** and press **Enter**. Now right-click again and select **Change Variable Name...** setting it to `nameLabel`.

Now use the same techniques to rename `jTextField1` to `nameField` and set its text to blank.

In the bottom left corner if the NetBeans frame you should see the **Navigator** window which shows a hierarchical view of the structure of your components as you add them to the form:

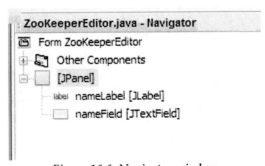

Figure 16.6: Navigator window

Place a new label underneath the first, rename it to addressLabel and set its text to **Address:**. Under the **Swing Containers** section of the palette drag a **Scroll Pane** next to the address label, sizing it to appear as follows:

Figure 16.7: JSrollPane added to form

There is no need to rename the scroll pane component. Drag a **Text Area** on top of the scroll pane and you will notice it take up all of the space inside of it. Rename the text area as addressArea.

Now drag across two more labels and two more text fields to represent the email address and salary, naming the text fields emailField and salaryField respectively[1] and blanking their text. Underneath these drag a **Button**, changing its text to **Save** and its variable name to saveButton. At this stage the screen should look like this:

---

1   There is no real need to rename the labels unless you want to.

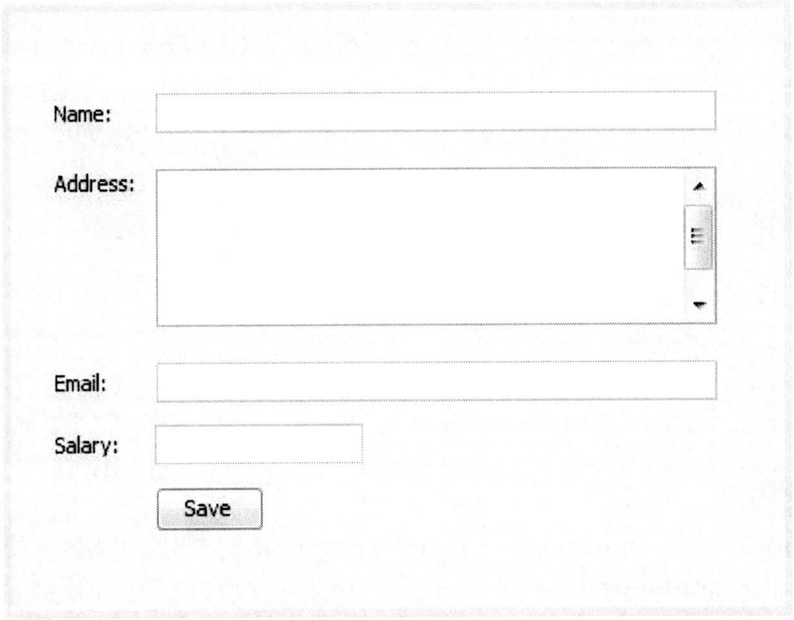

Figure 16.8: Completed form

The **Navigator** window should show this:

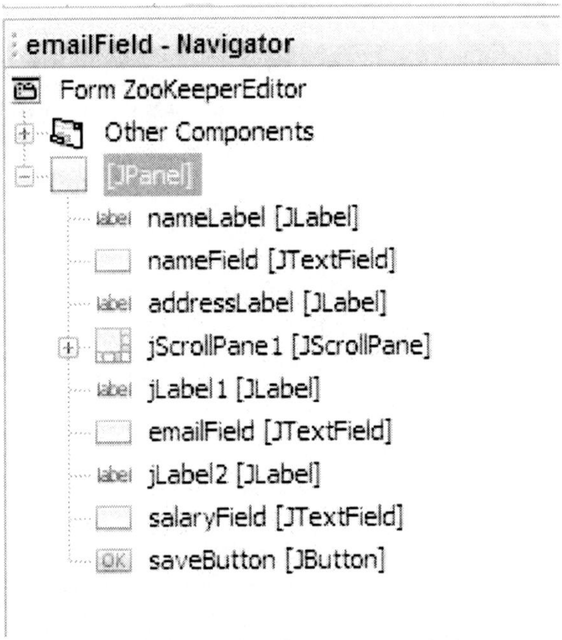

Figure 16.9: Updated Navigator window

Underneath the palette there is the **Properties** window which shows the available properties of the currently selected component. For example, if you click in `nameField` it will look similar to below:

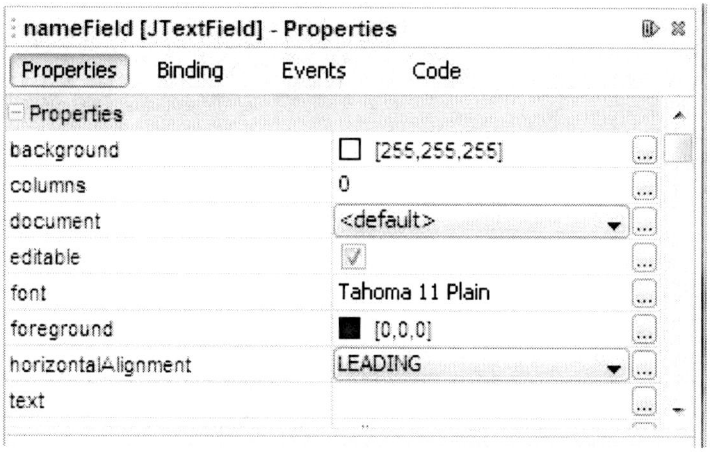

Figure 16.10: NetBeans Properties window

If you wanted to prevent the user from being able to type into the field you could un-check the `editable` check-box, for example. Here, you do need this field to be editable you should ensure the check-box remains checked.

Click the **Source** tab and scroll down to near the bottom of the Java source. You will see all of the instance variable declarations inside a shaded area that does not allow any editing.

If you click the **Design** tab again the third icon to its right is **Preview Design**, which provides an indication of how the panel will appear when in use.

There are in fact two more labels that need to be placed on the form, one above the existing components and one below. The top label will inform the user whether they are adding or editing a zoo keeper's details, and the bottom label will display a message confirming when the details have been saved. Drag two labels, one above and one below the current components so your form looks like this:

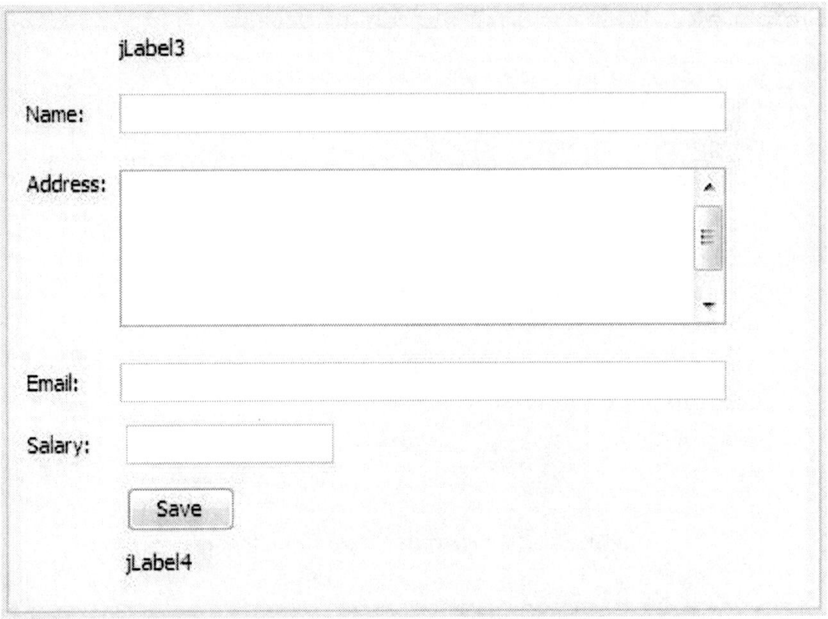

Figure 16.11: Updated form with addition JLabel components

Click in each of the new labels in turn and stretch them to the right to align with the longer text fields. Now rename `jLabel3` as `modeLabel` and set its text to **Mode will go here**. Underneath the palette you will see the **Properties** window showing the attributes of the currently selected component. Ensure `modeLabel` is still selected (by clicking on it on the form if necessary) and look at the `Properties` window:

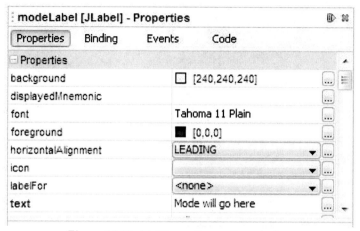

Figure 16.12: NetBeans Properties window

Locate the font attribute and notice that it is currently set to **Tahoma 11 Plain**. Click the little button to the right of this that contains three dots in order to open the customiser for this attribute. In this case you should see the font customiser in which you can change the **Font Style** from **Plain** to **Bold**:

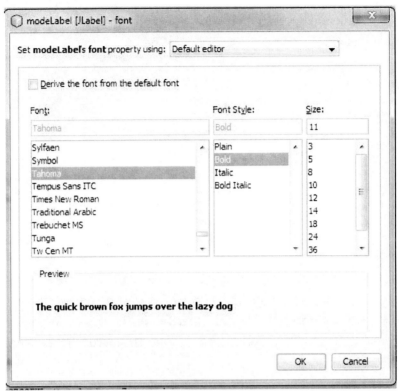

Figure 16.13: NetBeans font customizer dialog

Click **OK**.

Now rename `jLabel4` as `messageLabel` and set its text to **Message will go here**. Use the **Properties** window to change its font to bold and also have a size of 18. Also find the **Foreground** attribute in the **Properties** window and click the dots button to open the colour customiser:

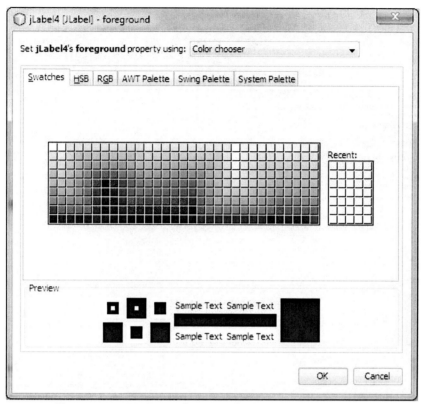

Figure 16.14: NetBeans foreground colour customizer dialog

Use your mouse to click on one of the shades of blue in the grid of colours, then click **OK**.

The form should now look similar to this:

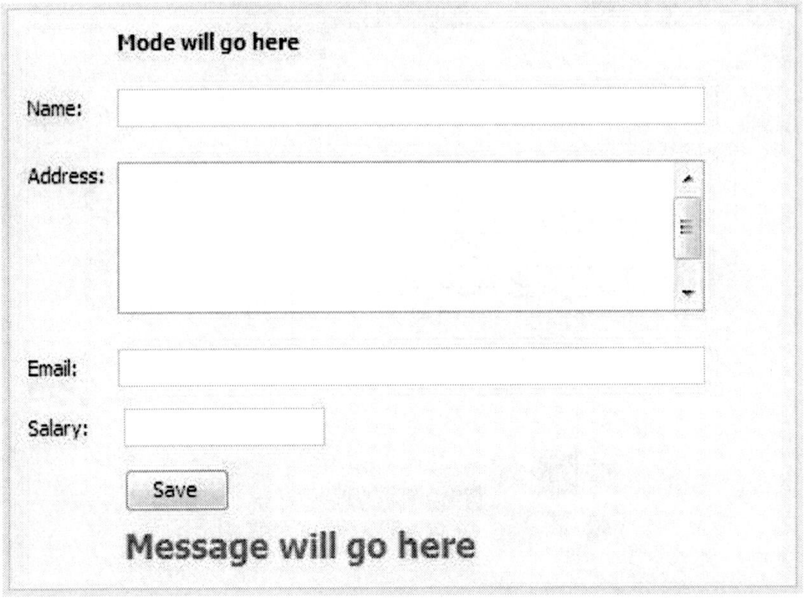

Figure 16.15: Updated form

> In the **Navigator** window the entries for `modeLabel` and `messageLabel` appear last in the list because they were the last to be added. Because `modeLabel` is actually the top component on the form you may prefer it to be listed first in the **Navigator** too. You can do this by right-clicking its node and selecting **Move Up**, repeating the process until it appears just above `nameLabel`.

Switch into source editing mode by clicking the **Source** button.

You should add imports for the core package and the Swing components:

```
import javax.swing.*;
import virtualzoo.core.*;
```

For `ZooKeeperEditor` to be any use it needs to know if it should be adding a new zoo keeper or editing an existing one. To this end, define a new instance variable to reference a `ZooKeeper` object:

```
private ZooKeeper zooKeeper;
```

> The instance variables generated by NetBeans (for the graphical components) appear at the bottom of the source file in an uneditable area. It is suggested that you define the above instance variable in the same position you have used in your other developed classes, i.e. just before the constructor, to distinguish it from the auto-generated variables.

If the `zooKeeper` instance variable is `null` then you will take this to mean that this panel should add a new zoo keeper using the values entered into the form fields. Conversely, if the variable is not `null` then it will reference the `ZooKeeper` object that should be used to pre-fill the entry fields to be potentially updated.

Define a new method in `ZooKeeperEditor` called `clearZooKeeper()` to handle the first of the above two scenarios:

```
void clearZooKeeper() {
    zooKeeper = null;
    nameField.setText("");
    addressArea.setText("");
    emailField.setText("");
    salaryField.setText("");
    modeLabel.setText("Add New Zoo Keeper");
    messageLabel.setText("");
}
```

- The `zooKeeper` instance variable is set to `null` and each of the text entry fields is emptied. The `modeLabel` is set to inform the user that they are adding a new zoo keeper.

Define another method called `setZooKeeper()` which accepts a `ZooKeeper` object as an argument representing the one that needs editing:

```
void setZooKeeper(ZooKeeper zooKeeper) {
    this.zooKeeper = zooKeeper;
    nameField.setText(zooKeeper.getName());
    addressArea.setText(zooKeeper.getAddress());
    emailField.setText(zooKeeper.getEmail().toString());
    salaryField.setText(zooKeeper.getSalary().toPlainString());
    modeLabel.setText("Change Zoo Keeper Details");
    messageLabel.setText("");
}
```

- The `zooKeeper` instance variable is set to the argument and each of the text entry fields is pre-filled with the existing values gleaned from the supplied zoo keeper. The `modeLabel` is set to inform the user that they are changing an existing zoo keeper;

- Note the use of `toString()` to get the `String` representation of the `Email` object, and the use of `toPlainString()` for the `String` representation of the `BigDecimal` object. While `BigDecimal` does have a `toString()` method, it might return the value in scientific notation, which would not be suitable for a monetary value.

By default, you want the editor to be in "add" mode when first instantiated, so add a call to `clearZooKeeper()` inside the constructor:

```
public ZooKeeperEditor() {
    initComponents();
    clearZooKeeper();
}
```

> Later, you will develop another class which will call either `clearZooKeeper()` or `setZooKeeper()` as appropriate.

You can now enter some code to handle the **Save** button being clicked. Click on the **Design** option to see the form, and then double-click the **Save** button. This will take you back into the source mode from which you will see an auto-generated method called saveButtonActionPerformed() as follows:

```
private void saveButtonActionPerformed(java.awt.event.ActionEvent evt) {
    // TODO add your handling code here:
}
```

Inside the above method you can enter the code to be executed whenever the **Save** button is clicked by the user. You should enter the following code:

```
private void saveButtonActionPerformed(java.awt.event.ActionEvent evt) {
    ZooAdministrator admin = ZooAdministrator.getInstance();

    if (zooKeeper == null) {
        // Adding a new zoo keeper
        admin.createZooKeeper(nameField.getText(),
                            addressArea.getText(),
                            emailField.getText(),
                            salaryField.getText());
        messageLabel.setText("New zoo keeper added");
    } else {
        // Changing an existing zoo keeper
        admin.changeZooKeeper(zooKeeper,
                            nameField.getText(),
                            addressArea.getText(),
                            emailField.getText(),
                            salaryField.getText());
        messageLabel.setText("Zoo keeper details changed");
    }
}
```

- A reference to the ZooAdministrator singleton object is firstly obtained, since you need to invoke either its createZooKeeper() or changeZooKeeper() method.

- A test is made to see whether the zooKeeper instance variable is null in order to know whether the zoo keeper is being added or changed;

Validating form input

In Chapter 7 you learned how Java exceptions can be used to indicate an error of come kind. You also learned that there are two types of exceptions, checked and unchecked:

- Use **checked** exceptions for errors from which you or the user can recover;

- Use **unchecked** exceptions for programming errors.

Thinking about how to apply this to your application it is helpful to review the sequence of actions when adding a new zoo keeper:

1. The user interface causes `createZooKeeper()` in `ZooAdministrator` to be invoked;

2. The `createZooKeeper()` method instantiates a `ZooKeeper` object.

It is the end user who effectively invokes the `createZooKeeper()` method (by clicking the **Save** button). It would therefore make sense for `createZooKeeper()` to throw a checked exception should an invalid entry be made. However, the `ZooKeeper` constructor is not directly invoked by the end user because it is called by the code within `createZooKeeper()`, so any invalid entries here could be considered as preventable (by the programmer) and will therefore throw unchecked exceptions.

For unchecked exceptions you could use either (or both) of the Java supplied `IllegalArgumentException` or `InvalidStateException`. For checked exceptions you can make use of the `ValidationException` class you created in Chapter 7. Because the attributes can be set in both the constructor and the individual setter methods, you need a way of validating their values in all cases.

You will now define some validation methods in the ZooKeeper class, so begin by defining a new protected[1] helper method called validateName() which performs some validation checks for the name argument:

```
protected void validateName(String name) {
    if (name.isEmpty()) {
        throw new IllegalArgumentException("Name must be specified");
    }
}
```

Now define similar methods to validate the other attributes:

```
protected void validateAddress(String address) {
    if (address.isEmpty()) {
        throw new IllegalArgumentException("Address must be
                                           specified");
    }
}


protected void validateEmail(Email email) {
    if (email.toString().isEmpty()) {
        throw new IllegalArgumentException("Email must be
                                           specified");
    }
}


protected void validateSalary(BigDecimal salary) {
    if (salary.compareTo(BigDecimal.ZERO) <= 0) {
        throw new IllegalArgumentException("Salary must be
                                           specified");
    }
}
```

• The validations performed have been deliberately kept simple. In a production level application more validation would be needed.

---

1   The validation methods are protected so that if you ever override the ZooKeeper class you will be able to override these methods if necessary.

The above validation methods can be called from inside each setter method:

```
void setName(String name) {
    validateName(name);
    this.name = name;
}

void setAddress(String address) {
    validateAddress(address);
    this.address = address;
}

void setEmail(Email email) {
    validateEmail(email);
    this.email = email;
}

void setSalary(BigDecimal salary) {
    validateSalary(salary);
    this.salary = salary;
}
```

Rather than the constructor having to invoke each individual validation method you can delegate to a new `private` helper method that does it for you:

```
protected void validate(String name, String address,
                                Email email, BigDecimal salary) {
    validateName(name);
    validateAddress(address);
    validateEmail(email);
    validateSalary(salary);
}
```

The constructor can now invoke `validate()`:

```
ZooKeeper(Person person, Email email, BigDecimal salary){
    validate(person.getName(), person.getAddress(), email, salary);
    this.person = new Person(person);
    this.email = email;
    this.salary = salary;
```

```
}
```

> Remember that if an exception is actually thrown then the statements that follow
> it are not performed. Instead, the exception is propagated back through the chain
> of calling methods until one of them catches it in a `try...catch` block.

If you return to the `createZooKeeper()` method in `ZooAdministrator` you find that as it stands it would simply propagate any thrown exception back to the user. However, these are of the unchecked type and it was decided earlier that this method should throw a checked exception. In Chapter 7 you developed the `ValidationException` class as a checked exception, so you can modify `createZooKeeper()` as follows:

```
public ZooKeeper createZooKeeper(String name, String address,
            String email, String salary) throws ValidationException {
    try {
        ZooKeeper zooKeeper = new ZooKeeper(new Person(name, address),
                                new Email(email),
                                new BigDecimal(salary));
        zooKeepers.add(zooKeeper);
        return zooKeeper;
    } catch (IllegalArgumentException ex) {
        throw new ValidationException(ex.getMessage());
    }
}
```

- By enclosing the statement which can give rise to an exception (the `ZooKeeper` constructor in this case) in a `try...catch` block you can trap it should it occur. If it does, the code generates suitable a `ValidationException` by retrieving the text of the caught exception and passing it to the constructor of `ValidationException`;

- Note that because `ValidationException` is a checked exception the method signature needs to specify that it can potentially be thrown. This was not needed for unchecked exception types.

There is another error that could occur that has not been handled yet; the BigDecimal constructor could throw the unchecked exception NumberFormatException if the passed String is not in a valid numerical format:

```
public ZooKeeper createZooKeeper(String name, String address,
        String email, String salary) throws ValidationException {
    try {
        ZooKeeper zooKeeper = new ZooKeeper(new Person(name, address),
                                    new Email(email),
                                    new BigDecimal(salary));
        zooKeepers.add(zooKeeper);
        return zooKeeper;
    } catch (NumberFormatException ex) {
        throw new ValidationException(salary + " is not a valid
                                            amount.");
    } catch (IllegalArgumentException ex) {
        throw new ValidationException(ex.getMessage());
    }
}
```

- Note that you must catch NumberFormatException before IllegalArgumentException since the former is a subclass of the latter.

Because the createZooKeeper() method can now potentially throw a checked exception the saveButtonActionPerformed() method within ZooKeeperEditor will no longer compile. You need to catch the exception should it occur and show an message dialog informing the user of the problem:

```
private void saveButonActionPerformed(java.awt.event.ActionEvent evt) {
    ZooAdministrator admin = ZooAdministrator.getInstance();

    try {
        if (zooKeeper == null) {
            // Adding a new zoo keeper
            admin.createZooKeeper(nameField.getText(),
                        addressArea.getText(),
                        emailField.getText(),
```

```
                          salaryField.getText());
            messageLabel.setText("New zoo keeper added");
        } else {
            // Changing an existing zoo keeper
            admin.changeZooKeeper(zooKeeper,
                            nameField.getText(),
                            addressArea.getText(),
                            emailField.getText(),
                            salaryField.getText());
            messageLabel.setText("Zoo keeper details changed");
        }
    } catch (ValidationException ex) {
        JOptionPane.showMessageDialog(null, ex.getMessage(), "Error",
                            JOptionPane.ERROR_MESSAGE);
    }
}
```

- Because the method can potentially throw a `ValidationException` the statements are enclosed within a `try...catch` block. If an exception is thrown, the `JOptionPane` class is used to inform the user of the problem.

You should change the `changeZooKeeper()` method inside `ZooAdministrator` to also catch and display to the user any exceptions which occur:

```
public void changeZooKeeper(ZooKeeper zooKeeper, String name,
                        String address, String email, String salary)
                                throws ValidationException {
    try {
        zooKeeper.setPerson(new Person(name, address));
        zooKeeper.setEmail(new Email(email));
        zooKeeper.setSalary(new BigDecimal(salary));
    } catch (NumberFormatException ex) {
        throw new ValidationException(salary + " is not a valid
                                                amount.");
    } catch (IllegalArgumentException ex) {
        throw new ValidationException(ex.getMessage());
    }
}
```

The ZooKeeperPanel class

If you look at again at Figure 16.1 at the beginning of this chapter you will see that the two classes you have developed so far, ZooKeeperList and ZooKeeperEditor, are set as the left and right components inside a JSplitPane, underneath which is a panel containing two centred buttons. You will now use NetBeans to create a new class called ZooKeeperPanel to model this.

You have seen how when using the form builder you can drag and drop components from the **Palette** window onto the form. You can even add your own components to the palette, and you will do this now by adding the ZooKeeperEditor panel you just created. Go into **Design** mode in ZooKeeperEditor so that the **Palette** window appears, and then right-click somewhere inside the **Palette** window and select **Palette Manager...** which should result in this dialog:

Figure 16.16: NetBeans Palette Manager dialog

Click the **New Category...** button and enter `Zoo Components` in the **New Category Name** field. After you click **OK**, click **Close** on the **Palette Manager** dialog. You should see the new category appear at the top of the **Palette** window.

Now right-click the `ZooKeeperEditor.java` node in the **Projects** window and select **Tools | Add to Palette...**, select **Zoo Components** from the list and click **OK**. If you now expand the **Palette** window's **Zoo Components** category (by clicking the small "plus" icon) you will see your component available:

Figure 16.17: NetBeans Palette window

You should now also add the `ZooKeeperList` class you created earlier to the palette.

You are now ready to create the new panel, so right-click on the `virtual.ui` package node and select **New JPanel Form...**, enter `ZooKeeperPanel` as the **Class Name**, and click **Finish**.

Enlarge the size of the blank design area to make it easier to see the components which will be added. Right-click the form and select **Set Layout | Border Layout**.

Now drag from the palette a **Panel** (from the **Swing Containers** category) and place it at the bottom of the form. As you are dragging, just above the form you will see some text which tells you where it will be placed, so you want it to say "Place the component into the Last area"[1].

Now right-click the panel you just placed at the bottom and select **Set Layout** | **Flow Layout**. Drag two **Button** objects from the palette onto the bottom panel, setting the first one's text to **Add** and variable name to `addButton`, and the second one's text to **Remove** and variable name to `removeButton`. To make the button panel stand out a bit more, click on it and inspect the **Properties** window:

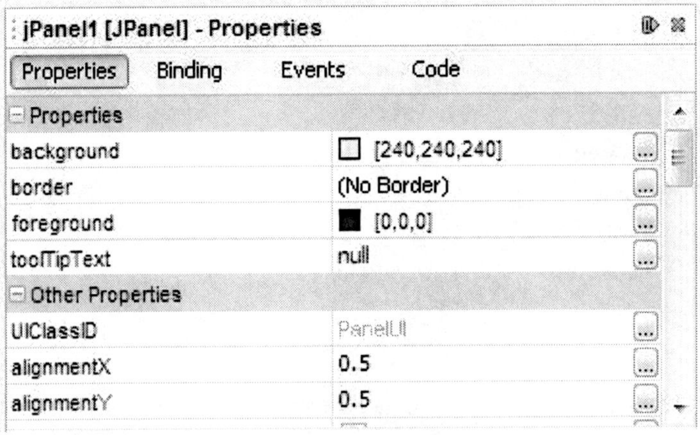

jPanel1 [JPanel] - Properties		
Properties	Binding	Events	Code

Properties		
background	☐ [240,240,240]	...
border	(No Border)	...
foreground	■ [0,0,0]	...
toolTipText	null	...
Other Properties		
UIClassID	PanelUI	...
alignmentX	0.5	...
alignmentY	0.5	...

Figure 16.18: NetBeans Properties window

Locate the **border** property, which is currently set to **(No Border)** and click the three-dotted icon to its right to open the customiser dialog. Select **Soft Bevel Border** and click **OK**.

From the **Swing Containers** section drag a **Split Pane** onto the centre area of the form. The form should now look as follows:

---

1   The "Last" area corresponds to `BorderLayout.SOUTH`.

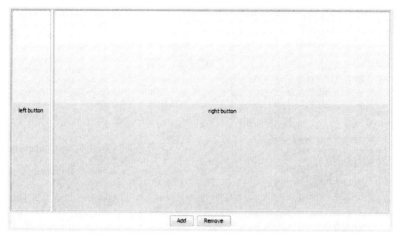

Figure 16.19: Form containing JSplitPane

The sections named **left button** and **right button** are just temporary placeholders. Under **Swing Containers** drag a **Scroll Pane** over the top of **left button** (which will replace it) and then under **Zoo Components** drag a **ZooKeeperList** component on top of the scroll pane (which will nest inside it). Change its variable name to `zooKeeperList`.

From **Zoo Components** drag **ZooKeeperEditor** over the top of **right button** to replace that too. Change its variable name to `zooKeeperEditor`.

The form should now look like this:

Figure 16.20: Updated form

Looking first at the list on the left, you will notice some dummy items listed (Item1 through Item5). You can delete these by clicking on the list to select it, and then ensuring the **Properties** button is selected in the **Properties** window:

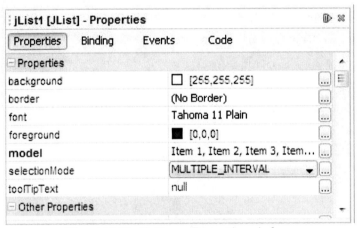

Figure 16.21: NetBeans Properties window

You can click in the area to the right of model and blank it out, remembering to press **Enter** on your keyboard. (Alternatively, you can click the button with three small dots to bring up a text editor).

The AdministratorFrame class

The frame now only needs to show ZooKeeperPanel inside a tab of a JTabbedPane. Create a class in virtualzoo.ui called AdministratorFrame:

```java
package virtualzoo.ui;

import java.awt.*;
import javax.swing.*;

public class AdministratorFrame extends JFrame {

    public AdministratorFrame() {
        super("Zoo Administrator");
        setLayout(new BorderLayout());
        setDefaultCloseOperation(DISPOSE_ON_CLOSE);

        // Create tabbed pane
        JTabbedPane tabPane = new JTabbedPane();

        // Create zoo keeper panel
        ZooKeeperPanel zooKeeperPanel = new ZooKeeperPanel();
        tabPane.addTab("Zoo Keepers", zooKeeperPanel);

        add(tabPane, BorderLayout.CENTER);

        // Set components to their preferred size
        pack();

        // Place in the centre of the desktop
        setLocationRelativeTo(null);

        // Make the frame visible
        setVisible(true);
    }
}
```

```
}
```

Change the main() method of VirtualZoo to instantiate AdministratorFrame (you will need to import virtualzoo.ui):

```
public static void main(String[] args) {
    AdministratorFrame frame = new AdministratorFrame();
}
```

At this point you can run the application to ensure it appears as below:

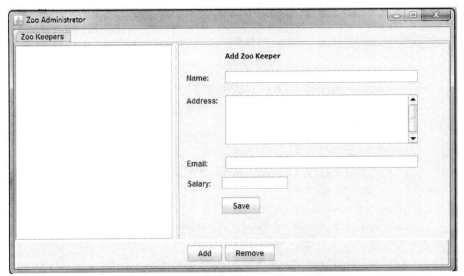

Figure 16.22: Zoo Administrator frame

You will note that after entering some details and clicking the **Save** button the added zoo keeper is not appearing in the list on the left. This will be addressed in the next section.

Updating ZooKeeperList automatically

The ZooKeeperList object needs some way of being notified whenever a change to the collection of zoo keeper objects held by the administrator changes, in order that it can update its model and thus be reflected in the list of items displayed. This can be accomplished by defining suitable event and listener objects, as follows:

Create a sub-package under `virtualzoo.core` called `event`, within which you will define the class `ZooKeeperEvent` and the interface `ZooKeeperListener`.

Define a `ZooKeeperEvent` class in package `virtualzoo.core.event`:

```
package virtualzoo.core.event;

import virtualzoo.core.*;
import java.util.*;

public class ZooKeeperEvent extends EventObject {

    public ZooKeeperEvent(ZooKeeper zooKeeper) {
        super(zooKeeper);
    }

    public ZooKeeper getZooKeeper() {
        return (ZooKeeper) getSource();
    }

}
```

- The class extends `EventObject`, which is a Java supplied class intended for sub-classing by different event types;

- The constructor requires a `ZooKeeper` object to be passed in and which is in turn passed to the superclass constructor (which accepts any `Object`);

- The `EventObject` class defines a `getSource()` method so client objects can determine the source of the event. Because `getSource()` returns it as an `Object` a cast is required to get it back into its `ZooKeeper` type which you know it has to be. To save client objects the inconvenience of having to do this cast you have defined a `getZooKeeper()` method that performs the cast here.

Define a `ZooKeeperListener` interface in package `virtualzoo.core.event`:

```
package virtualzoo.core.event;

import java.util.*;

public interface ZooKeeperListener extends EventListener {

    public void zooKeeperCreated(ZooKeeperEvent event);
    public void zooKeeperChanged(ZooKeeperEvent event);
    public void zooKeeperRemoved(ZooKeeperEvent event);

}
```

- The interface extends `EventListener`, which is a Java supplied interface intended for sub-classing by different event listeners;

- Separate methods are specified for when a `ZooKeeper` is created, changed or removed. Note the argument for each is `ZooKeeperEvent`.

Because `ZooAdministrator` stores the collection of `ZooKeeper` objects it is a natural place to maintain references to objects that want to know about new, changed or removed zoo keepers (i.e. `ZooKeeperListener`s) and to notify them whenever these events occur.

In `ZooAdministrator` define an `import` for `virtualzoo.core.event` and add the following instance variable to store a collection of listeners:

```
private Collection<ZooKeeperListener> zooKeeperListeners;
```

Instantiate the collection inside the constructor:

```
zooKeeperListeners = new ArrayList<ZooKeeperListener>();
```

Now define two new `public` methods so that client objects can register themselves as listeners:

```
public void addZooKeeperListener(ZooKeeperListener listener) {
    zooKeeperListeners.add(listener);
}

public void removeZooKeeperListener(ZooKeeperListener listener) {
    zooKeeperListeners.remove(listener);
}
```

- The above methods simply delegate to the `add()` and `remove()` methods of the collection.

Define a `private` helper method that notifies all registered listeners whenever a new zoo keeper is added:

```
private void fireZooKeeperCreated(ZooKeeper zooKeeper) {
    ZooKeeperEvent event = new ZooKeeperEvent(zooKeeper);
    for (ZooKeeperListener listener : zooKeeperListeners) {
        listener.zooKeeperCreated(event);
    }
}
```

- The above method creates a `ZooKeeperEvent` and then iterates over each registered listener notifying them of the fact that a new zoo keeper has been created.

Modify the `createZooKeeper()` method to invoke `fireZooKeeperCreated()` once the `ZooKeeper` object has been added to the collection:

```
public ZooKeeper createZooKeeper(String name, String address,
        String email, String salary) throws ValidationException {
    try {
        ZooKeeper zooKeeper = new ZooKeeper(new Person(name, address),
                                            new Email(email),
                                            new BigDecimal(salary));
        zooKeepers.add(zooKeeper);
        fireZooKeeperCreated(zooKeeper);
```

```
        return zooKeeper;
    } catch (NumberFormatException ex) {
        throw new ValidationException(salary + " is not a valid
                                              amount.");
    } catch (IllegalArgumentException ex) {
        throw new ValidationException(ex.getMessage());
    }
}
```

You can now define methods `fireZooKeeperChanged()` and `fireZooKeeperRemoved()`, each very similar to `fireZooKeeperAdded()`:

```
private void fireZooKeeperChanged(ZooKeeper zooKeeper) {
    ZooKeeperEvent event = new ZooKeeperEvent(zooKeeper);
    for (ZooKeeperListener listener : zooKeeperListeners) {
        listener.zooKeeperChanged(event);
    }
}

private void fireZooKeeperRemoved(ZooKeeper zooKeeper) {
    ZooKeeperEvent event = new ZooKeeperEvent(zooKeeper);
    for (ZooKeeperListener listener : zooKeeperListeners) {
        listener.zooKeeperRemoved(event);
    }
}
```

Modify `changeZooKeeper()` and `removeZooKeeper()` to invoke the respective "fire" methods:

```
public void changeZooKeeper(ZooKeeper zooKeeper, String name,
                            String address, String email, String salary)
                                    throws ValidationException {
    try {
        zooKeeper.setPerson(new Person(name, address));
        zooKeeper.setEmail(new Email(email));
        zooKeeper.setSalary(new BigDecimal(salary));
        fireZooKeeperChanged(zooKeeper);
    } catch (NumberFormatException ex) {
        throw new ValidationException(salary + " is not a valid
                                              amount.");
    } catch (IllegalArgumentException ex) {
        throw new ValidationException(ex.getMessage());
    }
```

```
}

public void removeZooKeeper(ZooKeeper zooKeeper) {
    zooKeepers.remove(zooKeeper);
    fireZooKeeperRemoved(zooKeeper);
}
```

> The purpose of `ZooAdministrator` maintaining a collection of listener objects is so that it need have no direct knowledge of any of the classes which are likely to want to be notified of when a zoo keeper is created, changed or removed. In this way, your classes are accomplish loose-coupling, meaning that they are not directly dependent upon any more classes than is strictly necessary.

The `ZooKeeperList` class can now be modified to implement the `ZooKeeperListener` interface (note you need to import `virtualzoo.core.event`):

```
package virtualzoo.ui;

import virtualzoo.core.*;
import virtualzoo.core.event.*;
import java.util.*;
import javax.swing.*;



public class ZooKeeperList extends JList implements ZooKeeperListener {
```

If you click the glyph that appears to the left of the class declaration statement above you can click the option to implement all abstract methods. The following code will appear:

```
@Override
public void zooKeeperCreated(ZooKeeperEvent event) {
    throw new UnsupportedOperationException("Not supported yet.");
}

@Override
public void zooKeeperChanged(ZooKeeperEvent event) {
    throw new UnsupportedOperationException("Not supported yet.");
}
```

```
@Override
public void zooKeeperRemoved(ZooKeeperEvent event) {
    throw new UnsupportedOperationException("Not supported yet.");
}
```

NetBeans generated the statements to throw an `UnsupportedOperationException` merely so that the code will compile. It is up to you to replace these lines with the actual code that should occur in response to the events. In all three cases you simply want the data in the list model (held in the `ZooKeeperListModel` inner class) to be reloaded. To do this you can invoke the `loadModel()` method from within the event listener methods, so make the following modifications:

```
@Override
public void ZooKeeperCreated(ZooKeeperEvent event) {
    model.loadModel();
}

@Override
public void ZooKeeperChanged(ZooKeeperEvent event) {
    model.loadModel();
}

@Override
public void ZooKeeperRemoved(ZooKeeperEvent event) {
    model.loadModel();
}
```

You now need to wire up the `ZooKeeperList` object which is referenced in `ZooKeeperPanel` so that it listens to events. In `ZooKeeperPanel` define a new instance variable to reference the `ZooAdministrator` object (you need to import import `virtualzoo.core`):

```
private ZooAdministrator admin;
```

Now change the constructor to obtain the `ZooAdministrator` object add call its `addZooKeeperListener()` method:

```
public ZooKeeperPanel() {
```

```
    initComponents();
    admin = ZooAdministrator.getInstance();
    admin.addZooKeeperListener(zooKeeperList);
}
```

You can now run the application, enter and save one (or several) zoo keepers, and you should find the list automatically updates itself:

Figure 16.23: Zoo Keeper added

It would be better to clear the editor form after adding a new zoo keeper ready for adding a new one, so add a call to `clearZooKeeper()` in the `saveButtonActionPerformed()` method of `ZooKeeperEditor`:

```
private void saveButtonActionPerformed(java.awt.event.ActionEvent evt) {
    ZooAdministrator admin = ZooAdministrator.getInstance();

    if (zooKeeper == null) {
        // Adding a new zoo keeper
        admin.addZooKeeper(nameField.getText(),
                           adressArea.getText(),
                           emailField.getText(),
                           salaryField.getText());
        messageLabel.setText("New zoo keeper added");
        clearZooKeeper();
    } else {
```

```
              // Changing an existing zoo keeper
              admin.changeZooKeeper(zooKeeper,
                                nameField.getText(),
                                addressArea.getText(),
                                emailField.getText(),
                                salaryField.getText());
              messageLabel.setText("Zoo keeper details changed");
          }

      }
```

Modifying existing zoo keeper details

Now that you have completed the code necessary to add new zoo keepers you need to enable their details to be changed. What you will do is detect whenever the user selects one of the names in `ZooKeeperList` and pass that selected `ZooKeeper` object to `ZooKeeperEditor` so that it transitions into "change" mode.

The `JList` class (of which `ZooKeeperList` is a subclass) supports the fact that client objects may wish to listen to selections in the list. All client objects need to do is implement the `ListSelectionListener` interface and provide the appropriate code in its required `valueChanged()` method. Then you can pass the client object as an argument to the `addListSelectionListener()` method of `JList`. You will now code these steps.

Firstly, change the class header of `ZooKeeperPanel` to implement `ListSelectionListener` (you will also need to import the `javax.swing.event` package):

```
package virtualzoo.ui;

import virtualzoo.core.*;
import javax.swing.event.*;

public class ZooKeeperPanel extends javax.swing.JPanel
                      implements ListSelectionListener {
```

Now you need to code the only method required by the interface:

```
@Override
public void valueChanged(ListSelectionEvent e) {
    // A zoo keeper has been selected from ZooKeeperList
    Object selected = zooKeeperList.getSelectedValue();
    if (selected != null) {
        ZooKeeper zooKeeper = (ZooKeeper) selected;
        zooKeeperEditor.setZooKeeper(zooKeeper);
    }
}
```

- The `valueChanged()` method will be called every time the user selects a zoo keeper from the list;

- The `getSelectedValue()` method retrieves the selected `Object`. This will be `null` if nothing is actually selected so it is tested to ensure that it is not `null` before continuing. Provided it is not `null` then it needs to be cast from `Object` to `ZooKeeper`;

- You then pass the `ZooKeeper` object to the `setZooKeeper()` method of `ZooKeeperEditor`, which you coded earlier.

You need to ensure you listen to the list events so invoke the registration in the constructor:

```
public ZooKeeperPanel() {
    initComponents();
    admin = ZooAdministrator.getInstance();
    admin.addZooKeeperListener(zooKeeperList);
    zooKeeperList.addListSelectionListener(this);
}
```

Run the application and enter two or three new zoo keepers. Now, select one of the names from the list and notice that the editor displays the selected one's details in "change" mode. You can edit the details and click

Save, and if you modified the name you should see this reflected in the list on the left.

Removing an existing zoo keeper

When you built the form for ZooKeeperPanel you included a **Remove** button. Before writing the code so that it removes the selected zoo keeper (after asking for confirmation) you will change the status of the button so that it is only enabled (i.e. available to be clicked) when a zoo keeper is actually selected in the list.

Open ZooKeeperPanel in **Design** mode and click the **Remove** button to select it. In the **Properties** window locate the **enabled** property (you may need to scroll to find it):

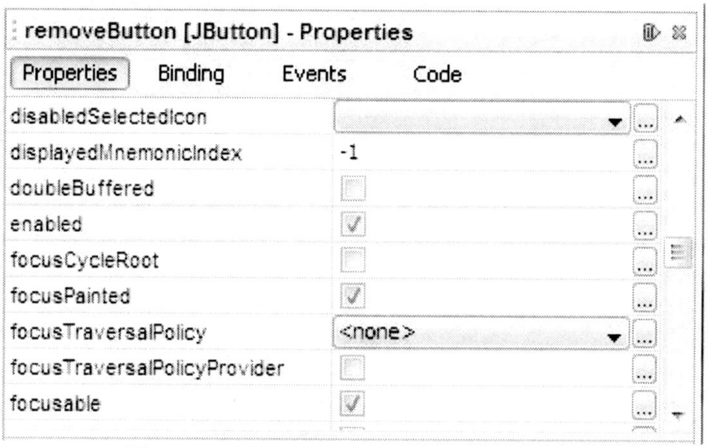

Figure 16.24: NetBeans Properties window

You will see that the check box for this attribute is checked, indicating that the button is enabled by default, so un-check this check box now. You will notice that the button becomes greyed out to indicate that it cannot be clicked.

Switch into **Source** mode and modify the `valueChanged()` method to enable the button whenever a zoo keeper is selected, or disable it again when nothing is selected:

```
@Override
public void valueChanged(ListSelectionEvent e) {
    // A zoo keeper has been selected from ZooKeeperList
    Object selected = zooKeeperList.getSelectedValue();
    if (selected != null) {
        ZooKeeper zooKeeper = (ZooKeeper) selected;
        zooKeeperEditor.setZooKeeper(zooKeeper);
        removeButton.setEnabled(true);
    } else {
        // Nothing selected
        removeButton.setEnabled(false);
    }
}
```

Now switch back to **Design** mode and double-click the **Remove** button to generate its `removeButtonActionPerformed()` method. This method needs to ask the user to confirm that they really do want to remove the zoo keeper and if so invoke the `ZooAdministrator` `removeZooKeeper()` method:

```
private void removeButtonActionPerformed(java.awt.event.ActionEvent evt)
{
    ZooKeeper zooKeeper = (ZooKeeper) zooKeeperList.getSelectedValue();
    int response = JOptionPane.showConfirmDialog(null,
            "Do you really want to remove " + zooKeeper.getName() + "?",
            "Confirm Remove", JOptionPane.YES_NO_OPTION);
    if (response == JOptionPane.YES_OPTION) {
        admin.removeZooKeeper(zooKeeper);
        zooKeeperEditor.clearZooKeeper();
    }
}
```

After the zoo keeper is removed the editor is placed back into "add" mode by calling `clearZooKeeper()`. You should also now ensure nothing is selected in the list of zoo keepers, so modify the `zooKeeperRemovedEvent()` of `ZooKeeperList` as follows:

```
@Override
public void zooKeeperRemoved(ZooKeeperEvent event) {
    model.loadModel();
    removeSelectionInterval(0, model.getSize());
}
```

- The `removeSelectionInterval()` method de-selects all items in a list between the range of indexes specified in the arguments;

- Also note that `removeSelectionInterval()` automatically triggers a `ListSelectionEvent` so you will find the **Remove** button becomes disabled.

Handling the Add button

All that remains now is to write some code for the **Add** button to enable the user to switch from "change" mode back into "add" mode. Go to the **Design** view of ZooKeeperPanel and double-click the **Add** button to generate its addButtonActionPerformed() method. All it needs to do is invoke clearZooKeeper() on the zooKeeperEditor instance:

```
private void addButtonActionPerformed(java.awt.event.ActionEvent evt) {
    zooKeeperEditor.clearZooKeeper();
}
```

After adding a new zoo keeper it would be best to ensure nothing is selected in the list, since the form remains in "add" mode. Update the zooKeeperCreated() method in ZooKeeperList:

```
@Override
public void zooKeeperCreated(ZooKeeperEvent event) {
    model.loadModel();
    removeSelectionInterval(0, model.getSize());
}
```

You will have noticed that this is the same line of code that you previously added to zooKeeperRemoved(). Even though it is only a single line of code, given its slightly involved argument values there is a case for refactoring it into its own helper method. Define a new method in ZooKeeperList called deselectListItems():

```
void deselectListItems() {
    removeSelectionInterval(0, model.getSize());
}
```

Now you can modify the zooKeeperCreated() and zooKeeperRemoved() methods to invoke the new method:

```
@Override
public void zooKeeperCreated(ZooKeeperEvent event) {
    model.loadModel();
    deselectListItems();
}
```

```
@Override
public void zooKeeperRemoved(ZooKeeperEvent event) {
    model.loadModel();
    deselectListItems();
}
```

Returning to the addButtonActionPerformed() method in ZooKeeperPanel, that should also cause any selected item in the list to be de-selected, and this is now possible since you have created the deselectListItems() method:

```
private void addButtonActionPerformed(java.awt.event.ActionEvent evt) {
    zooKeeperList.deselectListItems();
    zooKeeperEditor.clearZooKeeper();
}
```

That completes the coding for the zoo keeper panels, and you should now be able to add, change and remove as many zoo keepers as you wish. Bear in mind, however, that as it stands the data is only stored for as long as the application remains open. Saving the data to a disk file is covered in Chapter 19.

17. More User Interface Developments

This chapter continues the previous one to develop some additional interacting graphical components and panels.

In this chapter you will learn:

- *How to develop some additional types of interacting components and panels;*

- *How to prepare the core system for use by the graphical user interface;*

- *How to define a scrollable, selectable hierarchical tree of objects.*

Interacting components and panels for managing animals

This chapter continues the user interface development by creating the classes necessary to manage the addition, modification and removal of animals in the zoo. The classes will follow the same pattern as used in the previous chapter for zoo keepers, although some different components will be used in certain places.

This part of the application will look like this:

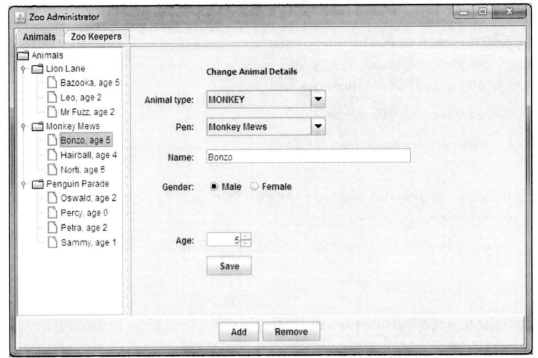

Figure 17.1: Zoo Administrator frame

Preparing the core system

Just as was done for the zoo keeper user interface components, the animal components will communicate with the core system through the ZooAdministrator class. You may recall that Animal objects are being stored inside Pen objects, and that ZooAdministrator has defined three of the latter named lionPen, monkeyPen and penguinPen. Although this book is, for simplicity, sticking to just these three types of animal, it makes sense to design the software to make it easier to enhance in the future for many more animal pens and types. To this end, rather than using three individually named Pen objects you will store a Collection of Pen objects.

In ZooAdministrator replace the following line:

```
private Pen lionPen, monkeyPen, penguinPen;
```

With this:

```
private Collection<Pen> pens;
```

In the constructor you need to instantiate an empty collection <u>before</u> the call to createExamplePens():

```
pens = new TreeSet<Pen>();
```

• The collection is sorted so that the pens will be listed alphabetically.

You should define a method that returns the collection:

```
public Collection<Pen> getPens() {
    return Collections.unmodifiableCollection(pens);
}
```

For the methods that generate sample data, since the individual Pen objects are no longer defined you can pass a reference to them as arguments:

```
private void acquireLions(Pen lionPen) {
    acquireAnimal(new Lion("Leo", Gender.MALE, 2), lionPen);
    acquireAnimal(new Lion("Mr Fuzz", Gender.MALE, 2), lionPen);
    acquireAnimal(new Lion("Bazooka", Gender.FEMALE, 5), lionPen);
}

private void acquireMonkeys(Pen monkeyPen) {
    acquireAnimal(new Monkey("Bonzo", Gender.MALE, 5), monkeyPen);
    acquireAnimal(new Monkey("Norti", Gender.FEMALE, 5), monkeyPen);
    acquireAnimal(new Monkey("Hairball", Gender.MALE, 4), monkeyPen);
}

private void acquirePenguins(Pen penguinPen) {
    acquireAnimal(new Penguin("Sammy", Gender.FEMALE, 1), penguinPen);
    acquireAnimal(new Penguin("Oswald", Gender.MALE, 2), penguinPen);
```

```
        acquireAnimal(new Penguin("Percy", Gender.MALE), penguinPen);
        acquireAnimal(new Penguin("Petra", Gender.FEMALE, 2), penguinPen);
    }
```

Now modify the `createExamplePens()` method to create the three required pens and add each to the collection:

```
    private void createExamplePens() {
        Pen lionPen = new Pen("Lion Lane");
        acquireLions(lionPen);
        pens.add(lionPen);

        Pen monkeyPen = new Pen("Monkey Mews");
        acquireMonkeys(monkeyPen);
        pens.add(monkeyPen);

        Pen penguinPen = new Pen("Penguin Parade");
        acquirePenguins(penguinPen);
        pens.add(penguinPen);
    }
```

In the `feedingTime()` method you need to replace these lines:

```
    animals.addAll(lionPen.getAnimals());
    animals.addAll(monkeyPen.getAnimals());
    animals.addAll(penguinPen.getAnimals());
```

With these:

```
    for (Pen pen : pens) {
        animals.addAll(pen.getAnimals());
    }
```

Because the zoo is restricting itself to only three types of animal it will prove helpful to define an enum for these types. Create a new enum inside the `Animal` class called `Type`:

```
    public abstract class Animal implements Comparable<Animal> {

        // The allowed animal types
```

```
public enum Type {LION, MONKEY, PENGUIN};

... rest of class omitted ...
```

It may be useful for client objects to easily find out what type a particular Animal object is, so define the following abstract getType() method in Animal:

```
// Return the animal's type
public abstract Animal.Type getType();
```

Now override this method in Lion to return the LION enum value:

```
@Override
public Animal.Type getType() {
    return Animal.Type.LION;
}
```

Now override this method in Monkey to return the MONKEY enum value:

```
@Override
public Animal.Type getType() {
    return Animal.Type.MONKEY;
}
```

Now override this method in Penguin to return the PENGUIN enum value:

```
@Override
public Animal.Type getType() {
    return Animal.Type.PENGUIN;
}
```

A useful technique when various subtypes of a class can be created is to provide a static **factory method** that determines what needs to be created and returns an object of that type. In the Animal class declare this method:

```java
// Factory method to create an animal of a specified type
static Animal create(Animal.Type type, String name,
                     Gender gender, int age) {
    Animal animal = null;
    if (type.equals(Animal.Type.LION)) {
        animal = new Lion(name, gender, age);

    } else if (type.equals(Animal.Type.MONKEY)) {
        animal = new Monkey(name, gender, age);

    } else {
        animal = new Penguin(name, gender, age);
    }
    return animal;
}
```

By defining the above method it makes it much easier for client objects to create a particular type of object without having to code their own `if...else...` statements. The method is `static` because it doesn't operate on any existing `Animal` object. You will make use of this method later in this chapter.

It would be prudent here to beef up the validation of new animal's. Currently, there is only a validation method for the age, so you will define new methods to validate the `name` and `gender`:

```java
protected void validateName(String name) {
    if (name.isEmpty()) {
        throw new IllegalArgumentException("Name must be specified");
    }
}

protected void validateGender(Gender gender) {
    if (gender == null) {
        throw new IllegalArgumentException("Gender must be specified");
    }
}
```

Call the above methods from the individual setter methods:

```
void setName(String name) {
    validateName(name);
    this.name = name;
}

void setGender(Gender gender) {
    validateGender(gender);
    this.gender = gender;
}
```

Define a `validate()` method that invokes the individual validation methods:

```
protected void validate(String name, Gender gender, int age) {
    validateName(name);
    validateGender(gender);
    validateAge(age);
}
```

Call `validate()` from the constructor:

```
Animal(String name, Gender gender, int age) {
    validate(name, gender, age);

    this.name = name;
    this.gender = gender;
    this.age = age;
    dateAdmitted = new Date(); // today's date is assumed

    // Add this animal's age to the combined age total
    combinedAge += this.age;
}
```

Because certain classes will be interested whenever an animal is added, changed or removed you can define an `AnimalEvent` class and `AnimalListener` interface in the `virtualzoo.core.event` package.

First, the `AnimalEvent` class:

```
package virtualzoo.core.event;

import virtualzoo.core.*;
import java.util.*;

public class AnimalEvent extends EventObject {

    public AnimalEvent(Animal animal) {
        super(animal);
    }

    public Animal getAnimal() {
        return (Animal) getSource();
    }

}
```

The `AnimalListener` interface:

```
package virtualzoo.core.event;

import java.util.*;


public interface AnimalListener extends EventListener {

    public void animalCreated(AnimalEvent event);
    public void animalChanged(AnimalEvent event);
    public void animalRemoved(AnimalEvent event);

}
```

In `ZooAdministrator` you need an instance variable to store a collection of `AnimalListener` objects:

```
private Collection<AnimalListener> animalListeners;
```

Instantiate the collection inside the constructor:

```
animalListeners = new ArrayList<AnimalListener>();
```

And methods to add or remove `AnimalListener` objects, and ones to fire the event changes:

```
public void addAnimalListener(AnimalListener listener) {
    animalListeners.add(listener);
}

public void removeAnimalListener(AnimalListener listener) {
    animalListeners.remove(listener);
}

private void fireAnimalCreated(Animal animal) {
    AnimalEvent event = new AnimalEvent(animal);
    for (AnimalListener listener : animalListeners) {
        listener.animalCreated(event);
    }
}

private void fireAnimalChanged(Animal animal) {
    AnimalEvent event = new AnimalEvent(animal);
    for (AnimalListener listener : animalListeners) {
        listener.animalChanged(event);
    }
}

private void fireAnimalRemoved(Animal animal) {
    AnimalEvent event = new AnimalEvent(animal);
    for (AnimalListener listener : animalListeners) {
        listener.animalRemoved(event);
    }
}
```

With the above in place you can define a `createAnimal()` method that adds a new animal into the specified pen:

```
public Animal createAnimal(Animal.Type animalType,
                           Pen pen,
                           String name,
                           Gender gender,
                           int age) throws ValidationException {
    try {
        Animal animal = Animal.create(animalType, name, gender, age);
```

```
            acquireAnimal(animal, pen);
            fireAnimalCreated(animal);
            return animal;
        } catch (IllegalArgumentException ex) {
            throw new ValidationException(ex.getMessage());
        }
    }
}
```

- Note the use of the `static` factory method `create()` you defined earlier, which will return either a `Lion`, `Monkey` or `Penguin` as appropriate.

You need a `changeAnimal()` method to update an animal's details:

```
public void changeAnimal(Animal animal,
                         Pen pen,
                         String name,
                         Gender gender,
                         int age) throws ValidationException {
    try {
        animal.setName(name);
        animal.setGender(gender);
        animal.setAge(age);
        if (! animal.getPen().equals(pen)) {
            relinquishAnimal(animal);
            acquireAnimal(animal, pen);
        }
        fireAnimalChanged(animal);
    } catch (IllegalArgumentException ex) {
        throw new ValidationException(ex.getMessage());
    }
}
```

- Note that there is no argument for the animal's type, since once set through the `createAnimal()` method it cannot be amended. (If you need to amend this because it was entered in error, then the user would need to remove and recreate the animal);

- Note also the check to see whether the animal has been moved to a different pen; if so, the relinquishAnimal() method removes it from its current pen and acquireAnimal() puts it into the new one.

You need a removeAnimal() method to remove an animal:

```
public void removeAnimal(Animal animal) {
    relinquishAnimal(animal);
    fireAnimalRemoved(animal);
}
```

You need a getAnimals() method that returns a collection of animals in a particular pen:

```
public Collection<Animal> getAnimals(Pen pen) {
    return Collections.unmodifiableCollection(pen.getAnimals());
}
```

Defining a selection tree of animals

The left hand section of the screen (see Figure 17.1) shows a scrollable tree of all of the animals in the zoo, categorised by the animal's type. The natural component to use for this is a JTree nested inside a JScrollPane.

The AnimalTree class

Create this class in virtualzoo.ui as follows:

```
package virtualzoo.ui;

import virtualzoo.core.*;
import java.util.*;
import javax.swing.*;
import javax.swing.tree.*;
```

```java
public class AnimalTree extends JTree {

    private ZooAdministrator admin;
    private DefaultTreeModel model;
    private DefaultMutableTreeNode root;

    public AnimalTree() {
        admin = ZooAdministrator.getInstance();
        root = new DefaultMutableTreeNode("Animals");
        model = new DefaultTreeModel(root);
        setModel(model);
        buildTree();
        getSelectionModel().setSelectionMode
                (TreeSelectionModel.SINGLE_TREE_SELECTION);
    }

    private void buildTree() {
        root.removeAllChildren();
        Collection<Pen> pens = new TreeSet<Pen>(admin.getPens());
        for (Pen pen : pens) {
            DefaultMutableTreeNode node =
                    new DefaultMutableTreeNode(pen);
            buildAnimalTreeNodes(pen, node);
            root.add(node);
        }
    }

    private void buildAnimalTreeNodes(Pen pen,
                                      DefaultMutableTreeNode node) {
        Collection<Animal> animals =
                    new TreeSet<Animal>(admin.getAnimals(pen));
        for (Animal animal : animals) {
            node.add(new DefaultMutableTreeNode(animal));
        }
    }

}
```

- The class extends `JTree` and uses the private helper methods `buildTree()` and `buildAnimalTreeNodes()` to create nodes for each animal, categorised by the pen they are in;

- The tree is set to only allow selection of a single node at a time;

- Note how after the collections of `Pen` objects and `Animal` objects are obtained from `ZooAdministrator` they are sorted into their natural ordering by passing the returned collections into a new `TreeSet` object.

An editor panel for an animal

In NetBeans, right-click on the `virtualzoo.ui` package node and select **New | JPanel Form...**, entering `AnimalEditor` as the **Class Name**. You will see the initially empty form.

The process of designing the form will be similar to that used for the zoo keeper's editor form in the previous chapter. The final screen should look like this:

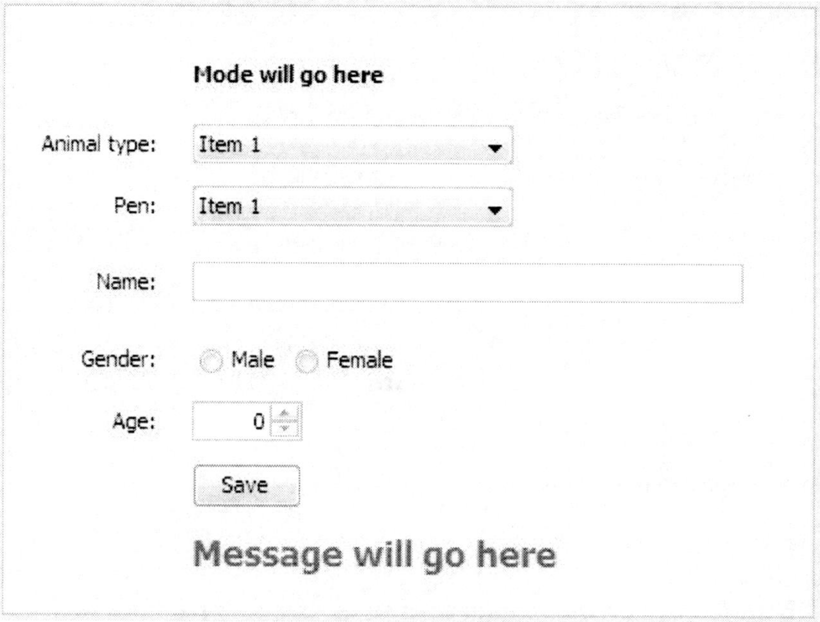

Figure 17.2: Animal editor form

There follows some guidance to help you create the above form:

- First switch into **Source** mode and `import` the following packages:

  ○ `virtualzoo.core.*;`

  ○ `com.example.util.*;`

  ○ `java.util.*;`

  ○ `javax.swing.*;`

- Switch back to **Design** mode;

- The top **Label** should be named `modeLabel` and set to have a bold font style with the text **Mode will go here;**

- Because there are three allowed animal types the user needs some way of telling the system which type each animal is. You may recall that you defined an enum called `Type` inside the `Animal` class, and you can use this to provide the options inside a `JComboBox` component. One of this component's constructors accepts an array of objects as its argument, and you can obtain an array from any enum through its `values()` method:

  ○ Use **Combo Box** under **Swing Controls** in the **Palette** window;

  ○ Rename the field as `animalTypeCombo;`

  ○ Under the **Properties** section of the **Properties** window empty the sample data (`Item 1`, etc.) from the `model` property;

  ○ Click the **Code** button in the **Properties** window and enter the following in the **Custom Creation Code** box: `new JComboBox(Animal.Type.values());`

- For the **Combo Box** of pens do the following:

  ○ Rename it to `penCombo;`

  ○ Under the **Properties** section of the **Properties** window empty the sample data (Item 1, etc.) from the `model` property;

○ Under the **Code** section of the **Properties** window click the 3-dotted button to the right of the **Pre-Creation Code** box to bring up a text entry dialogue, into which enter the following statements:

```
ZooAdministrator admin = ZooAdministrator.getInstance();
Collection<Pen> pens = admin.getPens();
Pen[] pensArray = pens.toArray(new Pen[pens.size()]);
```

▪ The above will obtain the `Collection` of `Pen` objects and convert them to an array. This is needed because there is no `JComboBox` constructor that accepts a collection, but there is one that accepts an array.

○ Under the **Code** section of the **Properties** window enter the following in the **Custom Creation Code** box: `new JComboBox(pensArray);`

• Rename the text field for the name as `nameField`, and empty its contents;

• For the gender you should firstly place a **Button Group** from the **Palette** window anywhere on the form. This is a non-visual component and you will see it listed under the **Other Components** node in the **Navigator** window;

○ Rename it as `genderButtonGroup` by right-clicking on its entry in the **Navigator** window;

○ Drag a **Radio Button** next to the **Gender** label, rename it `maleOption` with text of **Male**. You also need to attach it to the above button group, so locate the `buttonGroup` attribute in the **Properties** section of the **Properties** window. In the drop-down selector you can select `genderButtonGroup`. Check the `selected` property checkbox so that this option will be selected by default;

○ Repeat the above to create another radio button with text **Female**, named `femaleOption` and attached to genderButtonGroup, but don't check the selected property checkbox.

- For the age you will use a JSpinner component that restricts its values from zero to fifty. Use **Spinner** from the **Palette** window:

  ○ Rename it as ageSpinner;

  ○ Resize the component to make it slightly wider than its default width;

  ○ Under the **Code** section of the **Properties** window enter the following in the **Pre-Creation Code** box: SpinnerNumberModel ageSpinnerModel = new SpinnerNumberModel(0, 0, 50, 1);

  ○ Under the **Code** section of the **Properties** window enter the following in the **Custom Creation Code** box: new JSpinner(ageSpinnerModel);

- The button should be named saveButton, having the text **Save**;

- The bottom **Label** should be named messageLabel, and with a bold font of size 18, coloured blue, with text **Message will go here**.

For AnimalEditor to be any use it needs to know if it should be adding a new animal or editing an existing one. To this end, define a new instance variable to reference a Animal object:

```
private Animal animal;
```

If the animal instance variable is null then you will take this to mean that this panel should add a new animal using the values entered into the form fields. Conversely, if the variable is not null then it will reference the Animal object that should be used to pre-fill the entry fields to be potentially updated.

Define a new method in `AnimalEditor` called `clearAnimal()` to handle the first of the above two scenarios:

```
void clearAnimal() {
    animal = null;
    animalTypeCombo.setSelectedIndex(0);
    penCombo.setSelectedIndex(0);
    nameField.setText("");
    maleOption.setSelected(false);
    femaleOption.setSelected(false);
    ageSpinner.setValue(0);
    modeLabel.setText("Add New Animal");
    messageLabel.setText("");
}
```

- The `setSelectedIndex()` method of `JComboBox` makes the specified index of the box the selected one, where zero is the first entry.

Define another method called `setAnimal()` which accepts an `Animal` object as an argument representing the one that needs editing:

```
void setAnimal(Animal animal) {
    this.animal = animal;
    animalTypeCombo.setSelectedItem(animal.getType());
    penCombo.setSelectedItem(animal.getPen());
    nameField.setText(animal.getName());
    if (animal.isMale()) {
        maleOption.setSelected(true);
    } else {
        femaleOption.setSelected(true);
    }
    ageSpinner.setValue(animal.getAge());
    modeLabel.setText("Change Animal Details");
    messageLabel.setText("");
}
```

By default, you want the editor to be in "add" mode when first instantiated, so add a call to `clearAnimal()` inside the constructor:

```
public AnimalEditor() {
    initComponents();
    clearAnimal();
}
```

You can now enter some code to handle the **Save** button being clicked. In **Design** mode, double-click the **Save** button to bring up the saveButtonActionPerformed() method and edit it to be as follows:

```
private void saveButtonActionPerformed(java.awt.event.ActionEvent evt) {
    ZooAdministrator admin = ZooAdministrator.getInstance();

    try {
        // Prepare selected data
        Animal.Type selectedAnimalType =
                (Animal.Type) animalTypeCombo.getSelectedItem();
        Pen selectedPen = (Pen) penCombo.getSelectedItem();
        Gender selectedAnimalGender = null;
        if (maleOption.isSelected()) {
            selectedAnimalGender = Gender.MALE;
        } else {
            selectedAnimalGender = Gender.FEMALE;
        }
        int selectedAge = (Integer) ageSpinner.getValue();

        if (animal == null) {
            // Adding a new animal
            admin.createAnimal(selectedAnimalType,
                               selectedPen,
                               nameField.getText(),
                               selectedAnimalGender,
                               selectedAge);
            messageLabel.setText("New animal added");
            clearAnimal();

        } else {
            // Changing an existing animal
            admin.changeAnimal(animal,
                               selectedPen,
                               nameField.getText(),
                               selectedAnimalGender,
                               selectedAge);
```

```
            messageLabel.setText("Animal details changed");
        }
    } catch (ValidationException ex) {
        JOptionPane.showMessageDialog(null, ex.getMessage(), "Error",
                                JOptionPane.ERROR_MESSAGE);
    }
}
```

The AnimalPanel class

If you look at again at Figure 17.1 at the beginning of this chapter you will see that the two classes you have developed so far, `AnimalTree` and `AnimalEditor`, are set as the left and right components inside a `JSplitPane`, underneath which is a panel containing two centred buttons. You will now use NetBeans to create a new class called `AnimalPanel` to model this.

In the **Projects** window use **Tools** | **Add to Palette...** against both `AnimalTree.java` and `AnimalEditor.java` to add them to the **Zoo Components** section in the **Palette** window.

You are now ready to create the new panel, so right-click on the `virtual.ui` package node and select **New JPanel Form...**, enter `AnimalPanel` as the **Class Name**, and click **Finish**.

Enlarge the size of the blank design area to make it easier to see the components which will be added. Right-click the form and select **Set Layout** | **Border Layout**. Now drag from the palette a **Panel** (from the **Swing Containers** category) and place it at the bottom of the form. As you are dragging, just above the form you will see some text which tells you where it will be placed, so you want it to say "Place the component into the Last area".

Now right-click the panel you just placed at the bottom and select **Set Layout** | **Flow Layout**. Drag two **Button** objects from the palette onto the bottom panel, setting the first one's text to **Add** and variable name to `addButton`, and the second one's text to **Remove** and variable name to `removeButton`. To make the button panel stand out a bit more, click on it and inspect the **Properties** window. Locate the **border** property, which is currently set to **(No Border)** and click the three-dotted icon to its right to open the customiser dialog. Select **Soft Bevel Border** and click **OK**.

From the **Swing Containers** section drag a **Split Pane** onto the centre area of the form. Under **Swing Containers** drag a **Scroll Pane** over the top of **left button** (which will replace it) and then under **Zoo Components** drag a **AnimalTree** component on top of the scroll pane (which will nest inside it). Change its variable name to `animalTree`.

From **Zoo Components** drag **AnimalEditor** over the top of **right button** to replace that too. Change its variable name to `animalEditor`.

Modfying AdministratorFrame

The frame now needs to show `AnimalPanel` inside a new tab of the `JTabbedPane`:

```
package virtualzoo.ui;

import virtualzoo.core.*;
import java.awt.*;
import javax.swing.*;

public class AdministratorFrame extends JFrame {

    private ZooKeeperEditor zooKeeperEditor;

    public AdministratorFrame() {
        super("Zoo Administrator");
        setLayout(new BorderLayout());
        setDefaultCloseOperation(JFrame.DISPOSE_ON_CLOSE);
```

```
    ZooAdministrator admin = ZooAdministrator.getInstance();

    // Create tabbed pane
    JTabbedPane tabPane = new JTabbedPane();

    // Create animal panel
    AnimalPanel animalPanel = new AnimalPanel();
    tabPane.addTab("Animals", animalPanel);

    // Create zoo keeper panel
    ZooKeeperPanel zooKeeperPanel = new ZooKeeperPanel();
    tabPane.addTab("Zoo Keepers", zooKeeperPanel);

    add(tabPane, BorderLayout.CENTER);

    // Set components to their preferred size
    pack();

    // Place in the centre of the desktop
    setLocationRelativeTo(null);
  }

}
```

At this point you can run the application to ensure it appears as below:

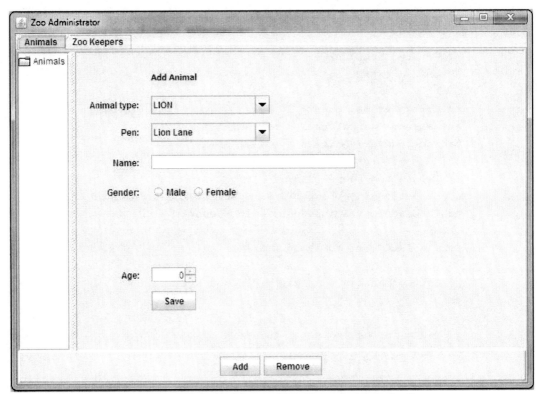

Figure 17.3: Add Animal form within Zoo Administrator frame

You can double-click the `Animals` node on the left to expand it, and then click the `Pen` sub-nodes that appear to see the animals in that pen. To make all of the nodes expanded when you start the application add the following method inside `AnimalTree`:

```
private void expandNodes() {
    for (int i = 0; i < getRowCount(); i++) {
        expandRow(i);
    }
}
```

- The `getRowCount()` method simply returns the total number of nodes in the tree, while `expandRow()` forces the specfied node to be expanded.

Now call `expandNodes()` from the constructor:

```
public AnimalTree() {
    admin = ZooAdministrator.getInstance();
    root = new DefaultMutableTreeNode("Animals");
```

```
    model = new DefaultTreeModel(root);
    setModel(model);
    buildTree();
    expandNodes();
    getSelectionModel().setSelectionMode
            (TreeSelectionModel.SINGLE_TREE_SELECTION);
}
```

You will note that after entering some details and clicking the **Save** button the added animal is not appearing in the list on the left. This will be addressed in the next section.

Updating AnimalTree automatically

For the `AnimalTree` object to get notified whenever a change to the collection of animal objects held by the administrator changes it can implement the `AnimalListener` interface, so you will need to import `virtualzoo.core.event`:

```
package virtualzoo.ui;

import virtualzoo.core.*;
import virtualzoo.core.event.*;
import java.util.*;
import javax.swing.*;
import javax.swing.tree.*;

public class AnimalTree extends JTree implements AnimalListener {
```

If you click the glyph that appears to the left of the class declaration statement above you can click the option to implement all abstract methods. The following code will appear:

```
@Override
public void animalCreated(AnimalEvent event) {
    throw new UnsupportedOperationException("Not supported yet.");
}

@Override
```

```
public void animalChanged(AnimalEvent event) {
    throw new UnsupportedOperationException("Not supported yet.");
}

@Override
public void animalRemoved(AnimalEvent event) {
    throw new UnsupportedOperationException("Not supported yet.");
}
```

To handle the `animalCreated()` method first, insert the following code:

```
@Override
public void animalCreated(AnimalEvent event) {
    DefaultMutableTreeNode animalNode =
                        new DefaultMutableTreeNode(event.getAnimal());
    Pen pen = event.getAnimal().getPen();
    DefaultMutableTreeNode parentNode = getTreeNode(pen);
    model.insertNodeInto(animalNode, parentNode,
                                parentNode.getChildCount());
    buildTree();
    model.reload();
    expandNodes();
}
```

- Firstly, a new `DefaultMutableTreeNode` is created for the new `Animal`;

- Then the `Pen` it should be in is determined;

- The `Pen` is passed as an argument to `getTreeNode()` (a method to be written shortly) which will return the node which relates to the `Pen`;

- The `insertNodeInto()` method is invoked on the model to cause the new animal to appear in the tree;

- The tree is then rebuilt in order that the nodes are correctly sorted.

The `getTreeNode()` method loops through each of the nodes under the root node until it finds the one in the argument, which it then returns:

```
private DefaultMutableTreeNode getTreeNode(Pen pen) {
    Enumeration penNodes = root.children();
    while (penNodes.hasMoreElements()) {
        DefaultMutableTreeNode penNode =
                    (DefaultMutableTreeNode) penNodes.nextElement();
        Pen penNodePen = (Pen) penNode.getUserObject();
        if (penNodePen.equals(pen)) return penNode;
    }
    throw new IllegalArgumentException(pen + " not found");
}
```

- An `Enumeration` is an alternative way of iterating over a group. The `hasMoreElements()` method returns true if there are more elements to process, and the `nextElement()` method returns the next element to be processed.

You now need to wire up the `AnimalTree` object which is referenced in `AnimalPanel` so that it listens to events. In `AnimalPanel` import `virtualzoo.core` and define a new instance variable to reference the `ZooAdministrator` object:

```
private ZooAdministrator admin;
```

Now change the constructor to obtain the `ZooAdministrator` object and call its `addAnimalListener()` method:

```
public AnimalPanel() {
    initComponents();
    admin = ZooAdministrator.getInstance();
    admin.addAnimalListener(animalTree);
}
```

You can now run the application, enter and save one (or several) animals, and you should find the tree automatically updates itself.

Modifying existing animal details

Now that you have completed the code necessary to add new animals you need to enable their details to be changed. What you will do is detect whenever the user selects one of the names in `AnimalTree` and pass that selected `Animal` object to `AnimalEditor` so that it transitions into "change" mode.

The `JTree` class (of which `AnimalTree` is a subclass) supports the fact that client objects may wish to listen to selections of nodes in the tree. All client objects need to do is implement the `TreeSelectionListener` interface and provide the appropriate code in its required `valueChanged()` method. Then you can pass the client object as an argument to the `addTreeSelectionListener()` method of `JTree`. You will now code these steps.

Firstly, change the class header of `AnimalPanel` to implement `TreeSelectionListener` (you will also need to import the `java.swing`, `javax.swing.event` and `javax.swing.tree` package):

```
package virtualzoo.ui;

import virtualzoo.core.*;
import javax.swing.*;
import javax.swing.event.*;
import javax.swing.tree.*;

public class AnimalPanel extends javax.swing.JPanel
                    implements TreeSelectionListener {
```

Now you need to code the only method required by the interface:

```
@Override
public void valueChanged(TreeSelectionEvent e) {
    // A node has been selected from AnimalTree
```

```
DefaultMutableTreeNode selectedNode = (DefaultMutableTreeNode)
                        animalTree.getLastSelectedPathComponent();
if (selectedNode != null) {
    Object selectedObject = selectedNode.getUserObject();
    if (selectedObject instanceof Animal) {
        Animal selectedAnimal = (Animal) selectedObject;
        animalEditor.setAnimal(selectedAnimal);
    }
}
}
```

- The `valueChanged()` method will be called every time the user selects an any node in the tree, which could be either an animal, a pen, or the root node;

- The `getLastSelectedPathComponent()` method retrieves the selected `Object`. This will be `null` if nothing is actually selected so it is tested to ensure that it is not `null` before continuing. Provided it is not `null` then it is checked to ensure that an animal node was selected, and if so this gets cast from `Object` to `Animal` (any other type of node will be ignored);

- You then pass the `Animal` object to the `setAnimal()` method of `AnimalEditor`, which you coded earlier.

You need to ensure you listen to the tree selection events so invoke the registration in the constructor:

```
public AnimalPanel() {
    initComponents();
    admin = ZooAdministrator.getInstance();
    admin.addAnimalListener(animalTree);
    animalTree.addTreeSelectionListener(this);
}
```

In `AnimalTree` you need to ensure the tree is updated:

```
@Override
```

```
public void animalChanged(AnimalEvent event) {
    model.reload();
    expandNodes();
}
```

Removing an existing animal

When you built the form for `AnimalPanel` you included a **Remove** button. Before writing the code so that it removes the selected animal (after asking for confirmation) you will change the status of the button so that it is only enabled (i.e. available to be clicked) when an animal is actually selected in the list.

Open `AnimalPanel` in **Design** mode and click the **Remove** button to select it. In the **Properties** window locate the **enabled** property (you may need to scroll to find it):

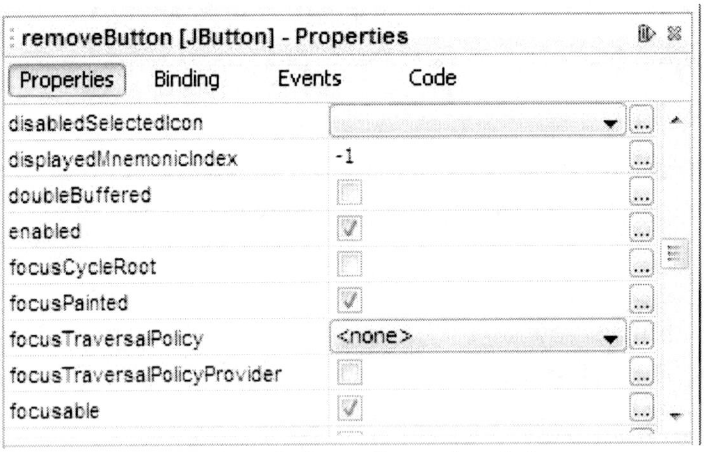

removeButton [JButton] - Properties	
Properties Binding Events Code	
disabledSelectedIcon	▼ ... ▲
displayedMnemonicIndex	-1 ...
doubleBuffered	☐ ...
enabled	☑ ...
focusCycleRoot	☐ ...
focusPainted	☑ ...
focusTraversalPolicy	<none> ▼ ...
focusTraversalPolicyProvider	☐ ...
focusable	☑ ... ▼

Figure 17.4: NetBeans Properties window

You will see that the check box for this attribute is checked, indicating that the button is enabled by default, so un-check this check box now. You will notice that the button becomes greyed out to indicate that it cannot be clicked.

Switch into **Source** mode and modify the `valueChanged()` method to enable the button whenever a zoo keeper is selected, or disable it again when nothing is selected:

```
@Override
public void valueChanged(TreeSelectionEvent e) {
    // A node has been selected from AnimalTree
    DefaultMutableTreeNode selectedNode = (DefaultMutableTreeNode)
                        animalTree.getLastSelectedPathComponent();
    removeButton.setEnabled(false);
    if (selectedNode != null) {
        Object selectedObject = selectedNode.getUserObject();
        if (selectedObject instanceof Animal) {
            Animal selectedAnimal = (Animal) selectedObject;
            animalEditor.setAnimal(selectedAnimal);
            removeButton.setEnabled(true);
        }
    }
}
```

Now switch back to **Design** mode and double-click the **Remove** button to generate its `removeButtonActionPerformed()` method. This method needs to ask the user to confirm that they really do want to remove the zoo keeper and if so invoke the `ZooAdministrator removeZooKeeper()` method:

```
private void removeButtonActionPerformed(java.awt.event.ActionEvent evt)
{
    DefaultMutableTreeNode selectedNode = (DefaultMutableTreeNode)
                        animalTree.getLastSelectedPathComponent();
    if (selectedNode != null) {
        Object selectedObject = selectedNode.getUserObject();
        if (selectedObject instanceof Animal) {
            Animal selectedAnimal = (Animal) selectedObject;
            int response = JOptionPane.showConfirmDialog(null,
                    "Do you really want to remove " +
                        selectedAnimal.getName() + "?",
                    "Confirm Remove", JOptionPane.YES_NO_OPTION);
            if (response == JOptionPane.YES_OPTION) {
                admin.removeAnimal(selectedAnimal);
                animalEditor.clearAnimal();
            }
```

```
            }
        }
    }
```

After the animal is removed the editor is placed back into "add" mode by calling `clearAnimal()`. You should also now ensure the entry is removed from the tree display, so modify `animalRemoved()` of `AnimalTree` as follows:

```
@Override
public void animalRemoved(AnimalEvent event) {
    buildTree();
    model.reload();
    expandNodes();
}
```

Handling the Add button

All that remains now is to write some code for the **Add** button to enable the user to switch from "change" mode back into "add" mode. Go to the **Design** view of `AnimalPanel` and double-click the **Add** button to generate its `addButtonActionPerformed()` method. All it needs to do is invoke `clearAnimal()` on the `animalEditor` instance and clear any selections in the tree:

```
private void addButtonActionPerformed(java.awt.event.ActionEvent evt) {
    animalEditor.clearAnimal();
    animalTree.getSelectionModel().clearSelection();
}
```

That completes the coding for the animal panels, and you should now be able to add, change and remove as many animals as you wish.

18. Finishing off the User Interface

This chapter puts the finishing touches to the graphical part of the application by creating a read-only table for the zoo's visitors, defining a menu-bar and toolbar, and by making the application adopt the running system's look-and-feel.

In this chapter you will learn:

- *How to develop a table of data;*

- *How to define a menu-bar;*

- *How to define a toolbar;*

- *How to adopt the running system's look-and-feel.*

A table of visitors

For simplicity the list of visitors, as defined in `ZooAdministrator`, will be displayed in a read-only table in a tab of the `AdministratorFrame`. First, you need to do some preparatory work in the `ZooAdministrator` class:

You will define a collection for the visitors, so replace the following line:

```
private Visitor mary, peter, richard, tanya;
```

With this:

```
private Collection<Visitor> visitors;
```

In the constructor you need to instantiate an empty collection, before the call to `createExampleVisitors();`

```
visitors = new TreeSet<Visitor>();
```

Define a method that returns the collection:

```
public Collection<Visitor> getVisitors() {
    return Collections.unmodifiableCollection(visitors);
}
```

Modify the `createExampleVisitors()` method to utilise the collection rather than the previously named variables:

```
private void createExampleVisitors() {
    visitors.add(new Visitor(new Person("Mary Roberts"),
                             new Email("mary@example.com")));
    visitors.add(new Visitor(new Person("Peter Harris"),
                             new Email("peter@example.com")));
    visitors.add(new Visitor(new Person("Richard York"),
                             new Email("richard@example.com")));
    visitors.add(new Visitor(new Person("Tanya West"),
                             new Email("tanya@example.com")));
}
```

In `virtualzoo.core` create a new class called `VisitorTable` which extends `JTable`:

```
package virtualzoo.ui;

import virtualzoo.core.*;
import java.util.*;
import javax.swing.*;
import javax.swing.table.*;

public class VisitorTable extends JTable {

    private TableModel model;

    VisitorTable() {
        model = new VisitorTableModel();
        setModel(model);
    }


    private class VisitorTableModel extends AbstractTableModel {

        private List<Visitor> visitors;
```

```java
public VisitorTableModel() {
    ZooAdministrator admin = ZooAdministrator.getInstance();
    visitors = new ArrayList<Visitor>(admin.getVisitors());
}


@Override
public int getRowCount() {
    return visitors.size();
}


@Override
public int getColumnCount() {
    return 3;
}


@Override
public Object getValueAt(int rowIndex, int columnIndex) {
    switch (columnIndex) {
        case 0:
            // First column - vistor's name
            return visitors.get(rowIndex).getName();
        case 1:
            // Second column - visitor's email
            return
                visitors.get(rowIndex).getEmail().toString();
        case 2:
            // Third column - visitors sponsored animal
            Animal sponsoredAnimal =
                visitors.get(rowIndex).getSponsoredAnimal();
            if (sponsoredAnimal != null) {
                return sponsoredAnimal;
            } else {
                return "";
            }
        default:
            // Should not happen
            throw new IllegalStateException();
    }
}


@Override
public String getColumnName(int columnIndex) {
```

```
            String[] columnHeaders =
                    {"Name", "Email Address", "Sponsored Animal"};
            return columnHeaders[columnIndex];
        }


    }


}
```

- The above class draws on very similar techniques to those shown in Chapter 14 for developing a `JTable` and associated `TableModel`:

  o The class extends `JTable` and includes an inner class that extends `AbstractTableModel` to manage the actual data;

  o The data is obtained from the `ZooAdministrator` into an `ArrayList`, and the `getRowCount()`, `getColumnCount()`, `getValueAt()` and `getColumnName()` methods are overridden to provide the various table values.

Create a new tab in the constructor of `AdministratorFrame`:

```
// Create visitor table
VisitorTable visitorTable = new VisitorTable();
tabPane.addTab("Visitors", new JScrollPane(visitorTable));
```

The application should now look like this:

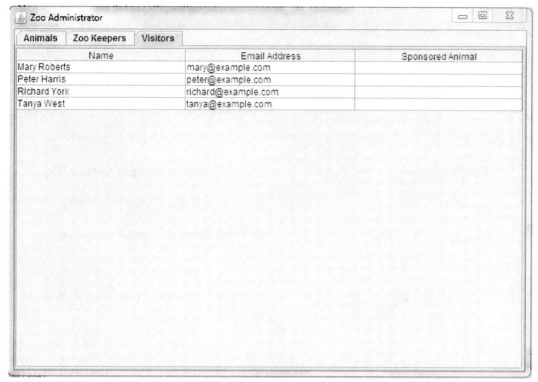

Figure 18.1: Visitor table

Creating a menu-bar

A menu-bar is constructed separately from the rest of the graphical layouts and components and once defined is attached to the frame.

There are three classes used in combination in building a menu-bar:

- JMenuBar: an object of this class defines the menu-bar as a whole, and is the component that will be attached to the frame. It needs to contain one or more JMenu objects.

- JMenu: an object of this class defines a separate menu category, such as **File**, **Edit**, **View**, **Help**, etc. Each JMenu object needs to contain one or more JMenuItem objects.

- JMenuItem: an object of this class defines each individual menu option, such as **Save**, **About**, **Exit**, etc.

You will now develop a simple menu-bar for the application, structured as follows:

- **File**

  o **Feeding Time...**   (will display a simple dialog box)

  o **--------------------**   (will display a separator line)

  o **Exit...**   (will prompt for confirmation)

- **Help**

  o **About Virtual Zoo...**   (will display a simple dialog box)

In sub-package virtualzoo.ui create a new class ZooMenuBar that extends JMenuBar with instance variables for the owning frame, the menu items, and a constructor to build it:

```java
package virtualzoo.ui;

import javax.swing.*;

public class ZooMenuBar extends JMenuBar {

    private AdministratorFrame owner;
    private JMenu fileMenu, helpMenu;
    private JMenuItem fileFeedingTime, fileExit;
    private JMenuItem helpAbout;

    ZooMenuBar(AdministratorFrame owner) {
        this.owner = owner;

        buildFileMenu();
        add(fileMenu);

        buildHelpMenu();
```

```
        add(helpMenu);
    }

    private void buildFileMenu() {
        fileMenu = new JMenu("File");

        fileFeedingTime = new JMenuItem("Feeding Time...");
        fileMenu.add(fileFeedingTime);

        fileMenu.addSeparator();

        fileExit = new JMenuItem("Exit...");
        fileMenu.add(fileExit);
    }

    private void buildHelpMenu() {
        helpMenu = new JMenu("Help");

        helpAbout = new JMenuItem("About Virtual Zoo...");
        helpMenu.add(helpAbout);
    }

}
```

- The constructor requires a reference to the `JFrame` object that will ultimately contain it. Although no use of is made of this as yet you will see how it comes into play as the options are coded later;

- The constructor then invokes helper methods to instantiate the `JMenu` and `JMenuItem` objects;

- Note how the individual menu items are added to the appropriate menu object, and then the menu objects are added to the `ZooMenuBar`.

To see the menu bar you need to attach it to the frame, so add the following line inside the `AdministratorFrame` constructor, just before the call to `pack()`:

```
// Set the menu bar
```

```
setJMenuBar(new ZooMenuBar(this));
```

If you run the application you should see the menu bar appear just under the title bar, although none of the options do anything at present:

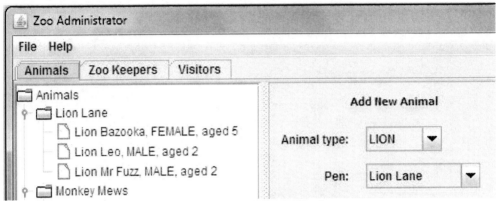

Figure 18.2: Menu-bar inside a frame

Coding the Help | About Virtual Zoo... Option

You now need to listen for the menu items being selected and take the appropriate action. The simpler item is **Help | About Virtual Zoo...** which just shows a dialog message. Inside ZooMenuBar define an inner class HelpAboutListener that implements ActionListener (you need to import java.awt.event):

```java
private class HelpAboutListener implements ActionListener {

    @Override
    public void actionPerformed(ActionEvent e) {
        JOptionPane.showMessageDialog
                (owner,
                "Sample application for the book " +
                "Java Programming Step-by-Step.",
                "About Virtual Zoo",
                JOptionPane.INFORMATION_MESSAGE);
    }

}
```

- You will see that use was made of the `owner` instance variable so that the dialog attaches to the owning `JFrame`.

You now need to attach the listener to the appropriate object, so after you have instantiated `helpAbout` (in the `buildHelpMenu()` method), add the following line:

```
helpAbout.addActionListener(new HelpAboutListener());
```

You should now find that the **Help | About VirtualZoo...** menu option causes the dialog to be displayed.

Coding the File | Exit... Option

The listener to handle **File | Exit...** is similar but this time uses the `showConfirmDialog()` static method of `JOptionPane` that prompts for a response and returns it as an `int`:

```
private class FileExitListener implements ActionListener {

    @Override
    public void actionPerformed(ActionEvent e) {
        // Prompt for confirmation
        int response = JOptionPane.showConfirmDialog
                        (owner,
                        "Are you sure you want to exit?",
                        "Exit Virtual Zoo",
                        JOptionPane.YES_NO_OPTION);

        // See what response is
        if (response == JOptionPane.YES_OPTION) {
            owner.dispose();
        }
    }
}
```

You now need to attach the listener to the `fileExit` object in the `buildFileMenu()` method:

```
fileExit.addActionListener(new FileExitListener());
```

The **File -> Exit...** menu option should now prompt for confirmation and exit if **Yes** is chosen.

There is, though, an inconsistency in that the user could still click the window's close button without it prompting for confirmation, due to the following statement in `AdministratorFrame`:

```
setDefaultCloseOperation(DISPOSE_ON_CLOSE);
```

To gain full control you first need to tell Java not to do anything automatically, so change the above to the following:

```
setDefaultCloseOperation(DO_NOTHING_ON_CLOSE);
```

You should now write a method inside `AdministratorFrame` called `confirmClose()` which prompts for confirmation, in a similar manner to the exit listener you wrote earlier:

```
void confirmClose() {
    // Prompt for confirmation
    int response = JOptionPane.showConfirmDialog(this,
            "Are you sure you want to exit?",
            "Exit Virtual Zoo",
            JOptionPane.YES_NO_OPTION);

    // See what response is
    if (response == JOptionPane.YES_OPTION) {
        dispose();
    }
}
```

Also inside `AdministratorFrame` define an inner class called `ExitListener` which extends the Java supplied `WindowAdapter` class (you will need to import `java.awt.event`):

```
private class ExitListener extends WindowAdapter {

    @Override
    public void windowClosing(WindowEvent e) {
        confirmClose();
    }

}
```

- The `WindowAdapter` class defines several empty event methods concerned with events that can happen with a window, and you just need to override the methods applicable. Above, you have overridden `windowClosing()`, being the method that gets called when a window is about to close. All your overridden method does in invoke the `confirmClose()` method you previously defined.

Because you have told the frame to do nothing when the close button is pressed you need to add a window listener to it, so insert this statement after the `setDefaultCloseOperation()` call in the constructor:

```
addWindowListener(new ExitListener());
```

Test the application to ensure that if you try and close the window using the window's close button you will be prompted for confirmation first.

Because you want to avoid code duplication you should now refactor the code in `ZooMenuBar` to use the frame's closing mechanism:

```
private class FileExitListener implements ActionListener {

    @Override
    public void actionPerformed(ActionEvent e) {
```

```
            owner.confirmClose();
        }
    }
```

Creating the File | Feeding Time... Option

For the **File | Feeding Time...** option you invoke the `feedingTime()` method of `ZooAdministrator`. At the moment that method sends its results to the **Output** window, which is only meant for the programmer's benefit. You will therefore modify the last part of the method to return a `Collection` of `String` objects instead. You can then obtain the collection from the user interface and display the messages in a list.

Change the `feedingTime()` method as follows:

```java
public Collection<String> feedingTime() {
    // Collect all the animals
    Collection<Animal> animals = new HashSet<Animal>();
    for (Pen pen : pens) {
        animals.addAll(pen.getAnimals());
    }

    Collection<Animal> sortedAnimals =
            new TreeSet<Animal>(new Animal.SortByAgeName());
    sortedAnimals.addAll(animals);

    // Feed them one at a time
    Collection<String> messages = new ArrayList<String>();
    for (Animal anAnimal : sortedAnimals) {
        messages.add(anAnimal.getName() +
                " is eating a " + anAnimal.favouriteFood());
    }
    return messages;
}
```

With that in place you can create a class in `virtualzoo.ui` that extends `JDialog` called `FeedingTimeDialog`:

```java
package virtualzoo.ui;
```

```java
import java.awt.*;
import java.util.*;
import javax.swing.*;
import virtualzoo.core.*;

public class FeedingTimeDialog extends JDialog {

    FeedingTimeDialog(AdministratorFrame owner) {
        super(owner, "Feeding Time", true);
        setLayout(new BorderLayout());

        ZooAdministrator admin = ZooAdministrator.getInstance();
        Collection<String> messages = admin.feedingTime();

        JList list = new JList(messages.toArray());
        add(new JScrollPane(list));

        setLocationRelativeTo(owner);
        pack();
    }

}
```

- The call to `super()` passes three arguments:

  ○ The owning frame;

  ○ The title for the dialog;

  ○ `true` means that the dialog will be modal.

- The retrieved messages are converted to an array for passing into a `JList`.

You can now create a new inner class within `ZooMenuBar` to show the dialog:

```java
private class FileFeedingTimeListener implements ActionListener {

    @Override
    public void actionPerformed(ActionEvent e) {
        JDialog d = new FeedingTimeDialog(owner);
```

```
        d.setVisible(true);
    }

}
```

You now only need to attach the listener to the `fileFeedingTime` object in `buildFileMenu()`:

```
fileFeedingTime.addActionListener(new FileFeedingTimeListener());
```

Verify that the **File | Feeding Time...** menu option results in a dialog being displayed, as follows:

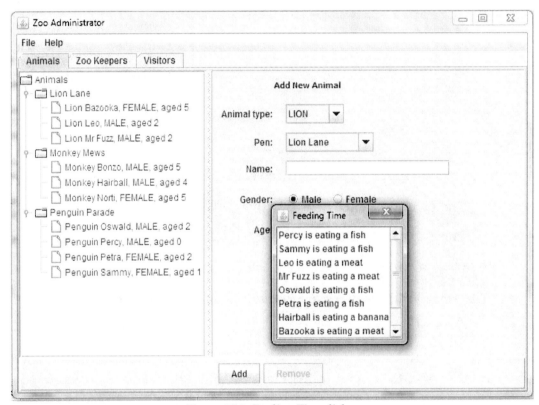

Figure 18.3: Feeding Time dialog

Creating a toolbar

Whereas the menu-bar provides selectable options for all of an application's functions, a toolbar provides a strip consisting typically of icons for the most frequently used facilities. Oracle provides a downloadable set of toolbar icons that you can use in applications from the following URL:

http://java.sun.com/developer/techDocs/hi/repository/index.html

Click the **Download** button on the above page to be taken to a second page. Locate the box headed **Java Look and Feel Graphics Repository 1.0**, click the radio button to accept the license agreement (assuming that you do) and then click the link called **jlfgr-1_0.zip** and save the file somewhere convenient.

Unzip the downloaded file to extract the file called **jlfgr-1_0.jar**, which is a **Java Archive** containing the icons. Now in NetBeans, right click on the VirtualZoo project node and select **Properties**. In the **Categories** list on the left select **Libraries**, and then click the **Add JAR/Folder** button. Browse to the extracted **jlfgr-1_0.jar** file and click **Open**. The dialog should now show the file listed under the **Utilities.jar** that you added in an earlier chapter:

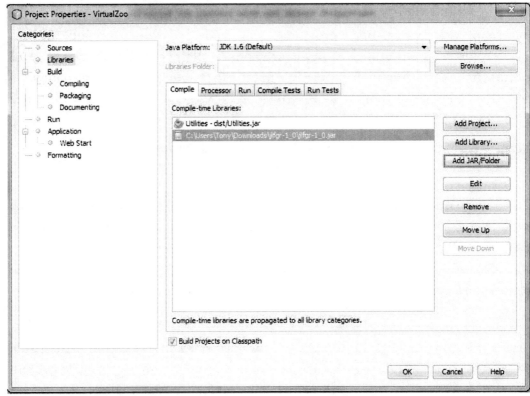

Figure 18.4: NetBeans Project Properties dialog

Click the **OK** button. If you now expand the **Libraries** node in the **Projects** window you will see the entry for **jlfgr-1_0.jar**, and you can also expand this file to see its folders and then the icons within these folders.

> You should now rebuild the project in order for the icons to be available when you run the application (right-click on the `VirtualZoo` project node and select **Clean and Build**).

You will shortly create a toolbar with an icon so the user can invoke the "feeding time" function, but before doing so it is worth considering the fact that the user will then have two separate ways of invoking that function; either through the menu option **File | Feeding Time...** or by clicking the toolbar icon. Because the action that needs to occur is identical in both cases it makes sense to utilise a single object that both the menu item and the toolbar icon can invoke. Java provides an interface called Action that enables this very facility, so create a new class under virtualzoo.ui called FeedingTimeAction, as follows:

```
package virtualzoo.ui;

import java.awt.event.*;
import javax.swing.*;

public class FeedingTimeAction extends AbstractAction {

    private AdministratorFrame owner;

    FeedingTimeAction(AdministratorFrame owner) {
        this.owner = owner;
    }

    @Override
    public void actionPerformed(ActionEvent e) {
        JDialog d = new FeedingTimeDialog(owner);
        d.setVisible(true);
    }

}
```

- The class extends the Java supplied AbstractAction class (which implements the Action interface). The AbstractAction class provides some useful facilities which you will use shortly;

- The constructor takes a reference to the owning JFrame;

- Because the Action interface itself extends ActionListener you have the familiar actionPerformed() method. Above, it has the same code as is defined in the inner class FeedingTimeListener in ZooMenuBar.

The constructor in `FeedingTimeAction` can be expanded to specify certain characteristics associated with this action, such as its text and icon. Import the `java.net` package and then add the following code to the constructor:

```
FeedingTimeAction(AdministratorFrame owner) {
    this.owner = owner;

    // Set the action's name
    putValue(Action.NAME, "Feeding Time...");

    // Set the action's hover help (used by toolbar)
    putValue(Action.SHORT_DESCRIPTION, "Feed the animals");

    // Set the action's small icon (used by menu bar)
    URL iconUrlSmall = getClass().getResource
            ("/toolbarButtonGraphics/development/Bean16.gif");
    putValue(Action.SMALL_ICON, new ImageIcon(iconUrlSmall));

    // Set the action's large icon (used by toolbar)
    URL iconUrlLarge = getClass().getResource
            ("/toolbarButtonGraphics/development/Bean24.gif");
    putValue(Action.LARGE_ICON_KEY, new ImageIcon(iconUrlLarge));
}
```

- The `AbstractAction` class you are inheriting allows you to set various settings using its `putValue()` method, where the first argument is the setting type and the second argument is the setting value:

  ○ The `Action.NAME` setting provides the text that will appear in the menu-bar;

  ○ The `Action.SHORT_DESCRIPTION` setting provides the hover help that appears when the user hovers the mouse over the icon in the toolbar;

  ○ The `Action.SMALL_ICON` setting provides the small icon to appear alongside the menu-bar text;

- ○ The `Action.LARGE_ICON_KEY` setting provides the large icon to appear in the toolbar.

- The technique to load an icon image is to firstly create a `URL` object using the `getResource()` method of any class, and then use the `URL` object to create an `ImageIcon` object. The argument to `getResource()` is the path inside the **jlfgr-1_0.jar** file of the icon you require.

Because ideally you want the same `Action` object to be used for both the menu-bar and the toolbar you will convert the `FeedingTimeAction` class to be a singleton.

Change the constructor visibility to `private`:

```
private FeedingTimeAction(AdministratorFrame owner) {
```

Declare a `static` variable of type `FeedingTimeAction` to hold a reference to the singleton object:

```
public class FeedingTimeAction extends AbstractAction {

    private static FeedingTimeAction instance;

    private AdministratorFrame owner;

    private FeedingTimeAction(AdministratorFrame owner) {
```

Define a `static` method called `getInstance()` that returns the singleton object, creating it if it is the first time:

```
public static FeedingTimeAction getInstance(AdministratorFrame owner) {
    if (instance == null) {
        instance = new FeedingTimeAction(owner);
    }
    return instance;
}
```

In `ZooMenuBar` delete the `FileFeedingTimeListener` inner class (as it is no longer needed), and then change the instantiation of the `fileFeedingTime` object to obtain the `FeedingTimeAction` singleton object rather that directly setting the text and a listener, since the `Action` object will take care of these things for you:

```
private void buildFileMenu() {
    fileMenu = new JMenu("File");

    fileFeedingTime =
            new JMenuItem(FeedingTimeAction.getInstance(owner));
    fileMenu.add(fileFeedingTime);

    fileMenu.addSeparator();

    fileExit = new JMenuItem("Exit...");
    fileExit.addActionListener(new FileExitListener());
    fileMenu.add(fileExit);
}
```

If you run the application you should see that the small icon now appears alongside the menu text for the option.

With the above now in place it is easy to reuse when creating a toolbar. In Java you can make use of the `JToolBar` class, so in `virtualzoo.ui` create a new class called `ZooToolBar` which extends it:

```
package virtualzoo.ui;

import javax.swing.*;

public class ZooToolBar extends JToolBar {

    ZooToolBar(AdministratorFrame owner) {
        add(FeedingTimeAction.getInstance(owner));
    }

}
```

In the constructor the `add()` method adds an `Action` object to the toolbar. In this case it just gets the `FeedingTimeAction` singleton object. You can have as many `add()` calls as you need, and you can use the `addSeparator()` method to separate them into groups with a vertical bar.

Finally, in the constructor of `AdministratorFrame` you can add an instance of `ZooToolBar` to the frame's `NORTH` position:

```
// Create toolbar
add(new ZooToolBar(this), BorderLayout.NORTH);
```

The resulting application should look like this:

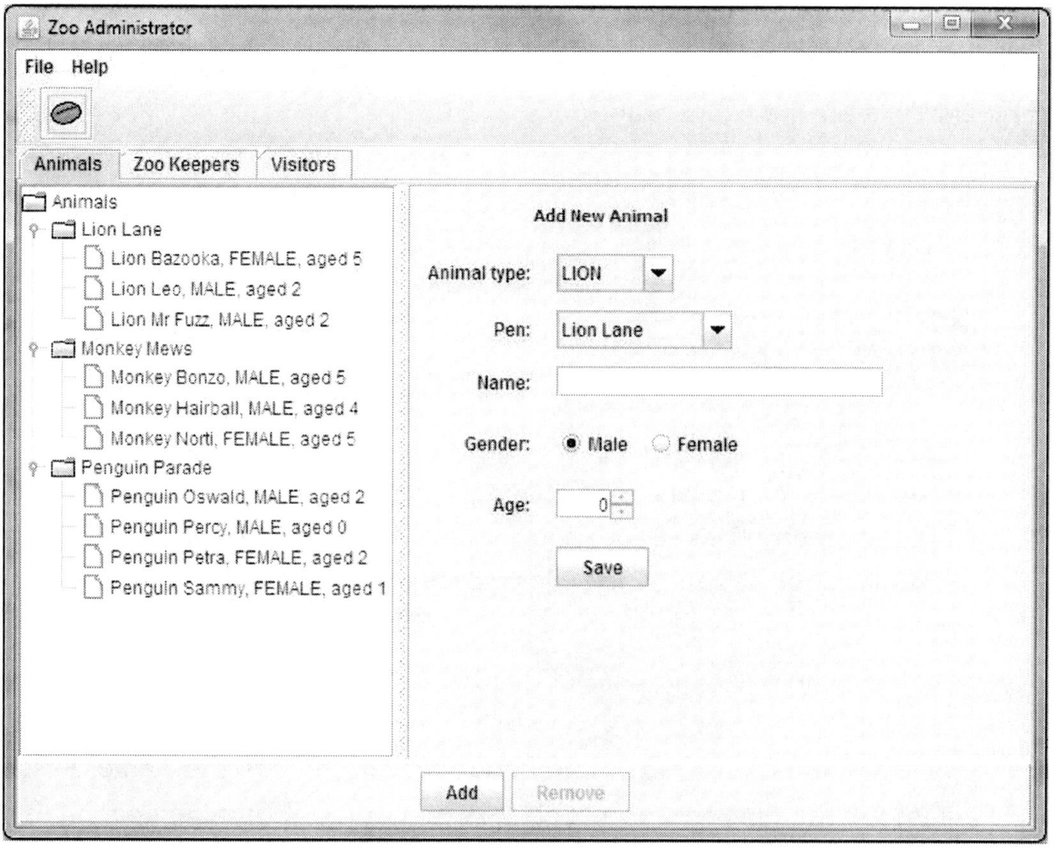

Figure 18.5: Toolbar inside frame

Note the large icon in the toolbar, which if you hover the mouse over provides the hover help as defined. The menu option and toolbar option will perform the same action.

Setting the look & feel

The Swing components are rendered directly by Java, and because Java is designed as a cross-platform language there are several implemented "look & feels" for the major target platforms, such as Windows, Mac and Motif (for Unix). There is also a default look & feel for Swing components, which is a cross-platform style called **Metal**, and NetBeans uses its own default. You will now modify the application so that it adopts the look & feel of the platform on which it is running.

Insert the following lines inside the `AdministratorFrame` constructor, immediately after the call to `super()`:

```
// Set to native look & feel
try {
    UIManager.setLookAndFeel
                    (UIManager.getSystemLookAndFeelClassName());
} catch (Exception e) {
    e.printStackTrace();
    // If unable just carry on with default look & feel
}
```

- `UIManager` is a class that manages look & feels. It contains the `static` method `setLookAndFeel()` that takes as a `String` argument the name of the class that controls the look & feel you want.

- The argument being passed is the `String` returned by another `static` method of `UIManager` called `getSystemLookAndFeelClassName()`. This returns the name of the class for the platform on which it is executing, if there is one, or the default look & feel otherwise.

- The `setLookAndFeel()` method can potentially throw one of several different exceptions (see the Javadoc API), so for simplicity the code above catches the superclass of all of these, being `Exception`.

- If an exception is thrown, it is hoped that the display will still render using the default look & feel, so the exception details are sent to the console and the application will continue anyway.

Here is how it looks on the Windows platform:

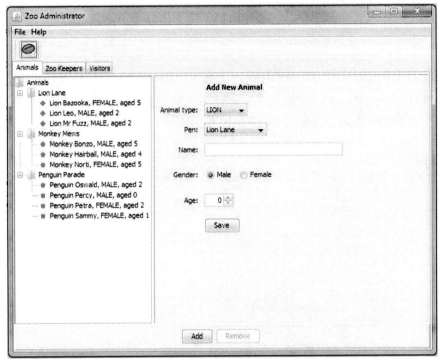

Figure 18.6: Windows look and feel

19. Persistence

Many applications are only of limited use if they are not able to save their state each time they run. Persistence enables you to store information to disk and to read it back at a later time.

In this chapter you will learn:

- *How to save data to a disk file;*

- *How to read saved data back from a disk file;*

- *An overview of different types of persistence.*

Saving data to disk

Thus far with the zoo application, every time you end the application any new, modified or deleted information about animals and zoo keepers is lost. **Persistence** refers to the action of storing data permanently, typically to a disk file or a database.

The use of a relational database is beyond the scope of this book, and is in any case better suited to larger scale applications with more sophisticated needs. It is worth mentioning, however, that Java is quite capable of connecting to many types of relational databases on various platforms.

The more straightforward approach used in this book will be to use **object serialization**; that is, writing the data of the appropriate objects to a binary file whenever the application is ended by the user, and then restoring that data from the file back into the application whenever it starts up again. To make use of object serialization you need to code each class that needs to be saved as implementing the `Serializable` interface. This interface, which is in the `java.io` package[1], is unusual in that it has no methods which you need to provide code for. It is simply a marker to

---

1   io stands for input/output.

Java in order to give it permission to save the values of its instance variables. A very useful feature that is built-in is that where a saved instance variable stores a reference to another object, which in turn may reference another, they will all be saved in one fell swoop, provided they are all marked as `Serializable`.

In the zoo application it is the `ZooAdministrator` object that holds references to the collections of `ZooKeeper`, `Visitor` and `Pen` objects. The `Pen` objects in turn hold references to collections of `Animal` objects. You only therefore need to **serialize** the `ZooAdministrator` object for them all to be saved. Before doing so, however, you need to change its class header to implement the the `Serializable` interface:

```
import java.io.*;

public class ZooAdministrator implements Serializable {
```

You should now also change the following classes to implement `Serializable`: `ZooKeeper`, `Visitor`, `Pen` and `Animal` (note that you don't need to change `Lion`, `Monkey` and `Penguin` since they inherit from `Animal`).

```
public class ZooKeeper implements Emailable,
                     Comparable<ZooKeeper>, Serializable {


public class Visitor implements Emailable,
                     Comparable<Visitor>, Serializable {


public class Pen implements Comparable<Pen>, Serializable {


public abstract class Animal implements Comparable<Animal>,
                     Serializable {
```

There are also references to the classes `Email` and `Person` that are in the `com.example.util` package, so these also need to be amended in the same way:

```
public final class Email implements Comparable<Email>, Serializable {
```

```
public class Person implements Serializable {
```

With the above in place you can now start the process of coding the serialization section of the application. You may recall from an earlier chapter the client-server approach that the application has adopted:

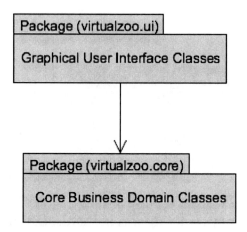

Figure 19.1: 2-tier client-server architecture

In the above figure, the `virtualzoo.ui` package is the *client* and the `virtualzoo.core` package is the *server*. Because this separation involves two levels the client-server approach is also known as **2-tier**. When you need to include a database of some description it is common to extend this into a **3-tier** structure:

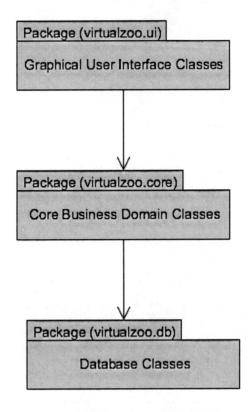

Figure 19.2: 3-tier architecture

Even though you will not be using a relational database it is still useful to separate out the persistence mechanism into its own layer, as indicated in the above figure. Create a sub-package under `virtualzoo` call `db`, and then create a class in `virtualzoo.db` called `ZooSerialization`, which will be a singleton:

```
package virtualzoo.db;

import java.io.*;
import virtualzoo.core.*;

public class ZooSerialization {

    public static final String ZOO_FILENAME = "zoo.ser";
```

```
    private static ZooSerialization instance;

    public static ZooSerialization getInstance() {
        if (instance == null) {
            instance = new ZooSerialization();
        }
        return instance;
    }

    private ZooSerialization() {
    }

    public void save(ZooAdministrator admin) throws IOException {
        // code will go here...
    }

    public ZooAdministrator restore() throws ClassNotFoundException,
                                    IOException {
        // code will go here...
    }

}
```

The above class is comprised of the two methods save() and restore() which will be used to save and restore the zoo application's data respectively. Because reading and writing to disk files may not always work (for example, you might try to read a non-existent or corrupted file) then exceptions will get thrown. These will be propagated back to the caller, as shown in the method signatures above.

For the save() method code the following:

```
public void save(ZooAdministrator admin) throws IOException {
    File f = new File(ZOO_FILENAME);                              // 1
    FileOutputStream fos = new FileOutputStream(f);               // 2
    BufferedOutputStream bos = new BufferedOutputStream(fos);     // 3
    ObjectOutputStream oos = new ObjectOutputStream(bos);         // 4
    oos.writeObject(admin);                                       // 5
    oos.close();                                                  // 6
```

```
System.out.println("Data has beeen saved to " +          // 7
                   f.getAbsolutePath());
}
```

- Statement 1 instantiates a `File` object using the `String` constant as its file path[1] and name. The instantiated `File` object does not have to exist on the disk and won't actually be created, so the object is just a pointer to either a file or directory that may or may not exist;

- Statement 2 instantiates a `FileOutputStream` object pointing to the above `File` object. Objects of type `FileOutputStream` can be used to save a series of bytes to a file;

- Statement 3 instantiates a `BufferedOutputStream` object which contains the above `FileOutputStream`. Creating a `BufferedOutputStream` is optional but recommended, since it uses a memory buffer to speed up the process of writing the data to the disk. You can think of it as a "wrapper" over the `FileOutputStream` that adds the additional capability of being buffered;

- Statement 4 instantiates an `ObjectOutputStream` object consisting of the above `BufferedOutputStream`. Objects of type `ObjectOutputStream` are used to for the actual serialization process. You can think of it as a "wrapper" over the `BufferedOutputStream` that adds the additional capability of allowing serialization of objects;

- Statement 5 invokes the `writeObject()` method on the `ObjectOutputStream` to save the `ZooAdministrator` object passed as the argument to the `save()` method. The `writeObject()` method is what actually performs the serialization of the object to the disk file;

- Statement 6 closes the `ObjectOutputStream` (which will result in the other stream objects being closed since they are wrapped inside

---

1   In the absence of a specified path the current directory will be used.

of it). It is important to remember to close your streams in order to ensure the data is actually written to the disk and to release its resources;

- Statement 7 writes the absolute path and file name to the **Output** window.

The code for the restore() method is similar except that it uses input streams instead of output streams and returns the restored object:

```
public ZooAdministrator restore() throws ClassNotFoundException,
                                          IOException {
    File f = new File(ZOO_FILENAME);
    FileInputStream fis = new FileInputStream(f);
    BufferedInputStream bis = new BufferedInputStream(fis);
    ObjectInputStream ois = new ObjectInputStream(bis);
    ZooAdministrator admin = (ZooAdministrator) ois.readObject();
    ois.close();
    System.out.println("Data has beeen loaded from " +
                    f.getAbsolutePath());
    return admin;
}
```

- You use the readObject() method of the ObjectInputStream class to read the serialized data from the disk back into the application. Because this methods returns an Object you need to cast it back into a ZooAdministrator.

As mentioned earlier, the act of serializing an object causes that object's instance (but not static) variables to be saved, so in your case it will save all instance variables in the ZooAdministrator class, plus all referenced objects, etc. There is a slight issue, however, since two of the instance variables are used by the UI as listeners, namely animalListeners and zooKeeperListeners. The upshot of this is that UI listeners don't get serialized, so special handling is required to cater for this, as follows:

1. Mark the listener instance variables as **transient**. Variables marked `transient` will be ignored by the serialization process;

2. As part of the restoration process, because the listener variables were not save you need to instantiate them again.

In `ZooAdministrator` add the `transient` keyword to the declaration of the two listener instance variables:

```
private transient Collection<ZooKeeperListener> zooKeeperListeners;
private transient Collection<AnimalListener> animalListeners;
```

Now add a method to `ZooAdministrator` called `readObject()`:

```
private void readObject(ObjectInputStream ois) throws IOException,
                                        ClassNotFoundException {
    ois.defaultReadObject();
    zooKeeperListeners = new ArrayList<ZooKeeperListener>();
    animalListeners = new ArrayList<AnimalListener>();
}
```

- The de-serialization process looks for a method with the above signature and if found executes it. As coded above, its first task is to call `defaultReadObject()` (which performs the normal de-serialization) followed by simply instantiating empty listener collections.

Because the UI should only converse with the core system you need to add another method to `ZooAdministrator` for that purpose:

```
public static void save() throws Exception {
    ZooSerialization zser = ZooSerialization.getInstance();
    zser.save(getInstance());
}
```

- Note that the method is `static` and that you need to import `virtualzoo.db`;

- The method simply invokes the `save()` method of `ZooSerialization`.

The restoration of the serialized data is most readily done in the static `getInstance()` method, so modify it as follows:

```
public static ZooAdministrator getInstance() {
    if (instance == null) {
        ZooSerialization zser = ZooSerialization.getInstance();
        try {
            instance = zser.restore();
        } catch (FileNotFoundException ex) {
            instance = new ZooAdministrator();
        } catch (Exception ex) {
            ex.printStackTrace();
        }
    }
    return instance;
}
```

- The above attempts to de-serialize the file, but if it wasn't found (as would be the case the very first time you run the application) then the constructor is called instead. If any other error occurs, the `printStackTrace()` method is invoked to send the details to the **Output** window.

Finally, you need to modify the `confirmClose()` method in `AdministratorFrame` to invoke the `save()` method of the `ZooAdministrator` object:

```
public void confirmClose() {
    // Prompt for confirmation
    int response = JOptionPane.showConfirmDialog(this,
            "Are you sure you want to exit?",
            "Exit Person Manager",
            JOptionPane.YES_NO_OPTION);
```

```
            // See what response is
            if (response == JOptionPane.YES_OPTION) {
                try {
                    // End the application
                    ZooAdministrator.save();
                } catch (Exception ex) {
                    ex.printStackTrace();
                    JOptionPane.showMessageDialog(this,
                            ex.getMessage(),
                            "Unable to save data.",
                            JOptionPane.ERROR_MESSAGE);
                } finally {
                    dispose();
                }
            }
        }
```

- You need to import `virtualzoo.core;`

- If an exception is thrown then a dialog will be displayed;

- Note the use of the `finally` block so that the frame's `dispose()` method is called whether or not an exception occurred.

Other types of persistence

You have seen how object serialization provides a relatively straightforward mechanism for saving the contents of one or more objects to a disk file. This section briefly mentions a few other ways in which data of various sorts can be saved to files.

Saving individual attribute values

The `DataOutputStream` class provides a wrapper that lets you save individual attribute values through the following methods:

```
writeBoolean(boolean b);
writeByte(int v);
writeChar(int c);
```

```
writeChars(String s);
writeDouble(double v);
writeFloat(Float v);
writeInt(int v);
writeLong(long v);
writeShort(short v);
```

An example of how you might use this class follows:

```
File myStream = new File("mystream.dat");
DataOutputStream myDataOutputStream = null;
try {
    myDataOutputStream = new DataOutputStream
                         (new BufferedOutputStream
                             (new FileOutputStream(myStream)));
    myDataOutputStream.writeInt(50);
    myDataOutputStream.writeBoolean(true);
    myDataOutputStream.flush();
} catch (FileNotFoundException ex) {
    System.out.println(ex.getMessage());
} catch (IOException ex) {
    System.out.println(ex.getMessage());
} finally {
    try {
        myDataOutputStream.close();
    } catch (IOException ex) {
        System.out.println(ex.getMessage());
    }
}
```

- The above wraps a `FileOutputStream` inside a `BufferedOutputStream`, which is in turn wrapped inside a `DataOutputStream`;

- It then invokes the `writeInt()` and `writeBoolean()` methods with the values 50 and `true` respectively;

- The `flush()` method forces the data to be written to the file, and the file is closed[1] inside the finally block.

---

1   Note that the `close()` method could itself throw an exception so there is a nested `try...catch` block inside

The `DataInputStream` class provides a wrapper with "read" methods corresponding to the `DataOutputStream` class's "write" methods. Here is some code that can read back the `int` and `boolean` values which were saved to the above file:

```
File myStream = new File("mystream.dat");
DataInputStream myDataInputStream = null;
try {
    myDataInputStream = new DataInputStream
                            (new BufferedInputStream
                                (new FileInputStream(myStream)));
    int i = myDataInputStream.readInt();
    boolean b = myDataInputStream.readBoolean();
    System.out.println("i=" + i + ", b=" + b);
} catch (FileNotFoundException ex) {
    System.out.println(ex.getMessage());
} catch (IOException ex) {
    System.out.println(ex.getMessage());
} finally {
    try {
        myDataInputStream.close();
    } catch (IOException ex) {
        System.out.println(ex.getMessage());
    }
}
```

Note how the above used the `readInt()` and `readBoolean()` methods to obtain the data from the file. You need to specify these in the same order they were written to the file because the read methods effectively positions to the next value each time.

Saving text files

So far in this chapter you have made use of **streams**, which you can think of as the mechanism for transmitting a series of bytes. For textual files Java provides the `Writer` class (and its subclasses) for when you want to

---

the outer `finally` block.

store character based files, and the `Reader` class (and its subclasses) to read them back again.

Here is an example that uses a `FileWriter` wrapped inside a `BufferedWriter` to save a file consisting of a well known piece of prose:

```
File myFile = new File("myfile.txt");
BufferedWriter myBufferedWriter = null;
try {
    myBufferedWriter = new BufferedWriter(new FileWriter(myFile));
    myBufferedWriter.write("To be, or not to be.");
    myBufferedWriter.newLine();
    myBufferedWriter.write("That is the question.");
    myBufferedWriter.flush();
} catch (IOException ex) {
    System.out.println(ex.getMessage());
} finally {
    try {
        myBufferedWriter.close();
    } catch (IOException ex) {
        System.out.println(ex.getMessage());
    }
}
```

- The `write()` method takes a `String` object and the `newLine()` method causes a line separator to appended, so that the next call to `write()` will cause its piece of text to appear on the next line in the file.

If you run the above you can see and open the created file by clicking on the **Files** window in NetBeans (immediately to the right of **Projects**) and look for the file named `myfile.txt`. This should display the following:

```
To be, or not to be.
That is the question.
```

> An alternative class that can be used for writing text files is `PrintWriter`, which has the method `println()` to save a `String` with an automatic line separator.

There follows some code that will read the file back from the disk and send each line to the **Output** window:

```
File myFile = new File("myfile.txt");
BufferedReader myBufferedReader = null;
String line = null;
try {
    myBufferedReader = new BufferedReader(new FileReader(myFile));
    line = myBufferedReader.readLine();
    while (line != null) {
        System.out.println(line);
        line = myBufferedReader.readLine();
    }
} catch (Exception ex) {
    System.out.println(ex.getMessage());
} finally {
    try {
        myBufferedReader.close();
    } catch (IOException ex) {
        System.out.println(ex.getMessage());
    }
}
```

- Note the use of the `while` loop so that as many lines will be read as appear in the file. Prior to the `while` loop the first line is read, and provided it is not `null` (which would indicate the end of the file has been reached) the loop is started;

- Inside the loop the current line is sent to the **Output** window and then the next line is read from the file. The loop continues until `null` is returned.

20. Other Java Features

The desktop application developed in this book used many, but not all, of the major facilities of the Java language. This final chapter provides a brief look at some of the other useful features.

In this chapter you will learn:

- *How you can distribute your application;*

- *How you can draw graphics and images to the screen;*

- *How to define an applet that runs a Java program inside a web browser;*

- *How to create JavaBeans;*

- *How to approach writing distributed client-server applications.*

Distributing your application

Now that you have completed the desktop application in this book, you may wonder how it might be possible to distribute it so that it can run on a different machine. When you run a **Clean and Build** for your project you will notice a number of lines sent to the **Output** window, at the end of which you should see the following:

```
To run this application from the command line without Ant, try:
java -jar "C:\path-to-project\VirtualZoo\dist\VirtualZoo.jar"
jar:
BUILD SUCCESSFUL (total time: 3 seconds)
```

The path-to-project will be different for your computer, and it points to the path on your system in which you will find the file VirtualZoo.jar. As briefly mentioned in an earlier chapter, a JAR file is a Java Archive consisting of all of the compiled classes that make up your application. It also contains a **manifest** file, being a simple text file which provides the

JVM with information about the JAR. Because the `VirtualZoo` application has a class with a `main()` method to start it off, the manifest will contain a pointer to this. NetBeans automatically generates this for you, and you can view it by doing the following steps:

1. Click on the **Files** tab (next to the **Projects** tab);

2. Under the `VirtualZoo` node expand the `dist` node;

3. Under the `dist` node expand the `VirtualZoo.jar` node;

4. Under the `VirtualZoo.jar` node expand the `META-INF` node;

5. Under the `META-INF` node open the `MANIFEST.MF` file.

You should see something resembling the following:

```
Manifest-Version: 1.0
Ant-Version: Apache Ant 1.8.2
Created-By: 1.6.0_26-b03 (Sun Microsystems Inc.)
Class-Path: lib/Utilities.jar lib/jlfgr-1_0.jar
X-COMMENT: Main-Class will be added automatically by build
Main-Class: virtualzoo.VirtualZoo
```

The **Main-Class** entry will tell the JRE the path to the class that contains the `main()` method to start the application.

If you locate the jar file on your system you should see that its file type is **Executable Jar File**. You can double-click on this to launch it independently of NetBeans, and you can distribute the JAR file to any other computer that has a JRE of at least the same version installed on it.

Graphics

There are facilities to draw graphics by overriding the `paint()` method of the component classes. Create a new class in `virtualzoo.ui` called `PenguinPicture`:

```java
package virtualzoo.ui;

import java.awt.*;
import javax.swing.*;

public class PenguinPicture extends JPanel {

    @Override
    public void paint(Graphics g) {
        super.paint(g);

        g.drawString("Percy", 105, 40);

        g.fillOval(105, 65, 30, 30);   // head
        g.fillOval(95, 90, 50, 100);   // body
        g.fillOval(85, 110, 20, 50);   // right wing
        g.fillOval(135, 110, 20, 50);  // left wing
        g.fillRect(95, 185, 20, 10);   // right foot
        g.fillRect(125, 185, 20, 10);  // left foot

        g.setColor(Color.WHITE);
        g.fillOval(111, 70, 8, 8);     // right eye
        g.fillOval(121, 70, 8, 8);     // left eye
        g.fillOval(105, 100, 30, 80);  // belly
    }

}
```

- The `paint()` method accepts a `Graphics` object as its argument. This is supplied by Java to provide a graphical context on which you can draw strings and shapes;

- You should typically call the `paint()` method of the superclass as the first statement when you override the method, so that it can

properly initialise the canvas area. This is done using
`super.paint(g);`

- The `Graphics` object allows a number of shape drawing methods. They require you to specify the x and y coordinates of where to place the shape together with the width and height. Some common ones are:

  - `drawString()` - draws a `String` at the specified x and y position;

  - `drawRect()` - draws a hollow rectangle at the specified x and y position and with the specified width and height;

  - `fillRect()` - draws a filled rectangle at the specified x and y position and with the specified width and height. The rectangle is filled with the currently set colour, which defaults to black;

  - `drawOval()` - draws a hollow oval at the specified x and y position and with the specified width and height. If the width and height are the same value you will create a circle;

  - `fillOval()` - draws a filled oval at the specified x and y position and with the specified width and height. If the width and height are the same value you will create a circle. The oval is filled with the currently set colour, which defaults to black;

  - `setColor()` - sets the colour to the argument, being one of the constants in the `Color` class. The colour remains set until you change it.

To see how the above looks you can put it inside a new tab in `AdministratorFrame`:

```
// Create drawing panel
PenguinPicture penguinPicture = new PenguinPicture();
tabPane.addTab("Penguin Picture", penguinPicture);
```

Which should look as follows:

Figure 20.1: Graphic of penguin

It is possible to create much better graphics than the rather unconvincing penguin generated above.

Suppose you have a graphics file (such as a JPG) that you want to show in a panel. Create a class `PenguinImage` as follows:

```
package virtualzoo.ui;

import java.awt.*;
import java.net.*;
import javax.swing.*;
```

```java
public class PenguinImage extends JPanel {

    @Override
    public void paint(Graphics g) {
        super.paint(g);
        URL penguin = getClass().getResource("images/penguin.jpg");
        Image image = new ImageIcon(penguin).getImage();
        g.drawImage(image, 10, 20, this);
    }

}
```

- The technique is similar to how you displayed a toolbar icon, although the `drawImage()` method of `Graphics` requires an object of type `Image`;

- The above assumes you have a file called `penguin.jpg` which exists in the folder `virtualzoo.ui.images`;

- The last argument passed to `drawImage()` is an `ImageObserver`, which for simplicity can be `this`.

Applets

An **applet** is a Java program which runs embedded inside a web page. Applets always execute inside a **sandbox**, which means that there are security restrictions built into the browser to prevent it from accessing files on the running computer or from connecting to hosts other than from where the applet was loaded[1]. An applet is composed of Java classes just like an application, and the compiled bytecode is loaded and run by a JVM built into the browser.

---

1 It is possible to overcome these restrictions by digitally signing the applet and by prompting the user to give permission to do so.

The applet life-cycle

To write an applet you need to extend the JApplet class which is in package javax.swing. The JApplet class includes empty implementations of several methods which you can override to accomplish your task, these methods being invoked for you by the browser when certain events happen.

The life-cycle methods are:

- init() - invoked by the browser when the applet is first loaded, such as when the web page containing the applet is navigated to. This method serves as a kind of constructor for the applet since it is invoked only once. There is therefore no need to write an actual constructor for applets;

- start() - invoked by the browser when the web page is viewed. This could occur multiple times if the user goes to another window and then back again;

- stop() - invoked by the browser whenever the applet page is made inactive. This could occur multiple times if the user goes to another window;

- destroy() - invoked by the browser as part of the unloading process when the user closes the browser;

- paint() - This method takes a Graphics object as its argument, working in a similar manner to that shown in the section on graphics earlier in this chapter. It is invoked by the browser as necessary to render graphics on screen.

You will now create a simple applet that makes use of the PenguinPicture class you developed earlier. Create a new class called PenguinApplet in the virtualzoo.ui package:

```
package virtualzoo.ui;

import java.awt.*;
```

```java
import javax.swing.*;

public class PenguinApplet extends JApplet {

    private PenguinPicture penguinPicture;

    @Override
    public void init() {
        penguinPicture = new PenguinPicture();
    }

    @Override
    public void paint(Graphics g) {
        super.paint(g);
        penguinPicture.paint(g);

        g.setColor(Color.BLUE);
        g.drawString("An unconvincing penguin", 50, 220);
    }

}
```

- The class extends `JApplet` and uses `PenguinPicture` as an instance variable;

- The `init()` method is overridden to instantiate the `PenguinPicture` object;

- The `paint()` method is overridden to delegate to the `paint()` method which was defined in `PenguinPicture`, after which another `String` is drawn on the same picture.

Now create an HTML file in the same package called `penguin.html`. You can do this in NetBeans by right-clicking on the `virtualzoo.ui` node in the **Projects** window and selecting **New | Other**, then choosing **Other** from the **Categories** list and **HTML File** from the **File Types** list, then enter `penguin` as the file name (the extension will be added automatically).

Modify the default code so that it appears as follows:

```
<html>
    <head>
        <title>Penguin Applet</title>
    </head>
    <body>
        <h1>Graphic of penguin</h1>
        <applet codebase="../.."
                code="virtualzoo.ui.PenguinApplet.class"
                width="400" height="400"></applet>
    </body>
</html>
```

- The `applet` tag above specifies four attributes:

  o `codebase` – this is the location where the class file exists relative to where this HTML file exists. Because the class file is in the same directory but the package name is an intrinsic part of a compiled class, the entry `../..` moves up two directories;

  o `code` – this specifies the package and compiled class name of the Java class that is an applet. Note that it ends in `.class`. If your classes are in a JAR file you could use the `archive` attribute in place of the `code` attribute;

  o `width`, `height` – these specify the dimensions in the browser window within which the applet runs.

The `applet` tag has been superseded by the `object` tag. However, `applet` is somewhat easier to use and is more widely supported by browsers.

At this point you should run a **Clean and Build** on the `VirtualZoo` project to ensure the HTML file is copied to the `build` folder.

To open the applet in your default browser, click in the `Files` tag in NetBeans and then open the **VirtualZoo | build | classes |**

virtualzoo | ui node. Then right-click on the `penguin.html` node and select **View**.

Instead of overriding the `paint()` method your applets can set a layout and make use of any of the Swing components such as `JButton`, `JTextField`, etc., just as you would do for an application. The most appropriate place to do this would generally be from within the `init()` method.

JavaBeans

A **JavaBean** is a reusable component that is written to conform to certain conventions. Although they don't have to be, JavaBeans are often graphical in nature and in fact all of the Swing graphical components are JavaBeans. This enables them to be used within builder tools such as NetBeans.

The essential conventions that mean that a class can be considered a JavaBean are:

- The class implements the `Serializable` interface;

- The class has a `public` constructor that takes no arguments. You can still optionally define other constructors which do have arguments, however;

- The instance variables which make up the **properties** of the bean are accessed using `public get`, `set` and `is`[1] as prefixes for the method names.

Here is a class called `Address` which you can create in the `Utilities` project. To keep things simple it only has two properties, `street` and `city`:

```
package com.example.util;
```

---

1   For `boolean` properties.

```
import java.io.*;

public class Address implements Serializable {

    private String street;
    private String city;

    public Address() {
        super();
    }

    public String getStreet() {
        return street;
    }

    public void setStreet(String street) {
        this.street = street;
    }

    public String getCity() {
        return city;
    }

    public void setCity(String city) {
        this.city = city;
    }

}
```

Although not essential, it is useful for a JavaBean to fire a **property change event** whenever a property value has changed (i.e. each time one of the setter methods is called). The `PropertyChangeSupport` class (which is in the `java.beans` package) provides a convenient way to do this:

```
package com.example.util;

import java.beans.*;
import java.io.*;

public class Address implements Serializable {
```

```java
    private PropertyChangeSupport changeSupport;
    private String street;
    private String city;

    public Address() {
        super();
        changeSupport = new PropertyChangeSupport(this);
    }

    public String getStreet() {
        return street;
    }

    public void setStreet(String street) {
        String oldValue = this.street;
        this.street = street;
        changeSupport.firePropertyChange("street", oldValue, street);
    }

    public String getCity() {
        return city;
    }

    public void setCity(String city) {
        String oldValue = this.city;
        this.city = city;
        changeSupport.firePropertyChange("city", oldValue, city);
    }

    public void addPropertyChangeListener
            (PropertyChangeListener listener) {
        changeSupport.addPropertyChangeListener(listener);
    }

    public void removePropertyChangeListener
            (PropertyChangeListener listener) {
        changeSupport.removePropertyChangeListener(listener);
    }
}
```

- The argument passed when instantiating the `PropertyChangeSupport` object is the object which is the source of the changes, which in this case is `this` object;

- In each setter method the old value is saved just before updating it, and finally the `firePropertyChange()` method is called to notify all listeners that a change to a property has occurred. There are three passed arguments:

  - A `String` which represents the property that has changed its value;

  - The old value of the property before the change took place;

  - The new value of the property after the change tool place.

- Note the two new methods to add and remove `PropertyChangeListener` objects, which just forward to the same methods within the `PropertyChangeSupport` object.

Client objects interested in being notified about property changes can implement the `PropertyChangeListener` interface and provide code for its `propertyChange()` method. Within that, you can call the `PropertyChangeEvent` object's `getPropertyName()`, `getOldValue()` and `getNewValue()` and process them as required.

Networking

Two of the main ways of programming networking applications in Java is through sockets and Remote Method Invocation (RMI):

Sockets

Java supports connection to other hosts through the use of sockets. You can use the `Socket` class (in package `java.net`) to connect to a remote host by specifying an IP address and port number:

```
Socket socket = new Socket("catalog.example.com", 4321);
```

You can then obtain an `InputStream` and `OutputStream` object from the socket to allow you to read and write (subject to any permissions) to the host:

```
InputStream is = socket.getInputStream();
OutputStream os = socket.getOutputStream();
```

In the above case you are the client and the host you are connecting to is the server. If you want to create a server application you can use the `ServerSocket` class:

```
ServerSocket serverSocket = new ServerSocket(80); // port 80 = http
```

You then need to wait for clients to connect to your server through the `accept()` method, which returns a `Socket` object:

```
Socket clientSocket = serverSocket.accept();
```

A typical way of coding server programs is to listen for client connections (via `accept()`) inside a while loop which continues until the server application is stopped. Each time a client connects, a new `Thread` would be created for that client so that multiple clients can connect simultaneously.

Remote Method Invocation (RMI)

Remote Method Invocation provides a means for you to create both a Java server and a Java client program that can communicate with each other without the need to create sockets. Your client object can invoke the methods of the server object just as if they were on the same physical machine, where the RMI mechanism takes care of the network connections for you.

On the server side, you need to define an interface that contains the methods which should be able to be invoked by a remote client. The interface must extend the `Remote` interface (in the `java.rmi` package), and because network connections are involved which could fail, your method must specify that they throw `RemoteException`. Here is a simple interface to convert a `String` to upper-case[1]:

```
package somepackage;

import java.rmi.*;

public interface WordUtilities extends Remote {

    public void makeUpperCase(String s) throws RemoteException;

}
```

Also on the server, you need to create a class which implements your interface and extends `UnicastRemoteObject`:

```
package somepackage;

import java.rmi.*;

public class WordUtilitiesImpl extends UnicastRemoteObject
                        implements WordUtilities {

    public void makeUpperCase(String s) throws RemoteException {
        return s.toUpperCase();
```

---

1   This could obviously be more easily done by the client object themselves, but the example is deliberately simple.

```
    }

}
```

Your server program needs to start the RMI registry, an instance of the WordUtilites object, and bind it to the registry:

```
try {
    LocateRegistry.createRegistry(1099); // 1099 is default RMI port
    WordUtilities wu = new  WordUtilitiesImpl();
    Naming.rebind("rmi://example.com/wordutilapp", wu);
    System.out.println("Server has started");

} catch (Exception ex) {
    ex.printStackTrace();
}
```

At the client end your application needs to connect to the server host before it can invoke the methods remotely:

```
try {
    WordUtilities wu =
        (WordUtilities) Naming.lookup("rmi://example.com/wordutilapp");
    String sUpper = wu.makeUpperCase("make this upper-case");
    System.out.println(sUpper);
} catch (Exception ex) {
    ex.printStackTrace();
}
```

Important:
In a real RMI application you need to protect against untrusted communication, and you would therefore need to set a SecurityManager object at both the server and the client end. This involves defining the files and addresses that are allowed to be accessed, and is beyond the scope of this book.

Appendix A.   Glossary

Abstract class: A class for which objects can only exist which are instances of one of its concrete (i.e. non-abstract) subclasses.

Abstract method: A method that only has its signature defined and which must be implemented by a concrete (i.e. non-abstract) subclass.

Aglet: A Java "mobile agent" program which can move between hosts.

Applet: A Java program which runs inside a web page.

Application: A program which could be of any type, though typically a desktop based graphical program.

Application Programming Interface (API): The available members of a collection of classes, such as those documented for the Java classes.

Argument: A value which is passed to a constructor or method. Sometimes also called a Parameter.

Array: A fixed-size collection of objects or primitives of a particular type. Each item in an array is known as an element.

Assertion: The statement that a certain condition should be true. Used as part of testing.

Attribute: A property of an object which references a value of some type.

Behaviour: A particular process that an object can perform, as defined in a method.

Breakpoint: A statement in a source file at which execution will pause when the program is run in debugging mode.

Bytecode: The code generated by the Java compiler from your source code.

Camel-case: A naming convention in which because compound words are not separated by a space, the initial letter of each new word is capitalised.

Casting: The conversion of one type to another. Only allowed for compatible types.

Class: A template or blueprint that models something from the real-world. It consists of attributes and methods.

Client-server: A system in which a "client" makes requests to a "server" which provides a response. Also known as a 2-tier architecture.

Collection: A group of related objects.

Concrete class: A class which is not abstract.

Compiler: A tool which converts Source Code into Bytecode (for java programs), or into Machine Code for non-Java programs. The generated Bytecode or Machine Code becomes a separate entity – contrast with Interpreter.

Constant: A variable whose value cannot vary once it has been defined. Created either by defining a variable which is both static and final, or by defining it within an enum.

Constructor: The part of a class definition which controls how an object of that class will be created.

Core system: A part of an application typically consisting of the business rules and logic. It is separated from the Graphical User Interface (GUI).

Data-hiding: The principle that an object's state is private (i.e. hidden) from direct access from client objects, in order to protect its integrity.

Debugging: The process of locating and correcting errors in a piece of software.

Defensive copy: A copy which is made of an object in order to protect its state from changes by other objects.

Eclipse: A popular IDE, similar to NetBeans.

Encapsulation: The concept that each individual object consists of both its state and its protocol; that is, they are *encapsulated* together as a unit.

Enum: An enumerated type consisting of constants.

Exception: An occurrence which can prevent the normal execution of a program.

Garbage collection: A process run automatically by the JVM during the execution of an application that reclaims the memory of objects which are no longer referenced. It runs in a separate thread.

IDE (Integrated Development Environment): A tool which simplifies the development and management of program applications. This book uses the NetBeans IDE.

Immutable class: A class whose objects have their state set during construction and whose state cannot be modified thereafter.

Inheritance: Where class B inherits from class A then class B has access to the non-private members of class A automatically.

Inner class: A class which is defined inside of another class.

Instance: A particular object.

Instance variable: A variable which is part of an object's state.

Interface: A definition of a type that differs from a class in that only the method signatures are defined. Classes which implement the interface must then provide the method bodies.

Interpreter: A tool which converts Source Code "on the fly" into Machine Code. The generated machine code is not stored as a separate entity and is instead re-generated each time the code runs – contrast with Compiler.

Iterative development: Developing an application in small, successive phases with frequent modifications and enhancements to existing code.

JAR file: A Java Archive file which contains the classes that make up an application together with a manifest file that describes it.

Java Card: A credit-card sized card with a Java enabled chip.

Java EE (Enterprise Edition): An extended version of Java used for large scale enterprise applications, often web-based.

Java ME (Mobile Edition): A cut-down version of Java used on mobile devices such as smartphones and PDAs.

Java SE (Standard Edition): The standard edition of Java as used in this book.

JavaBean: A class which conforms to the JavaBeans specification. Typically (but not always) a reusable graphical component.

Javadoc: A tool that can generate class and package documentation in HTML format.

JDK (Java Development Kit): A set of tools and utilities that you can download in order to write Java programs. It incorporates a JRE.

JRE (Java Runtime Environment): A downloadable tool that enables Java programs to run on a computer.

JUnit: A tool to facilitate the testing of your classes.

JVM (Java Virtual Machine): The component of the JRE which runs a Java program on a particular system.

Loose-coupling: A design goal that strives to reduce the dependencies between classes to only those that are strictly necessary.

Machine Code: A binary file which contains the instructions necessary to execute a program. It is generated from Source Code using a Compiler.

Member: Refers to a variable or a method of a class.

Method: A piece of code that manages a particular behaviour of an object.

MIDlet: A Java program developed using Java ME (Mobile Edition).

NetBeans: A popular IDE, similar to Eclipse.

Node: An item is a tree, such as a Java source file in the Projects tabs in NetBeans.

Object: A specific instance of a class.

Object-Oriented Programming: A style of programming which allows programs to more closely resemble the real-world world through the use of objects. Java is just one of several object-oriented programming languages.

Object class: The base class from which all other Java classes inherit.

Overloading: A constructor or method is said to be overloaded when there are more than one defined, each having a unique combination of the number and type of arguments.

Overriding: In an inheritance relationship, a method in a subclass may override a method from a superclass by redefining it.

Package: A location for a group of related class definitions, typically corresponds to a specific directory on the disk.

Parameter: Another name for Argument.

Persistence: Saving the state of an application to a file or a database.

Polymorphism: The capability of an object of a particular type to take the most appropriate action in response to a request, and which may be different to the action taken by an object of a different type to the same request.

Primitive variable: A type of variable which is built-in to the core of the Java language and which is not itself a class.

Privacy leak: A situation where a mutable instance variable which is declared private is still update-able by external objects because a defensive copy of it has not been made.

Property: Another name for an attribute, most commonly used to apply to attributes of a JavaBean.

Protocol: The behaviours (i.e. methods) of an object viewed as a whole.

Refactoring: The process of modifying the structure or coding an application to make it more efficient or easier to maintain, but which does not in itself change any of its functionality.

Reference variable: A variable which references a location in memory that stores an object.

Serialization: The process of storing an object's instance variables to a file.

Servlet: A Java program which generates a web-page.

Signature: On a method, the combination of its name and argument(s).

Singleton: A class which only allows one instance to exist.

Source code: The Java statements as entered by the programmer.

State: The values of an object's instance variables viewed as a whole.

Static member: A variable or method which does not depend upon any particular instance of the class in which it is defined. Also known as a Class member.

String: A commonly used class which stores a sequence of characters. It is immutable.

Subclass: In an inheritance relationship, the class which is doing the inheriting.

Superclass: In an inheritance relationship, the class which is inherited from.

Synchronisation: Used by a thread to lock an object until a block of code (such as a method) has completed.

Thread: A single line of execution within an application.

Unicode: A standardised character set which uses 16 bits.

Utility class: A class which is designed to be used by multiple applications.

Variable: A reference to a storage area in memory of an attribute.

Visibility: Describes whether client objects are able to access a member.

Appendix B.   Bibliography

Beck, Kent. *Extreme programming explained; embrace change.* Reading, MA: Addison-Wesley, 1999.

Bevis, Tony: *Java design pattern essentials.* Essex, England: Ability First Limited, 2010.

Bloch, Joshua. *Effective Java: programming language guide.* River, NJ: Addison-Wesley, 2001.

Court, Lindsey, et al. *Software development with Java.* Milton Keynes: The Open University, 2007.

Fowler, Martin, et al. *Refactoring: improving the design of existing code.* River, NJ: Addison-Wesley, 2000.

Fowler, Martin, and Kendall Scott. *UML distilled, second edition: a brief guide to the standard object modeling language.* River, NJ: Addison-Wesley, 1999.

Gamma, Erich, et al. *Design Patterns: Elements of Reusable Object-Oriented Software.* River, NJ: Addison-Wesley, 1995.

Gilbert, Stephen, and Bill McCarty. *Object-oriented design in Java.* Corte Madera, CA: Waite Group Press, 1998.

Langr, Jeff. *Java style: patterns for implementation.* River, NJ: Prentice-Hall PTR, 2000.

Index

Also available

Once you've learned the fundamentals of the Java programming language you need to be able to put that knowledge into practice. *Java Design Pattern Essentials* gives you a step-by-step guide to the world of object-oriented software development, using examples which have been deliberately kept simple. The pattern examples have been designed around a common theme, making it easier for you to see how they relate to each other and more importantly how you can adapt them to your applications.

ISBN 987-0-9565758-0-7

Coverage includes:

- All 23 of the design patterns described in the seminal work of Erich Gamma, Richard Helm, Ralph Johnson, John Vlissides; Design Patterns: Elements of Reusable Object-Oriented Software (Addison-Wesley, 1995).

- Additional patterns for use in real-world applications.

- Full, simple explanation of the Model-View-Controller (MVC) pattern.

- Easy to follow UML diagrams.

Available from Amazon USA, UK and worldwide.

For more information visit: www.abilityfirst.co.uk/books